Commercial Lending
Asset-Based lending, Crisis Management for Banking Professionals

BY PRADEEP K. BERRY

Dedication

To the unsung heroes of the financial world – the diligent analysts, the seasoned loan officers, the decisive risk

managers, and the resilient entrepreneurs who navigate the complexities of commercial and asset-based lending. This book is dedicated to those who strive for excellence amidst uncertainty, who make sound judgments under pressure, and who learn from both triumphs and failures. It's a tribute to their unwavering commitment to financial stability and their crucial role in the economic engine of our society. It's also dedicated to my family, whose unwavering support has made this work possible. Their patience and understanding have been the bedrock upon which this project has been built. This is to my mentors, colleagues, and friends who through their wisdom and experience have shaped my understanding and approaches, constantly challenging and educating me. To those who sought to push the boundaries of conventional thinking and embrace innovative techniques; through their endeavors we find a deeper understanding of the

complexities inherent within commercial and asset-based lending. To the countless individuals whose resilience in facing financial crises inspired me to focus on strategies for navigating such challenges.

Copyright Page
Commercial Based Lending

Written by Pradeep Berry

Copyright © [2025] by Pradeep Berry

Preface

The financial landscape is a dynamic environment,

constantly shifting due to economic fluctuations, regulatory changes, and technological advancements. This creates both opportunities and considerable challenges for those involved in commercial and asset-based lending. In the pursuit of sound financial practices, it's critical to understand that

challenges and risks often go hand-in-hand. The globalized economy has woven a complex web of interconnectedness, where a crisis in one sector can quickly cascade through others. Proactive and well-planned crisis management has become increasingly important, not as a reactive measure but as an integral aspect of strategic decision-making. This book is not merely a guide to the mechanics of lending; it's a comprehensive resource designed to equip banking

professionals with the tools and knowledge to navigate the complexities inherent in their roles. It emphasizes the

proactive nature of risk management and its importance in avoiding potentially catastrophic outcomes. We examine the best practices in lending techniques but then move beyond simply understanding the process to focus on the steps

required to effectively prevent, identify, and mitigate risks.

The real-world case studies illustrate not only successful crisis management strategies but also the critical lessons learned from unsuccessful attempts. These examples provide a practical framework for applying the principles discussed, enabling readers to adapt these strategies to their specific situations. The regulatory and compliance aspects are

thoroughly integrated throughout, ensuring readers

understand the legal and ethical responsibilities that underpin responsible lending and crisis management within the

banking industry. This book is not a theoretical exercise; it's a roadmap to success, emphasizing practical application and preparation in an unpredictable economic climate.

Introduction

The world of commercial and asset-based lending is a

multifaceted domain requiring a blend of analytical prowess, financial acumen, and a nuanced understanding of human behavior. This book delves into the intricacies of both

commercial and asset-based lending, guiding readers through the essential elements of credit analysis, loan structuring, risk assessment, and portfolio management. We explore the various types of commercial loans, from term loans and lines of credit to syndicated loans and leveraged buyouts,

outlining the unique characteristics and risk profiles of each.

The complexities of asset-based lending (ABL), with its focus on collateralized borrowing, are also addressed in depth, examining different ABL structures, the intricacies of collateral valuation, and the essential considerations for effective risk management. Beyond the core lending

functions, a considerable portion of this text is devoted to crisis management, recognizing that financial setbacks are an inherent risk within this field. We explore the development of proactive strategies for crisis prevention, early warning signs, and the critical role of communication in mitigating the impact of financial crises. This involves not only internal communication within the banking institution but also

effective engagement with stakeholders, such as borrowers, regulators, and investors. This book seeks to equip

professionals with the knowledge and skills needed to

navigate these scenarios with confidence and competence.

By understanding both the intricacies of lending and the proactive strategies for crisis management, professionals can approach the financial world with a well-rounded

perspective, prepared to make sound decisions in the face of uncertainty. The integration of real-world case studies and practical examples underscores the book's commitment to

Providing readers with actionable insights, bridging the gap between theory and practice and demonstrating the
effectiveness of the approaches discussed.

Understanding Commercial Loan Types

Understanding the diverse landscape of commercial loans is fundamental to successful lending practices. This section provides a detailed examination of the most prevalent

commercial loan types, highlighting their unique features, advantages, disadvantages, and suitability for various

borrower profiles and business circumstances. Effective loan structuring, aimed at optimizing risk and reward, is also a crucial aspect we will explore.

Term Loans:

A term loan is a straightforward loan structure where a borrower receives a lump sum of money upfront and repays the principal and interest over a predetermined

period, typically ranging from several months to several years. The repayment schedule is fixed, usually with regular installments, making it predictable for both the borrower and the lender. Term loans are often used to finance significant capital expenditures, such as purchasing equipment, real estate, or expanding operations.

The primary advantage of a term loan lies in its simplicity and predictability. Borrowers appreciate the fixed repayment schedule, allowing for better budgeting and financial

planning. Lenders benefit from a structured repayment plan minimizing uncertainty about cash flows. However, term loans can be inflexible. Once the loan terms are agreed upon, modifications can be challenging and potentially costly.

Further, borrowers must maintain sufficient cash flow to meet the regular repayment obligations throughout the loan term, which can be a significant constraint for businesses experiencing financial fluctuations.

Lines of Credit:

In contrast to term loans, a line of credit functions more like a revolving credit account. The lender provides a pre-approved credit limit, allowing the borrower to draw funds as needed up to that limit. Borrowers only pay interest on the outstanding balance, offering greater

flexibility in managing cash flow. Lines of credit are often utilized for working capital needs, covering short-term expenses like inventory purchases, operating costs, or

seasonal fluctuations in demand.

The flexibility of lines of credit is their greatest appeal.

Borrowers can access funds quickly and easily, and they only pay interest on the amount they borrow. This

adaptability is especially valuable for businesses with fluctuating cash flow demands. For lenders, lines of credit can lead to long-term customer relationships, fostering loyalty and repeat business. However, lines of credit

typically carry higher interest rates than term loans due to their inherent flexibility and increased risk for the lender. Further, the lender retains the right to alter or terminate the credit line, creating uncertainty for the borrower.

Asset-Based Lending (ABL):

Asset-based lending

represents a distinct category of commercial loans, where the loan is secured by the borrower's assets. This collateral

serves as a safety net for the lender, significantly reducing the risk of default. The loan amount is typically determined by the value of the collateral, creating a borrowing base that can fluctuate based on asset valuations. ABL is frequently used by businesses that lack substantial credit history or those operating in high-growth industries with volatile cash flows.

ABL offers several advantages for both borrowers and lenders. Borrowers with limited credit history or those experiencing rapid growth can access significant financing,

Leveraging their assets as collateral. The use of assets as collateral lowers the lender's risk, permitting the extension of loans that might otherwise be unavailable. However, ABL requires careful collateral management and monitoring, adding administrative complexity for both parties.

Maintaining accurate and up-to-date valuations of the

collateral is critical for both the lender's risk assessment and the borrower's access to funding. Liquidation of collateral in case of default presents complications that demand careful consideration in the loan structuring process.

Loan Structuring for Optimal Risk and Reward:

The structuring of a commercial loan is a complex process involving careful consideration of numerous factors. It's a crucial phase that significantly impacts the overall risk and reward profile of the loan for both the lender and the

borrower. Effective loan structuring demands a deep

understanding of the borrower's financial position, the business's industry, and the broader macroeconomic

environment.

Key aspects of loan structuring include:

Interest Rate:

The interest rate reflects the lender's perception of risk. Higher risk borrowers typically face higher interest rates. Variable interest rates offer flexibility but introduce uncertainty, while fixed rates provide predictability but may not reflect changes in the market.

Maturity Date:

The loan maturity date defines the repayment period. Longer maturities reduce short-term repayment pressure but increase the lender's exposure to longer-term risks.

Repayment Schedule:

The repayment schedule outlines the timing and amount of principal and interest payments.

Amortization schedules can be fully amortized (equal payments over the loan term), partially amortized (balloon payment at maturity), or interest-only payments.

Covenants:

Loan covenants are contractual agreements that impose certain restrictions or requirements on the borrower.

These can include maintaining specific financial ratios, limiting debt levels, or prohibiting certain business activities.

Covenants protect the lender's interests by mitigating risks and ensuring that the borrower operates in a manner

consistent with the loan agreement.

Collateral:

As previously discussed, collateral serves as security for the lender. The type and value of the collateral heavily influence the loan terms and interest rate.

Prepayment Penalties:

Prepayment penalties discourage borrowers from repaying the loan early, protecting the lender's anticipated interest income.

The optimal loan structure is a delicate balance between the borrower's needs and the lender's risk appetite. The lender must assess the borrower's creditworthiness, financial

projections, and the potential risks involved. A well-

structured loan protects the lender while providing the

borrower with accessible and manageable financing. The process is not a one-size-fits-all approach. Each loan requires careful tailoring to match the specific circumstances and mitigate the unique risks associated with each borrower and business scenario. Careful due diligence and a thorough understanding of the borrower's business model are

paramount in this process. A poorly structured loan can lead to significant financial losses for the lender, underscoring the critical importance of a comprehensive and meticulous

approach to loan structuring. The legal and regulatory

implications also need to be carefully considered during this

Phase. Ensuring compliance with all relevant regulations is not just a legal obligation; it is a cornerstone of sound lending practices.

This detailed analysis of commercial loan types provides a strong foundation for understanding the complexities of commercial lending. The next section will delve into the critical techniques of credit analysis, essential for informed decision-making in the lending process.

Credit Analysis Techniques

Credit analysis forms the bedrock of sound commercial lending. It's the meticulous process of evaluating a

borrower's creditworthiness, assessing their ability and willingness to repay a loan. This involves a comprehensive examination of financial statements, industry benchmarks, and qualitative factors that paint a complete picture of the borrower's financial health and future prospects. A thorough credit analysis minimizes the lender's risk while ensuring responsible lending practices.

The cornerstone of credit analysis rests on a deep

understanding of the borrower's financial statements. These statements—the balance sheet, income statement, and cash flow statement—provide a quantitative snapshot of the

borrower's financial position. The balance sheet presents a snapshot of assets, liabilities, and equity at a specific point in time. Analyzing the balance sheet helps to determine the borrower's capital structure, liquidity position, and overall financial leverage. A high level of debt relative to equity can signal increased financial risk, potentially making repayment more challenging. Similarly, low levels of current assets relative to current liabilities might indicate liquidity

concerns.

The income statement reveals the borrower's revenue,

expenses, and profitability over a specific period. Key

metrics like gross profit margin, operating income, and net income provide insights into the borrower's operational efficiency and profitability. Trends in these metrics over time reveal the trajectory of the business's financial performance. A consistent decline in profitability, for instance, raises a red

Flag, suggesting potential difficulties in meeting repayment obligations.

The cash flow statement is crucial as it tracks the movement of cash in and out of the business. It details cash from

operating activities, investing activities, and financing activities. Understanding the sources and uses of cash provides valuable insight into the borrower's ability to service debt. A healthy cash flow from operations is a critical indicator of the borrower's ability to generate sufficient funds to cover loan repayments. Insufficient operating cash flow, even with profitability, signals a potential problem, as the business may struggle to convert profits into readily available cash.

Beyond the individual statements, the interplay between them offers further insights. For example, a comparison of the income statement's net income with the cash flow

statement's cash from operations can reveal discrepancies, potentially highlighting issues such as aggressive accounting practices or timing differences in revenue recognition and cash collection. Analyzing these relationships allows for a more comprehensive understanding of the business's true financial health.

Ratio analysis transforms the raw data in financial

statements into meaningful metrics, facilitating comparisons across time and with industry peers. Key ratios provide insights into liquidity, profitability, solvency, and efficiency.

Liquidity ratios assess the borrower's ability to meet its short-term obligations. The current ratio (current assets divided by current liabilities) measures the ability to pay short-term debts with short-term assets. The quick ratio (liquid assets divided by current liabilities) is a more stringent measure, excluding less liquid current assets like

Inventory. A low current or quick ratio suggests potential difficulties in meeting immediate payment obligations.

Profitability ratios measure the borrower's ability to generate profits. Gross profit margin (gross profit divided by revenue) reflects the profitability of sales, while net profit margin (net income divided by revenue) indicates the overall profitability after all expenses. Return on assets (net income divided by total assets) measures how effectively the business utilizes its assets to generate profits. Declining profitability ratios can indicate weakening operational performance, raising concerns about the borrower's ability to repay the loan.

Solvency ratios assess the borrower's ability to meet its long-term obligations. The debt-to-equity ratio (total debt divided by total equity) reveals the proportion of financing from debt versus equity. A high debt-to-equity ratio indicates high financial leverage, increasing the risk of default. The times interest earned ratio (earnings before interest and taxes

divided by interest expense) measures the borrower's ability to cover its interest obligations. Low solvency ratios indicate a higher risk of default.

Efficiency ratios measure how efficiently the borrower utilizes its assets and manages its operations. Inventory turnover (cost of goods sold divided by average inventory) measures how quickly inventory is sold, and accounts receivable turnover (net credit sales divided by average accounts receivable) indicates the efficiency of collecting receivables. Inefficient operations can lead to reduced profitability and liquidity issues.

While quantitative analysis provides a significant

foundation, qualitative factors are equally important in credit analysis. These include an assessment of the borrower's management team, industry conditions, competitive

Landscape, and overall business strategy. A strong and experienced management team is crucial for successful business operations and debt repayment. Adverse industry trends or intense competition can significantly impact the borrower's financial performance and ability to repay. A well-defined and realistic business plan, clearly outlining strategies for growth and profitability, is also an essential factor in creditworthiness assessment.

In addition to financial statement and ratio analysis, lenders frequently employ cash flow projections to forecast the borrower's future cash flows. This involves creating a

detailed projection of the borrower's expected revenue, expenses, and cash flows over the loan term. These

projections are critical for assessing the borrower's ability to make loan repayments under various scenarios, including potential economic downturns or unforeseen events.

Sophisticated financial modeling software is often employed for this purpose, allowing for sensitivity analysis to test the impact of various assumptions on the projected cash flows. The accuracy and reliability of the projections hinge on the quality of the underlying assumptions and the historical financial data. A well-constructed cash flow projection is a powerful tool for identifying potential risks and

opportunities.

Credit scoring models, often used in conjunction with other analysis techniques, provide a quantitative assessment of creditworthiness. These models use statistical techniques to combine various financial and non-financial factors into a single credit score. While convenient, these scores should not be solely relied upon, as they may not capture the

nuances of individual business situations. They represent merely one piece of the comprehensive credit analysis puzzle.

In summary, effective credit analysis is a multifaceted process requiring a combination of quantitative and qualitative assessment. By thoroughly analyzing financial statements, utilizing ratio analysis, and evaluating qualitative factors, lenders can develop a comprehensive understanding of the borrower's creditworthiness, minimizing risk and facilitating responsible lending decisions. The process is iterative, often requiring further investigation and updates as new information becomes available. A well-executed credit analysis is paramount for success in commercial lending, safeguarding the lender's portfolio and supporting the growth of viable businesses.

Risk Assessment and Mitigation

Having established a robust framework for credit analysis, the next crucial step in commercial lending is a comprehensive risk assessment and mitigation strategy. This involves a multifaceted approach that goes beyond simply evaluating a borrower's financial statements. It encompasses a deeper dive into potential risks, implementing strategies to minimize those risks, and establishing a robust framework for ongoing monitoring and control. This process is iterative, constantly evolving as new information becomes available and market conditions shift.

One of the key tools employed in risk assessment is credit scoring models. These models utilize statistical techniques to combine various financial and non-financial data points into a single credit score, providing a quantitative measure of creditworthiness. While convenient and efficient for processing large volumes of applications, it's crucial to remember that these scores should never be the sole basis for lending decisions. They serve as one piece of a much larger puzzle. The model's limitations must be acknowledged. For instance, a model may not adequately capture the nuances of a unique business situation or account for unforeseen external factors like sudden changes in market demand or regulatory shifts.

Therefore, credit scoring should be supplemented by a thorough qualitative assessment. This includes a detailed review of the borrower's business plan, industry analysis, competitive landscape assessment, and an in-depth evaluation of the management team's experience and expertise. A strong management team with a proven track record is a key indicator of reduced risk. Conversely, a

Poorly conceived business plan, operating in a declining industry, or facing significant competitive pressures, should raise substantial concerns. The qualitative assessment helps contextualize the quantitative data provided by the credit score, revealing a more holistic and accurate picture of the borrower's creditworthiness.

Industry benchmarks play a crucial role in risk assessment. Comparing a borrower's financial performance to industry averages helps establish context and identify potential red flags. Analyzing key financial ratios—such as profitability, liquidity, and solvency ratios—against industry peers allows lenders to quickly identify outliers and potential areas of concern. For example, a borrower with significantly lower profitability margins than their competitors in the same industry might indicate operational inefficiencies or

underlying issues. Conversely, a company consistently exceeding industry averages on key metrics suggests a lower-risk profile. The selection of appropriate industry benchmarks requires careful consideration, ensuring that the comparison is made against truly comparable companies, accounting for factors like company size, geographical location, and business model nuances.

Stress testing is a crucial aspect of risk mitigation in commercial lending. This involves simulating various adverse economic scenarios to assess the borrower's resilience under pressure. This is especially vital in the current volatile global economic landscape. The process usually involves creating multiple scenarios, such as a

sudden economic downturn, a significant increase in interest rates, or a decrease in demand for the borrower's products or services. The lender then analyzes the borrower's financial projections under each scenario to determine the likelihood of loan repayment under stress. Stress testing enables lenders to proactively identify potential weaknesses and

Vulnerabilities in the borrower's financial position. This allows for more informed lending decisions and the implementation of appropriate risk mitigation strategies.

Collateral valuation is another critical component of risk management. In many commercial loans, especially asset-based lending (ABL), the loan is secured by the borrower's assets. Accurate valuation of this collateral is essential to accurately assess the lender's exposure in case of default.

The valuation process should be rigorous and objective, utilizing industry-standard methods and engaging qualified independent valuers when necessary. The type of collateral significantly influences the valuation process. Real estate, for example, requires a different approach than inventory or accounts receivable. The lender must understand the nuances of each asset class and employ appropriate valuation

techniques. Overvaluing collateral can create a false sense of security, potentially masking underlying credit risks.

Conversely, undervaluing collateral could lead to unnecessarily conservative lending practices.

Risk classification is an integral part of a comprehensive risk management framework. This involves categorizing

borrowers and loans based on their inherent risk profiles. This classification aids in portfolio management, allowing lenders to allocate resources effectively and implement appropriate risk mitigation strategies for each risk category. Different risk categories may require different levels of due diligence, monitoring, and collateral requirements. For

instance, a high-risk borrower may require a higher loan-to-value ratio (LTV), more stringent covenants, or additional security. A standardized risk classification system enhances consistency and transparency across the lending process.

Regulatory compliance is paramount in commercial lending. Lenders must adhere to all relevant regulations and

Guidelines, ensuring that their lending practices comply with both local and international laws. This includes meeting all reporting requirements, adhering to responsible lending practices, and maintaining accurate records. Failure to

comply with regulatory requirements can lead to significant penalties and reputational damage. Staying abreast of

regulatory changes is crucial, as regulations are constantly evolving to meet changing market conditions and to ensure the safety and soundness of the financial system. This often necessitates investment in training and technology to manage compliance effectively. A strong compliance framework is not merely a legal obligation but also a cornerstone of

building and maintaining trust with stakeholders.

The implementation of a formal risk management framework is crucial for commercial lenders. Such a framework should encompass a clear definition of risk appetite, a robust risk assessment process, effective risk mitigation strategies, and a well-defined reporting and monitoring system. Regular

review and updates of the risk management framework are essential to ensure its ongoing effectiveness in a constantly evolving economic landscape. The framework should be tailored to the specific characteristics of the lender's

portfolio, taking into account the types of loans offered, the borrower profiles, and prevailing market conditions. The framework should be transparent, readily accessible to all relevant personnel, and subject to regular audits to ensure its integrity and efficacy.

In summary, effective risk assessment and mitigation in commercial lending are not standalone processes but rather integral parts of a holistic approach to responsible lending. By carefully assessing creditworthiness, utilizing various risk mitigation strategies, and implementing robust risk management frameworks, lenders can minimize potential losses, manage their portfolios efficiently, and ensure long-

Term sustainability. This proactive approach safeguards both the lender and the borrower, fostering a healthy and

sustainable lending environment. The evolving nature of risk in the financial landscape necessitates continuous adaptation and refinement of risk management strategies. Staying

informed about emerging risks, refining assessment

methodologies, and embracing technological advancements are essential for success in commercial lending.

Loan Structuring and Documentation

Loan structuring is the art and science of crafting a lending agreement that balances the lender's need for security and return with the borrower's capacity to repay. It's a delicate dance, requiring a deep understanding of both the borrower's business and the legal and regulatory landscape. A poorly structured loan, regardless of the borrower's apparent

creditworthiness, can quickly morph into a costly problem for the lender. Conversely, a well-structured loan facilitates a healthy and mutually beneficial relationship, fostering

economic growth and stability.

The foundation of effective loan structuring lies in a

thorough due diligence process. This goes beyond the

financial statement analysis previously discussed. It

encompasses a comprehensive review of the borrower's business plan, industry analysis, competitive landscape, and management team. The due diligence process should also incorporate a detailed legal review, ensuring compliance with all applicable laws and regulations. This includes scrutinizing the borrower's legal structure, ownership, and any existing liens or encumbrances on their assets.

A key aspect of loan structuring involves defining the loan's terms and conditions. This includes specifying the loan amount, interest rate, repayment schedule, and any collateral securing the loan. The interest rate should reflect the

perceived risk associated with the loan, taking into account factors such as the borrower's creditworthiness, the loan's purpose, and prevailing market interest rates. The repayment schedule should be realistic and tailored to the borrower's cash flow projections. A rigid repayment schedule that doesn't account for seasonal fluctuations in revenue or

Unexpected business downturns can strain the borrower's finances and ultimately lead to default. Flexibility, within reason, can be a valuable asset.

Collateral plays a critical role in mitigating lending risk. The type and value of collateral significantly impact the loan structure. In asset-based lending (ABL), the loan is secured by the borrower's assets, such as inventory, accounts

receivable, or equipment. The lender will require a

comprehensive appraisal of this collateral to accurately determine its market value. The loan-to-value (LTV) ratio, representing the loan amount as a percentage of the

collateral's value, is a crucial determinant of lending risk. A lower LTV ratio indicates less risk for the lender, potentially leading to more favorable loan terms.

Real estate often serves as collateral for commercial real estate loans. The valuation of commercial real estate requires specialized expertise, often involving an independent

appraisal. Factors influencing valuation include location, property condition, market demand, and lease terms. The appraisal process should adhere to industry best practices and utilize appropriate valuation methodologies. A thorough due diligence process is crucial to ensure that the appraisal accurately reflects the property's true market value.

Overvaluation can lead to significant losses for the lender in the event of a default.

Beyond real estate and ABL, other types of collateral can be used, depending on the nature of the business and the

borrower's assets. Intellectual property, such as patents or trademarks, can be used as collateral, although valuation can be complex and requires specialized expertise. Similarly, franchise agreements or licenses can provide security for the loan, but their value depends on the strength of the franchise and the market demand for the franchisee's goods or

Services. The lender must carefully assess the value and enforceability of such collateral.

Loan documentation is the backbone of any successful lending agreement. The documentation should clearly and unambiguously define the terms and conditions of the loan, leaving no room for misinterpretation. It's crucial that the documentation is comprehensive, encompassing all aspects of the loan agreement, including details about repayment schedules, interest rates, fees, and any collateral involved.

The documentation should be legally sound, drafted by experienced legal counsel, and adhere to all applicable laws and regulations. A well-drafted loan agreement protects the lender's interests and minimizes potential disputes.

A key element of loan documentation is the inclusion of covenants. Covenants are specific conditions or restrictions imposed on the borrower that are designed to protect the lender's interests. These covenants can relate to various aspects of the borrower's operations, such as financial

reporting requirements, maintaining certain financial ratios, or restrictions on taking on additional debt. The specific covenants will vary depending on the nature of the loan, the borrower's risk profile, and the lender's risk appetite. Regular monitoring of the borrower's compliance with these

covenants is crucial for the lender to assess the health of the loan and to proactively address any potential issues.

Regulatory compliance is paramount in structuring and documenting commercial loans. Lenders must adhere to all applicable laws and regulations, including those related to consumer protection, fair lending practices, and anti-money laundering (AML) regulations. Failure to comply with these regulations can result in significant financial penalties and reputational damage. Staying informed about the constantly evolving regulatory environment is crucial for lenders to

Avoid legal pitfalls and ensure ethical and compliant lending practices. This necessitates ongoing training for lending staff and investment in compliance technology.

The loan structuring process is not a one-size-fits-all

proposition. The specific structure of each loan should be tailored to the unique circumstances of the borrower and the risk profile of the loan. This necessitates a thorough

understanding of the borrower's business model, its financial position, and the industry in which it operates. Furthermore, the lender's risk tolerance and the prevailing market

conditions must be considered. The loan structure should be flexible enough to adapt to unforeseen circumstances, but robust enough to protect the lender's interests.

In practice, loan structuring often involves negotiation

between the lender and the borrower. The lender aims to minimize risk and maximize return, while the borrower seeks the most favorable terms possible. This negotiation requires a balanced approach, acknowledging the legitimate interests of both parties. A successful outcome is one that benefits both parties and leads to a mutually beneficial, long-term relationship. A fair and transparent negotiation process builds trust and lays the groundwork for a successful lending partnership.

Effective loan structuring and documentation are critical for success in commercial lending. It's a process that requires expertise in finance, law, and risk management. By

meticulously planning the loan's structure, and meticulously documenting all terms and conditions, lenders can

significantly reduce their exposure to risk, safeguard their investments, and facilitate the growth and prosperity of their borrowers. A well-structured loan is a mutually beneficial arrangement, a cornerstone of a healthy and sustainable financial ecosystem. Neglecting this crucial aspect can have

Severe consequences, underscoring the importance of

prioritizing thoroughness and attention to detail throughout the entire lending process. The continuous evolution of the financial landscape requires lenders to stay abreast of

changes in regulations and best practices, ensuring that their loan structuring strategies remain current and effective.

Regulatory and Compliance Landscape

The regulatory landscape governing commercial lending is intricate and constantly evolving. Navigating this complex terrain requires a deep understanding of applicable laws and regulations, coupled with a commitment to maintaining unwavering compliance. Failure to do so can result in

significant financial penalties, reputational damage, and even criminal prosecution. This section delves into the key

regulatory areas that lenders must navigate, providing

practical guidance for ensuring compliance and mitigating potential risks.

One of the most crucial areas of regulatory concern is fair lending. Fair lending laws prohibit discrimination in lending based on factors such as race, color, religion, national origin, sex, marital status, age, or the receipt of public assistance.

These laws aim to ensure that all borrowers have equal access to credit, regardless of their protected characteristics.

Lenders must implement robust systems to prevent

discriminatory practices, including thorough training for loan officers, standardized lending criteria, and ongoing

monitoring for potential bias in lending decisions. The

consequences of violating fair lending laws can be severe, including substantial fines, legal action, and reputational damage that can severely impact a lender's ability to operate effectively. For example, a lender found to have

systematically denied loans to applicants from a particular ethnic group could face millions of dollars in fines, civil lawsuits, and a lasting negative impact on its public image.

Beyond fair lending, lenders must also comply with

regulations related to consumer protection. These regulations aim to safeguard borrowers from unfair or deceptive lending

Practices. This includes provisions requiring lenders to provide clear and concise disclosures to borrowers regarding loan terms, interest rates, fees, and other relevant information. Lenders must ensure that all loan documents are easily understandable and free of misleading or deceptive language. Regulations also typically mandate specific procedures for handling loan defaults, foreclosures, and other collection activities. Failure to comply with consumer protection laws can expose lenders to lawsuits, fines, and damage to their reputation. For instance, a lender failing to provide accurate information about loan terms or engaging in aggressive collection tactics could face significant penalties and litigation.

Anti-money laundering (AML) regulations are another critical aspect of the regulatory landscape for commercial lenders. These regulations aim to prevent the use of the financial system for illicit activities, such as drug trafficking, terrorism financing, and other forms of criminal enterprise. Lenders are required to implement robust AML compliance programs, including customer due diligence (CDD) procedures, transaction monitoring systems, and suspicious activity reporting (SAR) protocols. CDD involves verifying the identity of borrowers and understanding the nature of their businesses. Transaction monitoring involves analyzing loan transactions for unusual activity that may indicate money laundering. SAR involves reporting suspicious activity to the appropriate authorities. Non-compliance with AML regulations can result in significant fines, criminal charges, and reputational harm. A lender caught facilitating money laundering could face severe penalties, including hefty fines, license revocation, and criminal prosecution of its officers.

The regulatory environment surrounding commercial lending extends beyond these core areas. Lenders must also comply

With regulations related to data privacy and security, truth in lending, and various other state and federal laws depending on their lending activities and the types of loans offered. Staying abreast of these constantly evolving regulations is a continuous challenge. Lenders need to invest heavily in compliance infrastructure, which includes dedicated

compliance personnel, comprehensive training programs for employees, and sophisticated software systems to track and monitor compliance. This proactive approach minimizes the risk of non-compliance and strengthens the lender's ability to effectively manage its operations and reputation.

Furthermore, regulators frequently conduct examinations and audits to ensure compliance with all applicable laws and regulations. These examinations can be extensive and

rigorous, involving a comprehensive review of the lender's lending practices, compliance programs, and internal

controls. Preparing for these examinations requires

meticulous record-keeping, accurate documentation, and a thorough understanding of regulatory requirements. A well-structured compliance program demonstrates to regulators a lender's commitment to ethical and legal operations.

Conversely, shortcomings in a lender's compliance

infrastructure can trigger costly investigations, fines, and remediation efforts.

The consequences of regulatory non-compliance can be devastating for commercial lenders. Beyond the financial penalties, reputational damage can significantly hinder a lender's ability to attract new business, maintain existing relationships with clients and investors, and operate

effectively in the market. A strong reputation for compliance is essential for maintaining public trust and fostering a stable and sustainable business.

Effective compliance strategies go beyond simply reacting to regulatory changes. They involve a proactive approach to risk management, a commitment to ethical lending practices, and a robust internal control structure designed to prevent and detect compliance failures. Regular training, ongoing monitoring of regulatory changes, and independent audits are key components of a successful compliance program. This constant vigilance is not just about avoiding penalties; it is about safeguarding the integrity of the lending process, building a strong and trustworthy reputation, and

contributing to a stable and efficient financial system. By proactively embracing the requirements of the regulatory landscape, lenders build a foundation of stability and success in the dynamic world of commercial finance.

ABL Structures and Mechanisms

Asset-based lending (ABL) offers a flexible range of financing structures tailored to a borrower's specific needs and asset profile. Understanding these structures is crucial for both lenders and borrowers to ensure a successful and mutually beneficial arrangement. Three primary structures dominate the ABL landscape: borrowing base loans, revolving credit facilities, and term loans secured by assets.

Each possesses unique characteristics, advantages, and disadvantages that must be carefully considered.

Borrowing base loans are arguably the most common ABL structure. The loan amount is directly tied to the value of the borrower's eligible assets, often inventory, accounts receivable, or machinery and equipment. This "borrowing base" is regularly reviewed and adjusted to reflect fluctuations in asset values. A lender will typically assign a certain percentage of the eligible asset value as the available borrowing limit. For example, a lender might advance 70% of the value of eligible inventory and 85% of the value of eligible accounts receivable. This percentage, known as the advance rate, is determined by various factors, including the quality and liquidity of the assets, the borrower's creditworthiness, and market conditions. The lender will regularly conduct asset monitoring and valuation to ensure the loan remains adequately collateralized. The advantage of this structure is its flexibility. As the borrower's business fluctuates, so too can the borrowing capacity, offering a dynamic financing solution. However, this also presents a potential disadvantage: if asset values decline, the borrower's available credit line may be reduced, potentially leading to liquidity constraints if not properly managed. A further complication arises in determining the appropriate

Valuation methodology for different asset types. Inventory valuation, for example, may utilize cost, market, or net realizable value, each with its own complexities and

potential for dispute. Finally, the ongoing monitoring and valuation requirements can introduce administrative

overhead for both the lender and the borrower.

Revolving credit facilities provide borrowers with a readily available line of credit that can be drawn upon and repaid multiple times during the loan term. Similar to borrowing base loans, the credit limit is often linked to the value of the borrower's assets, though it may also incorporate other

factors, such as the borrower's cash flow. This structure provides significant liquidity and flexibility, allowing

businesses to manage short-term working capital needs effectively. For instance, a seasonal business experiencing a surge in demand could easily draw on the facility to fund increased inventory purchases or operational expenses. Once demand subsides, the borrower can repay the drawn amount and continue to utilize the remaining credit as needed. This structure is particularly advantageous for businesses with predictable but fluctuating operational cycles. However, revolving credit facilities typically come with higher interest rates and fees than term loans due to the inherent flexibility and ongoing monitoring requirements. Furthermore, lenders may impose covenants restricting the borrower's ability to incur additional debt or undertake significant capital

expenditures. These covenants, while protecting the lender's interests, can limit the borrower's operational flexibility. The ongoing interest payments can also represent a significant cost, particularly during periods of low utilization. Careful consideration must therefore be given to the potential cost of unused credit.

Term loans secured by assets provide financing for a specific purpose and a defined period, usually longer than revolving

Credit facilities. The repayment schedule is typically

amortized over the loan term, with regular installments of principal and interest. This structure is well-suited for

financing larger capital expenditures or long-term projects. For example, a manufacturing company might utilize a term loan secured by its plant and equipment to purchase new machinery. The stability and predictability of the repayment schedule are attractive to borrowers, providing a clear

financial roadmap. However, the rigid repayment terms may present a challenge for businesses experiencing unexpected financial difficulties. The longer-term nature of the loan also increases the risk for the lender, necessitating a more

thorough due diligence process and a potentially higher interest rate. Similarly, the fixed nature of the loan's terms may not be ideal for businesses facing unpredictable revenue streams or significant operational changes. Further

complicating matters is the potential for asset depreciation over the loan term. While the loan is secured by the assets, the value of those assets could decrease, increasing the

lender's risk.

Choosing the appropriate ABL structure requires a thorough understanding of the borrower's specific needs and

circumstances. Factors to consider include the borrower's asset profile, the intended use of funds, the borrower's

financial strength, and the length of financing required. For example, a rapidly growing company with a significant amount of liquid assets might be best served by a borrowing base loan or a revolving credit facility offering high

flexibility. Conversely, a mature company with a need for long-term capital investment might find a term loan more suitable. A comprehensive analysis of the borrower's

financial statements, including cash flow projections, is crucial in making this determination.

The selection process extends beyond simple financial considerations. The lender's risk appetite and internal lending policies must also play a significant role. Different lenders have varying risk tolerances and may favor particular ABL structures over others. Some lenders may have specialized expertise in certain asset classes, influencing their preferred structure. Ultimately, the optimal ABL structure is the one that best balances the needs of the borrower with the risk appetite and capabilities of the lender.

Beyond the core structures outlined above, hybrid structures are increasingly common, combining aspects of borrowing base loans, revolving credit facilities, and term loans to meet the specific requirements of complex transactions. These hybrid structures often involve multiple tranches of financing, each with its own terms and conditions, allowing for a more customized financing solution. For instance, a borrower might secure a revolving credit facility for working capital needs alongside a term loan for a significant capital expenditure, leveraging the strengths of both structures. The complexity of these hybrid arrangements necessitates careful negotiation and a deep understanding of the underlying principles governing each component of the structure.

Experienced legal and financial counsel are often required to navigate the nuances of these sophisticated financial instruments.

Successful ABL transactions rely heavily on transparent and effective communication between the lender and the borrower. Regular reporting on asset values, financial performance, and compliance with loan covenants is crucial in maintaining a healthy lending relationship. Proactive communication can help identify and mitigate potential risks early on, preventing crises and ensuring the continued success of the financing arrangement. This collaborative approach reinforces the mutually beneficial nature of ABL,

Where both parties share an interest in the borrower's success and the long-term viability of the financing agreement. The proactive monitoring of both the borrower's financial

performance and the value of the underlying assets is key to mitigating potential risks for both parties.

In conclusion, the selection of an appropriate ABL structure is a crucial element in securing successful financing. The decision should be a carefully considered process involving a thorough analysis of the borrower's financial profile, the nature of their assets, and the specific financing needs. The choice between a borrowing base loan, a revolving credit facility, a term loan, or a hybrid structure depends on a

multitude of interacting factors. The ongoing relationship between lender and borrower, characterized by transparent communication and proactive risk management, is equally crucial in ensuring the long-term success of the arrangement. A well-structured ABL agreement, coupled with responsible financial management by the borrower, forms the bedrock of a robust and beneficial financing partnership. The dynamic nature of the ABL market underscores the need for both lenders and borrowers to stay informed of evolving market trends and regulatory changes. The ability to adapt to these changes is essential in maintaining a sustainable and

productive relationship within the ABL landscape.

Collateral Evaluation and Management

Collateral evaluation is the cornerstone of any successful asset-based lending (ABL) transaction. The lender's ability to accurately assess and monitor the value of the borrower's assets directly impacts the loan's risk profile and the overall viability of the financing arrangement. The process is far from standardized, however, necessitating a nuanced

approach tailored to the specific characteristics of each asset class. This requires a deep understanding of valuation

methodologies, market conditions, and the borrower's

operational environment.

For inventory, the most common valuation methods include cost, market, and net realizable value. The cost method, as its name suggests, uses the historical cost of the inventory, adjusted for any subsequent write-downs. This approach is relatively straightforward but can be less accurate when inventory values fluctuate significantly. The market method, on the other hand, uses the current market price of similar inventory items. This is suitable for standardized, readily traded goods, but less so for specialized or customized inventory where comparable market data might be scarce. Finally, the net realizable value (NRV) method estimates the inventory's selling price less any associated costs of sale and disposal. This approach is generally favored by lenders as it reflects the actual value the inventory is expected to

generate, providing a more conservative estimate.

The selection of the appropriate valuation method depends on factors such as the inventory's nature, its liquidity, and the availability of reliable market data. For example, a retailer selling mass-produced consumer goods might use the market method, while a manufacturer with highly specialized

Components might opt for the NRV method. Lenders often require detailed inventory records, including item-level descriptions, costs, and quantities. Regular physical

inspections and independent audits may also be necessary to verify the accuracy of the inventory data and to ensure that the collateral remains adequately insured. The lender might even impose restrictions on inventory management practices such as minimum stock levels to minimize obsolescence risk.

Accounts receivable, another major component of ABL collateral, require a different valuation approach. The most common method focuses on the estimated amount that will be collected from outstanding invoices. Several factors influence this estimation, including the age of the

receivables, the creditworthiness of the debtors, and the industry's typical payment terms. Lenders often utilize aging schedules to categorize receivables based on their due dates, assigning different percentages to reflect the probability of collection for each category. Older receivables are typically assigned lower collection percentages, reflecting a higher risk of non-payment.

Further complicating matters is the presence of potential disputes or write-offs. Lenders will thoroughly review the borrower's credit and collection policies, examining the history of bad debts and customer payment patterns. The borrower may be required to provide detailed customer credit reports and evidence of proactive collection efforts.

The lender will typically impose restrictions on the

borrower's ability to extend credit to high-risk customers and may require the borrower to utilize credit insurance to

mitigate potential losses. The analysis extends beyond

simply aging schedules; sophisticated credit scoring models and predictive analytics can offer valuable insight.

Equipment and machinery represent a third significant asset class used as collateral in ABL. Their valuation typically involves a combination of approaches, factoring in the age, condition, and remaining useful life of the assets. Common methods include appraisals by independent experts, market comparison using similar used equipment sales, and the use of depreciation schedules. The condition of the equipment is crucial, affecting the assessed value and the lender's

willingness to offer a high advance rate. Regular

maintenance records, certifications, and inspections are essential to verify the equipment's operability and to assess its residual value. Depreciation schedules, while providing a standardized method, often need to be adjusted for specific circumstances based on factors such as obsolescence.

For specialized equipment with unique specifications,

finding comparable market data is challenging, making expert appraisals crucial. These appraisals consider factors like technological advancements, obsolescence risk, and the potential for future upgrades or modifications. The lender should always verify the legitimacy of appraisals through established valuation professionals and should ensure that the valuation methodology is in line with industry standards.

Beyond the specific valuation methods for each asset class, effective collateral management is equally crucial.

Maintaining accurate and readily accessible collateral records is essential for both the borrower and the lender.

These records should include detailed descriptions of the assets, their current market value, and any associated liens or encumbrances. Regular updates to these records are

necessary to account for changes in asset values, additions or deletions of assets, and any significant events affecting the assets' condition.

A robust collateral management system should also include mechanisms for monitoring the assets' physical condition and safeguarding against loss or damage. This may involve regular physical inspections, insurance policies, and security measures to protect the assets from theft or vandalism. In cases involving inventory, robust inventory management systems are critical, minimizing obsolescence and ensuring that the collateral remains adequately insured and protected.

Early detection of potential problems, such as damage to equipment or deterioration of inventory, allows for timely intervention to mitigate potential losses. Proactive

management also extends to the relationships with suppliers and customers; consistent, transparent communication can significantly impact the lender's ability to assess risk.

A sophisticated system also includes contingency plans for scenarios where collateral values decline or assets become impaired. This may involve implementing strategies such as accelerated collections, disposal of excess inventory, or negotiations with the borrower to strengthen their financial position. The goal is to minimize losses while preserving the ongoing viability of the financing relationship.

Case studies further highlight the importance of accurate collateral evaluation. A company specialized in the import and export of perishable goods experienced a sharp drop in inventory value due to a sudden market downturn.

Inadequate collateral evaluation and poor risk management left the lender with substantial losses when the company defaulted on its loan. In another instance, a manufacturer's failure to maintain proper equipment maintenance records led to inaccurate valuation and an underestimation of the equipment's depreciation, resulting in insufficient collateral to cover the loan. These examples demonstrate the need for lenders to implement rigorous evaluation and monitoring

Processes, focusing on both the asset's intrinsic value and the borrower's management capabilities.

Effective collateral management in ABL necessitates a proactive approach that combines rigorous valuation methodologies with stringent monitoring procedures.

Regular communication, transparent reporting, and a shared understanding of the risks involved between lender and borrower are paramount. The ultimate aim is to create a sustainable financing arrangement that protects the lender's interests while supporting the borrower's growth and

success. This ongoing dialogue and cooperative risk

management form the bedrock of a successful ABL

transaction. Failure in this critical area can lead to significant losses for the lender and financial distress for the borrower.

ABL Risk Management Strategies

Effective risk management is not merely a supplementary aspect of asset-based lending (ABL); it's the very foundation upon which successful and sustainable financing rests. While meticulous collateral evaluation, as discussed previously, forms the bedrock of ABL, it's only one piece of a significantly larger puzzle. A comprehensive risk management strategy encompasses a multifaceted approach, integrating advanced analytical tools, adherence to industry best practices, and strict compliance with regulatory requirements. Failure to adopt such a holistic approach can expose lenders to significant losses and jeopardize the entire financing arrangement.

One of the most crucial elements of ABL risk management is the continuous monitoring of borrower performance. This transcends simply reviewing financial statements; it involves a proactive and dynamic process of assessing various key performance indicators (kpis). These kpis can vary depending on the nature of the borrower's business, but they typically include metrics such as sales revenue, operating margins, inventory turnover, days sales outstanding (DSO), and debt service coverage ratio (DSCR). Regular monitoring of these kpis provides early warning signals of potential problems, allowing lenders to intervene proactively before situations escalate into major crises. For example, a consistent decline in sales revenue or a sharp increase in DSO might indicate weakening demand or deteriorating credit quality among the borrower's customers, both of which represent significant red flags.

Beyond basic financial ratios, lenders increasingly leverage advanced analytical tools to gain a deeper understanding of

Borrower risk. Sophisticated credit scoring models,

incorporating both quantitative and qualitative data, can provide a more nuanced assessment of creditworthiness than traditional methods. These models can incorporate factors such as the borrower's industry dynamics, competitive

landscape, and management expertise, leading to a more accurate prediction of default risk. Moreover, predictive analytics, utilizing machine learning algorithms and

historical data, can identify patterns and trends that might not be apparent through traditional financial analysis. These tools can forecast potential problems, providing valuable insights that enable lenders to make more informed decisions regarding loan structuring, pricing, and risk mitigation

strategies.

The application of these advanced tools, however, should not overshadow the importance of qualitative analysis. A

thorough understanding of the borrower's business model, operational efficiency, and management team is crucial. On-site visits, discussions with key personnel, and detailed industry research are essential to complement the

quantitative analysis. A skilled lender will not simply rely on numbers; they will seek to understand the context

surrounding those numbers, investigating potential risks and opportunities that might not be reflected in the financial statements.

Effective ABL risk management also necessitates stringent credit risk management practices. This includes a thorough due diligence process at the outset of the lending

relationship, involving a comprehensive review of the

borrower's financial history, credit reports, and legal

documentation. The lender should establish clear lending covenants and conditions to ensure that the borrower

maintains adequate financial health and adherence to agreed-upon terms. Regular reviews of these covenants are crucial,

Ensuring that they remain relevant and appropriate

throughout the life of the loan. The lender should establish clear triggers for increased monitoring or intervention, providing a structured response to escalating risks.

Managing the credit risk associated with ABL also involves actively mitigating potential losses. This can entail various strategies, including requiring adequate collateral coverage, imposing restrictions on the borrower's ability to incur

additional debt, and implementing appropriate insurance policies. Credit insurance, specifically, can significantly mitigate the risk of non-payment from accounts receivable. The lender might also insist on regular independent audits of the borrower's financial statements, ensuring the accuracy and reliability of the information provided. This combination of preventive measures and loss mitigation strategies forms a critical component of a robust ABL risk management

framework.

Regulatory compliance is another vital aspect of ABL risk management. Lenders must adhere to all applicable laws and regulations, which can vary depending on the jurisdiction and the nature of the transaction. This involves maintaining accurate and complete records, conducting thorough Know Your Customer (KYC) and Anti-Money Laundering (AML) checks, and complying with all relevant reporting

requirements. Failure to comply with these regulations can result in significant financial penalties and reputational damage. Staying abreast of evolving regulatory requirements is crucial for any ABL lender, demanding continuous

professional development and diligent internal compliance programs.

Furthermore, effective ABL risk management extends

beyond the individual loan level; it necessitates a broader consideration of portfolio risk. Lenders should diversify their

Loan portfolio across various industries and borrower types, mitigating the risk associated with concentration in any single sector. This strategic approach ensures that a

downturn in one sector doesn't disproportionately impact the lender's overall portfolio. Regular portfolio stress testing, simulating various economic scenarios, is crucial to assess the portfolio's resilience against unforeseen events. This helps in proactively identifying vulnerabilities and

implementing corrective actions.

Real-world scenarios underscore the critical importance of robust risk management in ABL. Consider a case involving a construction company that leveraged its inventory of

building materials and accounts receivable as collateral for an ABL facility. Due to a sudden downturn in the

construction sector, the value of the inventory declined

sharply and collections on accounts receivable slowed.

Because the lender lacked a comprehensive monitoring system and did not anticipate the industry downturn, they were caught off guard. The inadequate risk management left the lender with substantial losses when the construction company defaulted. Conversely, a well-managed ABL transaction would have incorporated monitoring of industry trends, regular reviews of the borrower's kpis, and

potentially, early intervention strategies to mitigate losses.

Another instructive scenario involved a manufacturing

company using its equipment as collateral. The lender,

relying solely on the borrower's provided depreciation

schedules, did not conduct independent assessments of the equipment's condition or market value. This oversight led to an inaccurate valuation of the collateral, significantly

underestimating the risk of default. A diligent lender would have independently verified the equipment's condition and market value, potentially employing independent appraisals to ensure the accuracy of the collateral valuation. This would

Have provided a more accurate risk assessment and informed better lending decisions. These examples highlight the

consequences of inadequate risk management and emphasize the need for a proactive and multifaceted approach.

In conclusion, effective ABL risk management is a

continuous process that demands vigilance, expertise, and a proactive approach. It's not a checklist to be completed but rather a dynamic system that adapts to changing

circumstances and leverages advanced analytical tools to mitigate potential losses. By combining rigorous monitoring of borrower performance, stringent credit risk management, strict regulatory compliance, and a holistic approach to portfolio risk, lenders can significantly reduce their exposure to defaults and maintain a strong and sustainable ABL

business. The cost of failing to implement such a

comprehensive risk management system significantly

outweighs the effort required to implement and maintain one, ultimately ensuring both the lender's and the borrower's financial well-being.

ABL Loan Documentation and Compliance

The bedrock of any successful asset-based lending (ABL) transaction lies not only in meticulous risk assessment but also in the comprehensive and meticulously crafted loan documentation. This documentation serves as the legal contract governing the entire lending relationship, outlining the rights and responsibilities of both the lender and the borrower. A poorly drafted or incomplete agreement can lead to significant legal disputes, financial losses, and reputational damage for all parties involved. Therefore, the creation and negotiation of ABL loan documentation require a high degree of legal expertise and a thorough understanding of the intricacies of ABL transactions.

The core components of ABL loan documentation typically include a comprehensive loan agreement, security agreements, borrowing base certificates, and various other supporting documents. The loan agreement itself forms the foundational legal contract, detailing the terms and conditions of the loan, including the amount of credit extended, the interest rate, the repayment schedule, and any other relevant financial covenants. It is crucial that this agreement be unambiguous and precisely worded to avoid any potential misunderstandings or disagreements down the line. A clear and comprehensive loan agreement will minimize the risk of litigation, offering a solid framework for the loan's execution and repayment.

Security agreements are equally crucial, defining the collateral pledged by the borrower to secure the loan. In ABL, this collateral typically consists of accounts receivable, inventory, equipment, or other assets. The security agreement must clearly describe the collateral, its location,

And the lender's rights to seize and sell the collateral in the event of default. Precision in defining the collateral is

paramount; ambiguity could lead to disputes about the extent of the lender's security interest. This meticulousness extends to ensuring the agreement covers all potential collateral, including any after-acquired assets generated during the loan term. The inclusion of after-acquired property clauses

prevents disputes should the borrower acquire new assets relevant to the loan's purpose.

Borrowing base certificates are critical instruments in ABL transactions, providing a periodic assessment of the

borrower's eligible collateral. These certificates, often

prepared by independent accountants or specialists, provide a detailed evaluation of the borrower's accounts receivable and inventory, determining the amount of credit available under the lending facility. The frequency of these

certifications is typically determined within the loan

agreement, usually reflecting a balance between managing risk and the borrower's operational capacity. The process of calculating the borrowing base often entails adhering to specific industry standards and methodologies, ensuring consistency and transparency. Any deviations from the standard approach must be clearly documented and justified.

The use of standardized templates for these certificates minimizes ambiguity and aids consistency across multiple transactions.

Beyond these core documents, ABL loan documentation typically includes a range of supporting agreements and schedules, such as personal guarantees from the borrower's principals, collateral management agreements, insurance policies, and financial statements. The scope and complexity of these additional documents depend on the particular circumstances of each loan and the risk profile of the

borrower. For instance, in high-risk transactions, the lender

May require more comprehensive insurance coverage or stricter financial reporting requirements.

The drafting and negotiation of ABL loan documentation is a complex and iterative process, demanding a deep

understanding of both legal and financial principles.

Experienced banking professionals play a vital role in

ensuring that the documentation accurately reflects the terms of the transaction, protects the interests of the lender, and complies with all applicable laws and regulations. This process goes beyond merely filling out pre-printed forms; it requires skillful negotiation between the lender and the borrower to achieve a mutually agreeable outcome that effectively manages risks while simultaneously facilitating a healthy business relationship. This process often involves multiple revisions and back-and-forth communication

between legal counsel for both parties.

Compliance with relevant laws and regulations is a critical aspect of ABL loan documentation. Lenders must ensure that all aspects of the loan, from the initial underwriting to the final repayment, comply with applicable federal and state laws, as well as any industry-specific regulations. Non-compliance can result in significant penalties, ranging from financial fines to legal action and reputational damage. The consequences of non-compliance can be severely

detrimental, potentially eroding investor confidence and harming the lender's financial health. Staying current on regulatory changes is therefore an ongoing and vital

responsibility for any ABL lender. Dedicated compliance departments often manage this ongoing challenge, ensuring that lenders remain up to date with any amendments or new legislation.

Specific regulatory considerations are varied and include, but are not limited to, Truth in Lending Act (TILA)

Compliance for consumer loans, Fair Credit Reporting Act (FCRA) adherence for credit reporting practices, and state-specific usury laws regarding permissible interest rates.

These, along with the often-complex and evolving

requirements surrounding anti-money laundering (AML) and Know Your Customer (KYC) regulations, need meticulous attention. The consequences of failing to fulfill these

compliance requirements extend beyond financial penalties to include potentially severe reputational harm and damage to customer relationships.

One crucial aspect of ABL loan documentation involves the definition of events of default. These are specific

circumstances that, upon occurrence, allow the lender to accelerate the loan, demand immediate repayment, and exercise its rights over the pledged collateral. These events of default are often tailored to the specifics of each loan and may include such factors as the borrower's failure to make timely payments, a significant decline in the value of the collateral, material breaches of financial covenants, or

instances of bankruptcy or insolvency. Clearly defining these default events mitigates the potential for disputes in the event of a borrower default. The language used must be clear, unambiguous and easily interpretable to minimize the chance of later conflict.

Another critical element in ABL loan documentation is the precise articulation of the lender's remedies upon default. These remedies might include the right to seize and sell the collateral, file lawsuits for the recovery of outstanding debt, or pursue other legal actions to recoup losses. The

documentation must clearly delineate the procedures and processes the lender will follow in the event of a default, minimizing potential disputes and ensuring a fair and

transparent process. This clarity also assists in preserving the lender's reputation within the industry. In practice, a

Carefully considered default process minimizes the disruption and uncertainty for both the borrower and the lender.

The legal ramifications of poor or inadequate ABL loan documentation can be severe, leading to protracted and costly legal battles. Ambiguity, incompleteness, or inconsistencies in the documentation can create fertile ground for disputes over the terms of the loan, the value of the collateral, or the lender's rights upon default. Such disputes not only consume considerable time and resources but also can significantly impair the lender's ability to effectively recover its debt, potentially leading to substantial financial losses. The cost of litigation extends beyond legal fees to encompass the expense of delayed debt recovery and potential reputational harm.

In conclusion, the meticulous crafting and thorough negotiation of ABL loan documentation are indispensable aspects of a successful ABL transaction. The clarity, completeness, and compliance with relevant regulations are not mere formalities; they are critical safeguards that protect the interests of both the lender and the borrower. By employing experienced legal counsel and adhering to best practices, lenders can mitigate the potential for disputes and ensure a smooth and efficient lending process. The investment in comprehensive and well-drafted documentation far outweighs the potential costs associated with poor documentation, ultimately contributing to the stability and success of the ABL market.

Case Studies in Successful ABL Transactions

This section delves into specific examples of successful asset-based lending (ABL) transactions, providing concrete illustrations of the principles discussed earlier. These case studies highlight best practices in originating, structuring, and managing ABL loans, offering valuable insights for lenders navigating the complexities of this specialized

financing arena. Each example will focus on distinct aspects of a successful transaction, emphasizing the crucial role of thorough due diligence, robust loan documentation, and proactive risk management.

Our first case study involves a mid-sized manufacturing company, "Precision Parts Inc.", experiencing rapid growth but facing limitations in accessing traditional bank financing.

Their existing lines of credit were insufficient to support their expanding production needs and burgeoning order book. Precision Parts possessed substantial inventory and a strong history of on-time collections from its accounts

receivable. Recognizing this, a specialized ABL lender

conducted a thorough assessment of their assets, including detailed inventory valuations and an analysis of the aging of their receivables. This due diligence process identified a robust and reliable borrowing base. The lender subsequently structured a revolving credit facility secured by the

company's inventory and accounts receivable. Crucially, the loan documentation meticulously defined the borrowing base methodology, ensuring transparency and minimizing

potential disputes. The agreement also included clear

covenants regarding financial reporting and maintenance of appropriate insurance coverage. This transparent and well-structured approach fostered a strong lender-borrower

relationship, enabling Precision Parts to secure the necessary

Funding to meet their growth objectives. The regular

reporting and consistent communication between lender and borrower facilitated early detection of potential issues, allowing for proactive adjustments to the credit line and risk mitigation strategies. This case demonstrates the

effectiveness of a collaborative approach, emphasizing the importance of a clearly defined borrowing base and

proactive communication in fostering successful ABL

transactions. The loan was successfully repaid ahead of schedule, underscoring the borrower's financial strength and the effectiveness of the ABL facility.

In contrast, our second case study showcases the advantages of ABL in a more challenging environment. "Coastal

Distribution," a company operating in the highly volatile seafood industry, experienced a significant disruption to its supply chain due to an unforeseen environmental event. While their accounts receivable were historically strong, the immediate impact on their inventory significantly reduced their traditional borrowing capacity. A conventional lender would likely have curtailed or withdrawn credit, potentially forcing Coastal Distribution into insolvency. However,

through a well-structured ABL facility, Coastal Distribution secured financing based on the robust nature of their existing receivables. The ABL lender, understanding the industry's volatility, incorporated flexibility into the loan agreement, allowing for adjustments to the borrowing base calculation in response to the temporary inventory shortfall. This

flexibility, coupled with a strong focus on consistent

reporting and open communication, allowed the lender to monitor the evolving situation and adjust its risk assessment accordingly. The lender also leveraged its expertise in the industry to provide valuable insight and support to Coastal Distribution during this challenging period, helping them to navigate the supply chain disruptions and to secure

alternative sourcing channels. The successful navigation of

This crisis demonstrates the resilience and adaptability of ABL in managing unexpected events. The lender's

understanding of the specific industry challenges, combined with the flexibility of the loan structure, proved crucial to the survival and eventual recovery of Coastal Distribution. This exemplifies the benefit of choosing an ABL lender with industry expertise and the ability to adapt to unforeseen circumstances.

Our third case study examines the importance of proactive risk management in an ABL transaction. "Tech Solutions LLC," a rapidly growing software development firm,

secured an ABL facility to finance its operations. While their accounts receivable showed strong growth, the lender

identified a potential risk in their reliance on a limited

number of major clients. The lender proactively addressed this risk by incorporating clauses in the loan agreement requiring diversification of their client base and setting

minimum levels of receivable concentration. Regular

monitoring of these key risk indicators, coupled with

ongoing dialogue about the company's business strategy, allowed the lender to monitor progress and take necessary actions if needed. The agreement also included a detailed description of events of default related to client

concentration, giving the lender clear mechanisms for

managing potential risk. This meticulous approach to risk assessment and mitigation, embedded within the loan

documentation and the lender-borrower relationship, proved vital in securing the long-term success of the financing. This case emphasizes the benefits of proactive risk management, highlighting how a well-structured ABL facility can address potential vulnerabilities and protect both the lender and the borrower. The successful outcome underscores the

importance of a collaborative approach that integrates risk assessment into the ongoing management of the loan.

A fourth example illustrates the significance of accurate and timely financial reporting in maintaining a healthy ABL relationship. "Green Energy Solutions," a renewable energy company, used an ABL facility to fund the purchase of

specialized equipment. The loan agreement included strict financial reporting requirements, with regular submissions of audited financial statements and detailed borrowing base certificates. This transparency allowed the lender to closely monitor the borrower's financial performance, enabling prompt identification and management of potential issues before they escalated into major problems. The consistent and accurate reporting facilitated a smooth and efficient lending process, strengthening the trust and confidence between lender and borrower. The emphasis on transparent and accurate reporting underscores the critical role of

detailed documentation and regular communication in

maintaining the integrity and sustainability of an ABL

relationship. This case highlights the benefits of strong

financial governance and the importance of establishing clear expectations for reporting requirements from the outset of the transaction. The smooth repayment of the loan

demonstrated the success of this collaborative approach, emphasizing the value of transparency and mutual

accountability.

These case studies demonstrate the versatility and

effectiveness of ABL financing across diverse industries and circumstances. The successful outcomes highlight the

significance of careful due diligence, comprehensive loan documentation, proactive risk management, and open

communication between lender and borrower. The lessons learned from these examples are valuable for all parties involved in ABL transactions, reinforcing the importance of a structured and collaborative approach to ensure successful outcomes and foster long-term, mutually beneficial

partnerships. By understanding these best practices and

Adapting them to specific circumstances, lenders can

effectively mitigate risks and maximize the benefits of this specialized form of financing, while simultaneously

supporting the growth and stability of their client base. The consistent theme across all these examples is the crucial interplay between a thorough understanding of the

borrower's business, a well-structured loan agreement, and proactive monitoring to ensure a positive outcome for all involved. The future of ABL rests on the ability to continue to refine these best practices, adapting them to an evolving financial landscape and leveraging technology to enhance efficiency and risk mitigation.

Developing a Proactive Crisis Management Plan

Developing a robust crisis management plan is not merely a compliance exercise; it's a strategic imperative for any lending institution, especially those heavily involved in commercial and asset-based lending. The inherent risks within these sectors—economic downturns, sudden market shifts, borrower defaults, and unforeseen events like natural disasters—demand a proactive and comprehensive approach to crisis management. A well-defined plan mitigates potential losses, protects the institution's reputation, and ensures business continuity.

The first step in developing a proactive crisis management plan is a thorough risk assessment. This involves identifying potential threats that could significantly impact the lending institution's operations and financial stability. This should not be a superficial exercise; it demands a deep dive into various aspects of the business. Consider both internal and external factors. Internal risks might include weaknesses in internal controls, inadequate technology infrastructure, or a lack of skilled personnel in key areas like credit risk management or legal compliance. External risks, on the other hand, could encompass macroeconomic factors such as interest rate hikes, inflation, or recessionary pressures.

Industry-specific risks also need careful consideration. For example, in asset-based lending, a significant drop in commodity prices could impact the collateral value of inventory-based loans, triggering a cascade of potential problems. Similarly, a sudden change in government regulations or a major geopolitical event could disrupt supply chains and negatively affect borrower performance.

Beyond identifying specific risks, the institution needs to assess the likelihood and potential impact of each threat. This involves assigning probabilities and potential financial losses to each identified risk. This probabilistic approach allows the institution to prioritize its efforts on the most critical threats. This assessment should leverage historical data, industry benchmarks, and expert opinions to create a realistic risk profile. Furthermore, a "what-if" analysis should be employed, considering scenarios that may not have occurred previously but are plausible given current market conditions and industry trends.

Once potential risks are identified and assessed, the next critical step is to develop specific mitigation strategies for each. This involves designing actions and processes to

reduce the likelihood or impact of these risks. For example, if a key risk is identified as a significant decline in the value of collateral securing loans, a mitigation strategy could

involve implementing more stringent collateral valuation processes, diversifying collateral types, or increasing the loan-to-value ratio cushions. Similarly, if the risk assessment identifies a dependence on a few major borrowers, the

mitigation strategy could focus on diversifying the loan portfolio by expanding the client base and reducing exposure to any single borrower or industry sector.

Effective communication is the lifeblood of a successful crisis management plan. A clear communication protocol must be established, defining roles, responsibilities, and escalation procedures. This protocol should outline who is responsible for communicating with key stakeholders—such as borrowers, regulators, and investors—during a crisis. The plan should also specify the methods of communication (e.g., email, phone calls, press releases) and the frequency of updates. It is essential to prepare pre-written templates for communication materials to ensure timely and consistent

Messaging during a crisis. These templates should cover various scenarios and be adaptable to evolving situations. It's crucial to include a designated spokesperson to manage external communications and ensure a consistent message is relayed to the public.

The plan should also incorporate clear escalation procedures, defining the process for escalating issues to senior

management and potentially external experts as needed. This ensures that decisions are made efficiently and effectively, considering all relevant information and expertise. The

escalation procedures should detail the channels for

escalation, the criteria for escalation, and the responsibilities of different levels of management. Regular drills and

simulations are vital to test the plan's effectiveness and

ensure that all stakeholders understand their roles and

responsibilities. These simulations should cover various scenarios, allowing the team to practice their responses and identify any weaknesses or gaps in the plan.

A crucial component of the crisis management plan is the development of a comprehensive recovery plan. This

outlines the steps to be taken to restore normal operations after a crisis. The recovery plan should include procedures for restoring damaged systems, resuming lending activities, and communicating with clients and stakeholders. This might also involve contingency plans for accessing backup systems or relocating operations in the event of a major disruption. The recovery plan should also address the

potential long-term impacts of a crisis, outlining strategies for rebuilding relationships, repairing reputations, and ensuring the institution's long-term stability.

The crisis management plan should not be a static document; it requires regular review and updates. The plan should be reviewed at least annually, or more frequently if necessary,

To ensure that it remains relevant and effective. Updates should reflect changes in the institution's business

operations, the regulatory environment, and the overall risk landscape. The plan should be easily accessible to all

relevant staff and should be presented in a clear, concise, and user-friendly format.

A template for a crisis management plan might include the following sections:

Risk Assessment:

Detailed identification and assessment of potential threats, including both internal and external factors.

This section should clearly articulate the likelihood and potential impact of each risk.

Mitigation Strategies:

Specific actions and processes designed to reduce the likelihood or impact of each identified risk. This section should include both preventative and reactive measures.

Communication Protocol:

Clear guidelines for communicating with various stakeholders during a crisis.

This should specify roles, responsibilities, communication methods, and message templates.

Escalation Procedures:

Detailed steps for escalating issues to senior management and external experts as needed. This should include clear triggers for escalation and the responsibilities of different individuals.

Recovery Plan:

Specific steps to restore normal operations after a crisis. This should cover system restoration, business resumption, and communication with stakeholders.

Roles and Responsibilities:

A clear delineation of roles and responsibilities of all individuals involved in the crisis management process.

Contact List:

A list of essential contact information for all key individuals involved in the crisis response.

Finally, it is imperative to conduct regular training exercises for all staff members to familiarize them with the crisis

management plan. These exercises should simulate various crisis scenarios and test the effectiveness of the

communication protocol and escalation procedures. This ensures that the plan is not merely a document on a shelf but a living, breathing tool ready to be deployed when needed. The goal is to create a culture of preparedness, enabling the institution to respond effectively and efficiently to any crisis, safeguarding its financial stability and maintaining its

reputation. A proactive and well-executed crisis management plan transforms a potential disaster into a manageable

challenge, preserving the institution's long-term success and stability.

Communication Strategies During a Crisis

Effective communication is not merely a component of a crisis management plan; it is the very lifeblood that sustains its efficacy. During a financial crisis, the speed and clarity of communication can be the difference between successfully navigating the turbulent waters and capsizing. This section delves into the best practices for communicating with a multitude of stakeholders, emphasizing the critical need for transparency and a consistent message across all platforms.

The initial hours and days of a crisis are often the most critical. Rapid, accurate information dissemination is paramount to preventing rumors and speculation from gaining traction, which can quickly escalate the situation and erode confidence in the institution. A pre-defined communication protocol, detailed within the crisis management plan, is essential. This protocol should not be a generic template but a meticulously crafted document that outlines the specific roles and responsibilities of each team member. Designated spokespeople, equipped with training in crisis communications, should be identified well in advance.

These individuals need to be capable of delivering clear, concise, and accurate information to a wide range of audiences, handling difficult questions with professionalism and composure.

The communication protocol must clearly define the channels to be used for different stakeholders. For example, direct communication with borrowers might be prioritized through personal phone calls or secure online platforms, ensuring personalized attention and the timely address of individual concerns. Investors, on the other hand, might require more formal communication via press releases,

Investor calls, or SEC filings, depending on the severity and nature of the crisis. Regulators, due to their oversight role, demand transparent and timely updates, usually through official channels, adhering strictly to regulatory requirements and reporting deadlines. Finally, media communication requires a strategic approach, potentially through press

conferences or prepared statements, focusing on delivering key messages accurately and efficiently while protecting the institution's reputation.

A crucial element of the communication protocol is the preparation of pre-written templates for various scenarios.

These templates should not be rigid scripts but rather

adaptable frameworks that can be quickly modified to fit the specifics of the unfolding crisis. This preemptive work saves valuable time during a crisis, ensuring swift and consistent messaging without compromising accuracy. These templates should cover a range of scenarios, from minor operational disruptions to major financial setbacks, encompassing

potential impacts on borrowers, investors, and the broader community. They should be clear, concise, and easily

understandable to the lay public, avoiding jargon and

technical language that might confuse or misinform.

Maintaining transparency is paramount in crisis

communication. While complete disclosure of every detail might not always be feasible or advisable (considerations of ongoing investigations or market sensitivities), a

commitment to openness and honesty is crucial for

rebuilding trust and mitigating reputational damage.

Withholding information or attempting to spin events

negatively will only further erode public and stakeholder confidence. Open communication fosters a sense of

collaboration and shared understanding, fostering

cooperation amongst stakeholders. This transparent approach

Can be instrumental in fostering collaborative problem-solving and reducing negative consequences.

Maintaining consistency in messaging across all

communication channels is vital to prevent conflicting narratives from emerging. Internal inconsistencies in communications can not only confuse employees but also undermine credibility with external stakeholders. The designated spokesperson plays a pivotal role here,

coordinating all communication efforts to ensure a unified and coherent message is conveyed. This coordination extends to various media platforms, ensuring consistency across press releases, social media updates, and any other external communication channels.

The crisis communication protocol should also include procedures for handling misinformation and rumors. During a crisis, speculation can spread rapidly, fuelled by social media and other channels, potentially exacerbating the

situation. Having a designated team to monitor these

channels and proactively address inaccurate information or rumors is crucial. This might involve preparing fact-sheets, publishing clarifying statements, or even engaging with social media users directly to correct misconceptions. A reactive approach to misinformation can be detrimental, so a proactive strategy is essential to counter misleading

narratives.

Beyond external communication, robust internal

communication is equally critical during a crisis. Keeping employees informed about the situation, the institution's response, and their individual roles is essential for

maintaining morale and ensuring business continuity.

Regular updates, whether through internal email

announcements, town hall meetings, or dedicated intranet sites, should provide staff with accurate information and

Clear guidance. Open dialogue and addressing concerns promptly can help prevent anxiety and maintain productivity during a difficult time. This internal communication should also include the ongoing implementation of the crisis

management plan itself, providing continuous feedback and adjusting communication strategies as necessary.

Regular testing and review of the crisis management communication plan are just as vital as its creation.

Simulations, including mock crisis scenarios, should be conducted regularly to refine communication strategies and address potential gaps. These drills provide valuable

experience for team members, allowing them to practice their roles and improve coordination. The plan should not be a static document; it must be reviewed and updated

periodically to adapt to changing circumstances, internal organizational changes, and evolving regulatory

requirements. This includes refining messaging, reviewing communication channels, and adjusting roles and

responsibilities as needed. The goal is to create a dynamic, evolving system that is consistently refined and improved to ensure that the institution can respond effectively to any future crisis.

Finally, beyond the formal protocols and communication strategies, a strong emphasis on ethical conduct and empathy is critical. A crisis often brings human hardship and financial distress to many. Treating stakeholders with respect and empathy, showing compassion during difficult

circumstances, is not only morally correct but also

strategically sound. It helps build and maintain trust, which is invaluable during a crisis. This sensitivity underscores the human element of crisis management, reminding us that behind the financial figures and regulatory frameworks are individuals facing real-life consequences. A genuinely

compassionate approach not only reinforces positive

Relationships but also strengthens the institution's long-term reputation. A crisis, while undeniably challenging, presents an opportunity to demonstrate an organization's true

character and its commitment to its stakeholders. Effective communication, therefore, must be driven by both technical proficiency and profound human understanding.

Stakeholder Engagement and Management

Stakeholder engagement during a financial crisis is not merely a reactive measure; it's a proactive strategy that can significantly influence the outcome. Building strong relationships *before* a crisis hits is crucial for effective management during the turbulent times that follow. This involves understanding the needs, concerns, and priorities of each key stakeholder group – borrowers, investors, regulators, employees, and the broader community. Regular communication, even in the absence of a crisis, lays the groundwork for trust and cooperation when the inevitable storm arrives. This proactive approach allows for the development of tailored communication strategies designed to resonate with each group's specific needs and concerns.

For borrowers, who are often directly impacted by financial distress, maintaining consistent and transparent communication is paramount. This necessitates proactively anticipating their concerns and addressing them preemptively through clear, accessible updates on the institution's stability and any potential implications for their loans. Personal outreach, tailored to individual circumstances, can make a critical difference in minimizing anxiety and maintaining confidence. This might involve dedicated phone lines staffed by experienced personnel equipped to answer questions patiently and empathetically.

Providing regular updates on any restructuring options or forbearance programs, presented in clear and understandable terms, can minimize defaults and safeguard the financial health of both the institution and its borrowers. Furthermore, the availability of personalized financial counseling can prove invaluable in navigating the complexities of the crisis and fostering a sense of partnership.

Investors require a different approach, demanding

transparency and demonstrably sound risk management practices. Regularly scheduled investor calls, comprehensive financial reports, and meticulously crafted press releases are crucial for maintaining confidence and investor relations.

During a crisis, these channels become even more critical, conveying not only the current situation but also the

institution's strategic response, mitigating measures being employed, and a realistic outlook on the recovery process.

It's crucial to present a clear and comprehensive narrative that acknowledges the challenges while highlighting the institution's strength, resilience, and commitment to

overcoming the crisis. Maintaining open communication with rating agencies to proactively address concerns is vital to avoid downgrades that could trigger a further escalation of the crisis. Transparency in addressing financial

vulnerabilities, while safeguarding sensitive information, strengthens the institution's credibility and helps maintain investor confidence during turbulent periods.

Regulators are key stakeholders requiring immediate,

accurate, and complete reporting as per regulatory

requirements. Prompt communication, adhering to stringent reporting deadlines and providing all necessary

documentation, is non-negotiable. Open and collaborative communication with regulatory bodies is crucial to avoiding penalties and ensuring continued compliance. Proactively engaging with regulators, keeping them informed of the institution's response plan, demonstrates a commitment to transparency and responsible conduct. This proactive

approach can foster a collaborative relationship with

regulatory bodies, preventing misunderstandings and easing compliance processes during a stressful period. Maintaining open communication channels and adhering strictly to

Regulations are essential to preserving the institution's reputation and avoiding potential sanctions.

Employees, the backbone of the institution, need constant reassurance and clear directives during a crisis. Internal communication must be swift, accurate, and consistent, fostering a sense of solidarity and collective purpose.

Regular updates, town hall meetings, and open forums allow employees to voice concerns and obtain clear instructions regarding their roles in navigating the crisis. Transparency in communication fosters a sense of trust and reinforces the management's commitment to the well-being of its

workforce. Maintaining a positive internal atmosphere is critical in preserving morale, productivity, and employee retention during stressful circumstances. A well-informed and supportive workforce is essential in navigating and overcoming the crisis.

Community engagement is crucial in maintaining public trust and reputation during a crisis. Proactive communication with local media, community leaders, and concerned citizens can help mitigate misunderstandings and avoid harmful misinformation. This involves actively addressing public concerns, providing accurate information, and demonstrating a commitment to the community's well-being. Building bridges of communication and trust before the crisis will significantly reduce reputational damage when the

unexpected happens. Transparency and empathy in

communicating with the broader community helps avoid panic and maintain social stability during difficult times.

Effective stakeholder management requires a multifaceted strategy encompassing multiple communication channels. A comprehensive crisis communication plan should detail roles and responsibilities, communication protocols, and

escalation procedures. The plan should clearly outline

Designated spokespeople, ensuring consistent messaging across all platforms, and detail procedures for handling misinformation and rumors. This integrated approach

ensures a cohesive and coordinated response, minimizing confusion and maximizing effectiveness. Regular testing and review of the crisis communication plan are crucial to refine strategies and adapt to evolving circumstances.

Building trust is central to effective stakeholder engagement.

Transparency, honesty, and empathy are invaluable in

maintaining positive relationships. Demonstrating a genuine commitment to addressing stakeholder concerns, providing timely and relevant information, and proactively seeking feedback builds long-term confidence and cooperation. The establishment of feedback mechanisms allows for

continuous improvement of communication strategies and the address of ongoing concerns. This focus on building and nurturing relationships strengthens the institution's resilience and enhances its capacity to weather future crises.

Beyond technical proficiency in communication, a profound understanding of the human element is critical. A crisis often brings personal hardship and financial distress. Empathy, compassion, and a commitment to treating stakeholders with respect are essential not only for ethical reasons but also for strategic advantages. A compassionate approach fosters trust, strengthens relationships, and promotes cooperation.

This human-centered approach builds a positive long-term reputation that strengthens the institution's resilience and capacity for future challenges.

Finally, a successful stakeholder engagement strategy must be rooted in a comprehensive understanding of the specific needs and expectations of each stakeholder group. A tailored approach, considering the unique concerns and priorities of each group, allows for more effective and targeted

Communication. This individualized approach strengthens trust, fosters cooperation, and contributes significantly to the overall success of crisis management efforts. By actively listening, responding empathetically, and consistently

delivering on commitments, institutions can build and

maintain strong relationships that prove invaluable during times of crisis. This proactive, multifaceted approach

significantly enhances the ability to navigate the challenging circumstances presented by a financial crisis.

Practical Application of Crisis Management Strategies

The preceding discussion established the foundational principles of stakeholder engagement during a financial crisis. Now, we delve into the practical application of these principles within the specific contexts of commercial and asset-based lending. Understanding how these strategies translate into real-world actions is crucial for effective crisis management.

Let's consider a scenario involving a significant downturn in the commercial real estate market. A regional bank with a substantial commercial real estate loan portfolio finds itself facing increasing loan defaults. The initial response involves swiftly activating its crisis management plan. This plan, pre-established and regularly tested, outlines clear communication protocols, designates spokespeople, and details escalation procedures for various scenarios, including a market downturn of this magnitude.

The bank immediately initiates proactive communication with its borrowers. This isn't a blanket email; it's a tailored, multi-pronged approach. For borrowers facing imminent default, the bank offers personalized financial counseling and explores restructuring options. This might involve extending loan terms, modifying interest rates, or converting short-term loans into longer-term ones. The bank utilizes a dedicated team of experienced loan officers, trained in empathetic communication and financial restructuring, to navigate these sensitive conversations. These officers don't just present solutions; they actively listen to the borrowers' concerns, understand their individual circumstances, and collaborate to find mutually beneficial solutions. The aim is

Not merely to avoid default, but to maintain a long-term, positive relationship with the borrower.

Simultaneously, the bank engages with its investors through meticulously prepared investor calls and press releases.

These communications are transparent and factual,

acknowledging the challenges presented by the market downturn while emphasizing the bank's robust risk

management practices and its strategic response to mitigate potential losses. The bank highlights its diversification strategy, stress testing results, and its capital adequacy

position to reassure investors about its long-term viability. This proactive approach helps maintain investor confidence, preventing a panic selloff that could further destabilize the bank's financial position. Furthermore, the bank maintains open lines of communication with credit rating agencies, proactively addressing their concerns and providing all necessary information to prevent downgrades.

In parallel, the bank meticulously adheres to its regulatory reporting requirements. This is not just a matter of

compliance; it's a crucial element of building trust with regulatory bodies. The bank proactively engages with

regulators, providing regular updates on the situation and the bank's mitigation efforts. This open communication fosters a collaborative relationship and prevents misunderstandings that could lead to penalties or increased regulatory scrutiny.

The bank's commitment to transparency reinforces its

reputation as a responsible financial institution, even during times of stress.

Internally, the bank maintains consistent and transparent communication with its employees. Regular town hall meetings and internal communications keep employees informed about the situation, the bank's response, and its long-term outlook. This fosters a sense of solidarity and

Reduces uncertainty among the workforce. The bank

emphasizes the importance of teamwork and collaboration in navigating the crisis, reinforcing its commitment to

employee well-being.

Public communication is also carefully managed. The bank works with local media outlets to provide accurate

information and address public concerns, mitigating the risk of misinformation and panic. The bank's commitment to community engagement, even during a crisis, reinforces its reputation and strengthens its relationships with the

community it serves.

This scenario showcases the practical application of a

comprehensive crisis management framework. The bank's proactive communication strategy, its commitment to

transparency, and its focus on building relationships with all stakeholders were critical to successfully navigating the crisis.

Now, let's consider another scenario within the context of asset-based lending. A company heavily reliant on inventory financing finds itself experiencing a sharp decline in sales due to unforeseen supply chain disruptions. The lender, a specialized finance company, must again apply a robust crisis management framework. The initial response involves immediate communication with the borrower to assess the situation and understand the impact of the supply chain disruption.

Unlike commercial real estate, where the underlying asset is relatively illiquid, asset-based lending relies on readily available collateral. However, the rapidly changing market conditions require swift action. The lender, in consultation with the borrower, may agree to temporarily increase the borrowing base to accommodate the increased inventory

Levels. This requires meticulous monitoring of the inventory value and rigorous adherence to the terms of the loan agreement. Furthermore, the lender might negotiate a temporary reduction in interest rates or extend the loan maturity to provide the borrower with additional breathing room. This proactive approach prevents a potential default and preserves the lender's relationship with a valued client.

Communication with investors and regulators mirrors the scenario above. Transparency, factual reporting, and proactive engagement are crucial in maintaining confidence and compliance. However, in the asset-based lending context, the lender needs to provide detailed information on the collateral value, the borrower's sales trends, and the ongoing management of the borrowing base. This ensures that investors and regulators have a clear understanding of the lender's risk exposure and mitigation strategies.

Internal communication is essential. The lending team requires constant updates on the borrower's situation and the evolving market conditions. The lender must actively monitor its portfolio and identify potential problem loans before they become major issues. This requires a proactive approach to risk management and a vigilant monitoring of market indicators.

Public communication, while less critical in this instance compared to a commercial real estate crisis, remains important. Maintaining the lender's reputation for responsible lending and robust risk management is crucial for attracting new business and maintaining investor confidence.

The lessons learned from both scenarios underscore the importance of a proactive, multi-faceted crisis management approach. A pre-established plan, regular testing, and a

Strong emphasis on stakeholder engagement are crucial for navigating crises effectively. The emphasis on proactive communication, tailored to the specific needs of each

stakeholder group, is key to maintaining trust and

cooperation. Furthermore, the ability to adapt to changing circumstances and employ creative solutions is crucial for success. While the specific strategies may vary depending on the type of lending and the nature of the crisis, the

underlying principles of transparency, communication, and relationship management remain constant. Regular review and refinement of crisis management plans are essential to maintain their effectiveness in the constantly evolving

financial landscape. This proactive and flexible approach, combined with a deep understanding of the human element involved, is essential for navigating the complex challenges presented by financial crises and ensuring the long-term sustainability of lending institutions. Ultimately, the success of crisis management isn't just about mitigating losses; it's about preserving relationships and maintaining confidence in the long-term viability of the institution.

Postcrisis Analysis and Lessons Learned

The successful navigation of a financial crisis, as illustrated in the previous scenarios, is only half the battle. Equally crucial is the meticulous process of post-crisis analysis and the subsequent integration of lessons learned into future crisis management plans. This post-mortem examination is not simply an exercise in assigning blame or identifying individual failures; rather, it's a systematic process designed to strengthen the institution's resilience and preparedness for future challenges. The goal is to transform crisis experiences into valuable opportunities for continuous improvement, enhancing the effectiveness and efficiency of crisis

management strategies.

A robust post-crisis analysis begins with a comprehensive review of the events leading up to, during, and after the crisis. This involves gathering data from multiple sources, including internal communications, financial records,

regulatory reports, and stakeholder feedback. The analysis should meticulously examine the effectiveness of the crisis management plan, identifying both strengths and

weaknesses. Did the plan adequately address the specific challenges presented by the crisis? Were communication protocols effective in disseminating timely and accurate information to all stakeholders? Were decision-making processes efficient and transparent? Did the institution's risk management framework adequately identify and mitigate potential vulnerabilities?

The answers to these questions, gleaned from a thorough data analysis, form the basis for identifying areas for

improvement. For instance, an analysis might reveal

deficiencies in communication protocols, leading to delays

In information dissemination or inconsistencies in

messaging. It could highlight weaknesses in the risk

management framework, revealing a failure to adequately anticipate or assess specific risks. The analysis might also uncover shortcomings in the institution's technological infrastructure, hindering its ability to rapidly access and process critical information during the crisis. Equally, the analysis might reveal unforeseen dependencies or

vulnerabilities within the institution's operational processes.

Crucially, the analysis must extend beyond simply

identifying weaknesses. It must also explore the factors that contributed to the institution's successful response. What aspects of the crisis management plan worked effectively?

What strategies proved particularly valuable in mitigating losses or maintaining stakeholder confidence? What internal resources or external relationships were instrumental in navigating the crisis? Identifying these successes allows for the reinforcement of best practices and the development of more robust and effective strategies for future crises.

The integration of lessons learned involves translating the findings of the post-crisis analysis into concrete actions designed to enhance future crisis response capabilities. This may involve revising the crisis management plan, updating communication protocols, strengthening risk management frameworks, investing in new technologies, or improving internal training programs. It may also necessitate the

development of new policies and procedures designed to address specific vulnerabilities identified during the crisis. These modifications are not merely cosmetic changes; they are fundamental adjustments designed to enhance the

institution's overall resilience and its ability to withstand future shocks.

Let's consider a real-world example: the 2008 financial crisis exposed significant vulnerabilities within many financial institutions, particularly in their exposure to subprime

mortgages. Post-crisis analyses conducted by various

institutions and regulatory bodies revealed weaknesses in risk assessment models, inadequate oversight of derivative products, and insufficient capital reserves. In response, many institutions implemented stricter lending standards,

strengthened their risk management frameworks, and

increased their capital reserves. Regulatory reforms, driven by lessons learned during the crisis, also resulted in

increased oversight of the financial industry and the

implementation of new regulations designed to mitigate systemic risks. The subsequent establishment of the

Financial Stability Oversight Council in the U.S., for

instance, exemplifies this regulatory response to the lessons learned.

Another compelling example can be drawn from the

response to the COVID-19 pandemic. Many businesses faced unprecedented challenges, prompting the need for quick adaptation. Those who effectively leveraged digital tools for remote work and communication fared better than those who lagged. Post-crisis analysis in various sectors revealed the critical role of technology in crisis management, leading to increased investment in digital infrastructure and the adoption of remote work policies. Businesses that had pre-existing disaster recovery plans and robust

communication systems were better equipped to handle the abrupt shift to remote operations. Analyzing the successes and failures highlighted the importance of flexible business continuity planning and underscored the value of digital agility.

The post-crisis analysis should also involve detailed

evaluation of the effectiveness of communication strategies

Across various stakeholder groups. This includes investors, regulators, employees, customers, and the broader

community. Did the institution effectively manage

expectations and maintain transparency? Were

communication channels adequately utilized to ensure timely and accurate information dissemination? Were responses to stakeholder concerns adequate and responsive? The

feedback gathered from various stakeholders should be incorporated into the refinement of the institution's

communication strategies, strengthening its ability to

manage public perception and mitigate reputational risks in future crises.

Furthermore, a critical aspect of post-crisis analysis is the evaluation of the institution's internal culture and its impact on crisis response. Did the institution's culture of

collaboration and transparency support an effective crisis response? Were employees adequately trained and

empowered to respond effectively? Were internal

communication channels clear and effective? The post-crisis analysis should assess the efficacy of leadership and

management decisions throughout the crisis and identify opportunities to enhance team cohesion, leadership training, and employee empowerment.

The process of documenting and disseminating lessons learned is vital. This goes beyond internal reports; it requires the creation of structured documents, case studies, and

presentations that are easily accessible and understood by staff at all levels. This process ensures the institutional

memory of the crisis is preserved, and the hard-won

knowledge gained is not lost as personnel change or time passes. Sharing lessons learned with peer institutions,

through industry associations or conferences, further fosters a collective learning environment and strengthens the overall resilience of the financial sector. This collaboration is

Crucial, as crises often share common themes or underlying vulnerabilities that can be addressed proactively across institutions.

In conclusion, the post-crisis analysis is not a mere

formality; it is a critical component of a robust crisis

management framework. By systematically reviewing the events, identifying areas for improvement, and integrating lessons learned into future plans, financial institutions can significantly enhance their resilience and preparedness for future challenges. The emphasis on thorough documentation, transparent communication, and the active sharing of

knowledge across the industry builds a collective learning environment, strengthening the stability and sustainability of the financial sector as a whole. This continuous cycle of learning and adaptation is essential for navigating the

complex and ever-evolving landscape of financial markets.

The ability to learn from past experiences and proactively adapt to future uncertainties is the hallmark of a truly resilient and successful financial institution.

Responding to Economic Downturns

Responding to economic downturns presents unique challenges to lenders, demanding a proactive and adaptable approach to mitigate losses and maintain portfolio stability.

The severity of an economic downturn, whether a mild recession or a deep depression, significantly impacts the ability of borrowers to service their debt obligations. This necessitates a shift in lending strategies from a focus on growth to one emphasizing risk mitigation and portfolio protection.

The first critical step is a thorough assessment of the lending portfolio's vulnerability to economic shocks. This involves a granular analysis of borrowers' financial health, industry sector performance, and geographic concentration of loans. Key indicators to scrutinize include debt-to-income ratios, cash flow projections, and sensitivity to interest rate changes. Specific industries particularly susceptible to economic downturns, like construction, retail, and hospitality, require heightened scrutiny. Geographic areas experiencing higher unemployment rates or property value declines present additional risks.

Once vulnerabilities are identified, a proactive approach to risk management is vital. This may involve tightening credit standards for new lending, limiting exposure to high-risk borrowers or sectors, and increasing loan loss reserves. The goal is to proactively reduce the potential for defaults and to strengthen the institution's capital position to withstand potential losses. Diversification of the loan portfolio across various sectors and geographic regions can also help to mitigate overall risk.

However, simply tightening lending standards isn't always enough. An economic downturn can significantly impact even previously strong borrowers. This necessitates the development of robust workout strategies for borrowers facing financial difficulties. Early intervention is crucial.

Lenders should proactively engage with struggling borrowers to understand their challenges and explore potential solutions before defaults occur. This often involves open communication and a collaborative approach to restructuring loan terms. This could include extending loan maturities, reducing interest rates, or modifying payment schedules to align with the borrower's revised cash flow projections.

Renegotiating loan terms requires careful consideration of the borrower's financial situation and the lender's risk tolerance. A thorough analysis of the borrower's financial statements, including cash flow projections and collateral valuation, is crucial. The goal is to find a mutually beneficial agreement that allows the borrower to remain current on their obligations while protecting the lender's investment.

Negotiations must be documented meticulously, with all agreed-upon terms clearly outlined in legally binding amendments to the original loan agreement.

In situations where renegotiation proves insufficient, more aggressive workout strategies may be necessary. This could include the assignment of loans to specialized debt recovery agencies or the initiation of foreclosure proceedings on secured loans. While such measures are often a last resort, they are sometimes necessary to minimize losses and protect the lender's financial interests. However, even in these instances, a pragmatic approach is warranted. The cost of pursuing legal action often outweighs the potential recovery, particularly in cases where collateral values have significantly declined.

The efficient management of loan defaults requires

sophisticated systems and processes. This necessitates the use of advanced analytical tools and technologies to identify early warning signs of borrower distress, enabling proactive intervention. This may include the use of credit scoring models, financial statement analysis software, and early warning systems that track key performance indicators.

Moreover, dedicated teams of experienced credit analysts and workout specialists are critical for effectively managing the entire default process, from initial contact with the borrower to the final resolution.

Let's consider the impact of the 2008 financial crisis on the commercial real estate lending sector. Many lenders

experienced a significant increase in loan defaults as

property values plummeted. Successful responses involved a combination of strategies, including loan modifications, foreclosures, and the creation of special purpose vehicles to manage distressed assets. Lenders who proactively engaged with borrowers, demonstrating flexibility and a willingness to negotiate, were often more successful in mitigating losses. Conversely, those who adopted a rigid approach faced higher default rates and greater financial losses.

The COVID-19 pandemic presented another significant challenge. Government-backed loan programs such as the Paycheck Protection Program (PPP) in the United States played a crucial role in supporting businesses and preventing widespread defaults. Lenders who actively participated in these programs and worked closely with borrowers to

navigate the economic uncertainty often maintained better portfolio performance. They were able to adapt quickly, implementing new processes and technologies to manage the increased demand for loan modifications and forbearance agreements.

The successful navigation of economic downturns requires more than simply reacting to defaults; it demands a

proactive, strategic approach that anticipates challenges and prepares for potential losses. This starts with a robust risk management framework that continually monitors portfolio vulnerabilities, allowing for timely adjustments to lending strategies. Regular stress testing of the loan portfolio under various economic scenarios is crucial for identifying

potential weaknesses and developing contingency plans.

This should incorporate a range of potential economic shocks, including interest rate hikes, recessions, and industry-specific crises.

Effective communication is paramount. Open dialogue with borrowers is crucial, allowing for early identification of potential problems and fostering collaborative solutions.

Transparent communication with investors and regulators builds trust and confidence, essential for maintaining

stability during times of economic stress. Internally, clear communication channels and well-defined roles and

responsibilities ensure efficient and coordinated responses to emerging challenges.

Technological advancements offer significant opportunities to improve the management of lending portfolios during economic downturns. Advanced analytical tools can enhance the identification of early warning signs of borrower distress, allowing for proactive intervention. Automated systems can streamline loan modification and workout processes,

improving efficiency and reducing costs. The integration of data analytics and artificial intelligence can improve credit risk assessment and enhance the overall accuracy of

forecasting models.

In conclusion, the ability to successfully navigate economic downturns hinges on a combination of factors: proactive risk management, robust workout strategies, efficient default management processes, effective communication, and the leveraging of technological advancements. By integrating these elements into a comprehensive crisis management framework, lending institutions can significantly enhance their resilience and protect their portfolios during periods of economic uncertainty. The experience gained during past crises, meticulously documented and analyzed, provides valuable lessons for future preparedness and strengthens the overall stability of the financial system. Continuous learning and adaptation are crucial, recognizing that economic

downturns are an inevitable part of the business cycle, and the ability to effectively respond defines the success and long-term sustainability of any lending institution.

Managing Loan Defaults and Recoveries

Effective management of loan defaults is paramount to the financial health of any lending institution. It's not merely a reactive process of dealing with delinquent accounts; it's a proactive, strategic function requiring a multi-faceted approach. This begins long before a loan enters default, starting with robust underwriting and ongoing monitoring of borrower performance. The earlier a potential problem is identified, the greater the likelihood of successful intervention and minimizing losses. Regular review of financial statements, industry trends, and macroeconomic indicators provides early warning signs. Changes in key performance indicators (kpis), such as declining revenue, increased debt-to-equity ratios, or missed payments, should trigger immediate action. Advanced analytical tools and predictive modeling can significantly enhance this early detection process.

Early intervention is the cornerstone of effective default management. This involves engaging with borrowers exhibiting signs of financial distress before they formally default. The goal here isn't to initiate legal action but to foster open communication and explore mutually beneficial solutions. This may involve a collaborative approach to restructuring the loan terms. Examples of such restructuring could include extending the loan maturity date, modifying the payment schedule to better align with the borrower's cash flow, or temporarily reducing the interest rate. This approach requires a delicate balance: the lender must protect its financial interests while acknowledging the borrower's difficulties and working towards a sustainable solution.

The restructuring process must be meticulously documented. All agreed-upon terms should be clearly outlined in a legally binding amendment to the original loan agreement. This ensures clarity and minimizes the potential for future disputes. This amendment should explicitly define the new payment schedule, interest rate, and any other relevant terms. It should also include clauses addressing potential breaches of the amended agreement and the consequences thereof.

The lender should retain comprehensive documentation of all communications and negotiations with the borrower, including emails, meeting minutes, and financial statements.

Forbearance, another crucial tool in the default management arsenal, provides temporary relief to borrowers facing temporary financial hardship. This could involve temporarily suspending or reducing loan payments for a defined period.

It often requires a thorough assessment of the borrower's situation, including a detailed analysis of their financial statements and a realistic projection of their future cash flow.

The lender must assess whether the temporary hardship is likely to be overcome, and whether the borrower possesses the capacity to resume payments once the hardship abates. Unlike restructuring, forbearance typically does not alter the fundamental terms of the loan agreement; it merely offers a temporary reprieve. However, it should also be documented thoroughly with a clear plan for resuming regular payments.

Should early intervention and forbearance prove insufficient, more assertive measures may be necessary. This could involve the assignment of the loan to a specialized debt recovery agency. These agencies possess the expertise and resources to pursue more aggressive collection strategies, including legal action. The decision to assign a loan rests on a cost-benefit analysis. The potential recovery must justify the cost of engaging a debt recovery agency, considering legal fees, collection costs, and the time involved. The value

Of the collateral and the borrower's ability to repay must be carefully evaluated.

In situations where collateral is secured, foreclosure

proceedings may become necessary. This is a legally

complex process that varies by jurisdiction and involves the legal seizure and sale of the collateral to recover the

outstanding debt. Foreclosure is a last resort, given its time-consuming and expensive nature. Lenders must carefully weigh the potential recovery against the legal and

administrative costs involved. The value of the collateral, the market conditions, and the potential for delays in the

foreclosure process are all critical factors to consider.

Liquidation of assets, a related strategy, involves the sale of assets owned by the borrower to repay the outstanding loan.

This may be a voluntary agreement reached during the

workout process or a court-ordered action as part of the foreclosure proceedings. Effective asset liquidation requires a thorough understanding of the assets' market value and the optimal strategy for their sale. This may involve engaging professional appraisers and auction houses to maximize the recovery value. The timing of the asset sale is also crucial, as market conditions can significantly impact the sale price.

Maximizing recovery rates requires a strategic, multi-

pronged approach. This starts with proactive risk

management and early intervention but also necessitates efficient processes for managing the default cycle. Effective communication is crucial throughout the process, with open dialogue between the lender and the borrower to foster mutual understanding and facilitate a smooth resolution. Transparent and consistent communication also builds trust with regulators and investors, essential for maintaining the stability of the institution.

Technological advancements play a vital role in improving default management. Sophisticated data analytics and

predictive modeling can identify high-risk borrowers early, allowing for proactive intervention. Automated systems can streamline the workflow of loan modifications, forbearance agreements, and asset liquidation, reducing costs and

improving efficiency. The integration of artificial

intelligence can further enhance the accuracy of credit risk assessment and forecasting models.

The successful management of loan defaults hinges on a combination of proactive strategies, efficient processes, effective communication, and the utilization of technological advancements. By implementing a comprehensive default management framework, lenders can mitigate losses, protect their portfolios, and ensure the long-term financial health of their institutions. Regular review and refinement of these strategies, informed by lessons learned from past

experiences, are crucial for adapting to evolving economic conditions and maintaining resilience in the face of

unexpected challenges. The ultimate aim is not simply to recover outstanding debt but to minimize losses and

maintain strong, healthy relationships with borrowers, even during times of significant financial stress. This approach fosters a culture of trust and cooperation that ultimately benefits both the lender and the borrower.

Dealing with Fraud and Financial Misrepresentation

Fraud and financial misrepresentation pose significant

threats to the stability of commercial and asset-based lending (ABL) portfolios. The potential for losses is substantial, and the reputational damage to the lending institution can be severe. Effective mitigation strategies require a multi-layered approach encompassing robust preventative measures,

sophisticated investigative techniques, and decisive legal recourse.

A critical first line of defense is the establishment of robust internal controls. This goes beyond simple compliance

checks; it involves a comprehensive system of checks and balances designed to detect irregularities at every stage of the lending process. This begins with thorough due diligence during the loan application stage. Independent verification of financial statements is crucial, particularly for larger

transactions. This often involves engaging external auditing firms to scrutinize the borrower's financial records, ensuring their accuracy and completeness. The scope of this

verification should extend to assessing the underlying assets used as collateral, confirming their ownership and market value. Inconsistencies or questionable entries should trigger further investigation.

Furthermore, continuous monitoring of borrower activity is essential. Regular reviews of financial performance, cash flow statements, and other key performance indicators (kpis) can reveal early warning signs of potential fraud.

Significant deviations from projected performance or unusual transactional patterns should prompt immediate scrutiny. The use of advanced analytics and predictive

Modeling can significantly enhance this monitoring process, identifying subtle indicators of fraudulent activity that may otherwise go unnoticed. These analytical tools can flag

unusual transactions, inconsistent data patterns, and other red flags that warrant closer examination.

In the context of ABL, where collateral plays a central role, meticulous inventory management is paramount. Regular physical inspections of the collateralized assets, coupled with independent valuations, are vital to verify their

existence and market worth. Discrepancies between the borrower's reported inventory and the physical count can indicate fraudulent activities such as inflated asset values or outright asset misappropriation. Sophisticated tracking systems, utilizing technology such as RFID tags or

blockchain, can enhance inventory accuracy and

transparency, thereby reducing the risk of misrepresentation.

Beyond the technological advancements, a strong internal culture of ethics and compliance is critical. Employees

should be trained to recognize and report suspicious activity. Clear reporting mechanisms should be established, ensuring that employees feel comfortable raising concerns without fear of retribution. Regular compliance training,

encompassing ethics and fraud detection, is necessary to ensure that all staff are equipped to identify and address potential issues. This training should be tailored to the

specific risks associated with commercial and ABL lending, including common fraud schemes and best practices for reporting. Regular updates and refresher courses should keep employees abreast of evolving fraud techniques.

When suspicions of fraud or financial misrepresentation arise, a thorough investigation is necessary. This may involve internal audit teams working in conjunction with external forensic accounting specialists. The investigation

Should be methodical and comprehensive, leaving no stone unturned. Evidence gathering should be conducted according to strict legal protocols, ensuring the admissibility of any findings in subsequent legal proceedings. This includes securing relevant financial documents, interviewing key personnel, and analyzing electronic data. The use of data analytics tools can prove invaluable in this process, enabling investigators to identify complex patterns and anomalies indicative of fraudulent behaviour.

The scope of the investigation should extend beyond the immediate financial records. It should delve into the

borrower's business operations, scrutinizing the flow of funds, relationships with key suppliers and customers, and any unusual external connections. This broader perspective can reveal deeper aspects of potential fraud, including

collusion or the involvement of third parties. Information sharing with other lenders, credit bureaus, and law

enforcement agencies, where appropriate, can prove valuable in uncovering a wider pattern of fraudulent activity.

Should the investigation confirm fraudulent activity, the lender must pursue appropriate legal recourse. This may involve civil litigation to recover the outstanding debt and any related losses. The strength of the lender's case will depend heavily on the quality and completeness of the

evidence gathered during the investigation. Experienced legal counsel specializing in commercial lending and fraud litigation is essential to navigate the complexities of the legal process. This includes carefully crafting legal pleadings, managing evidence disclosure, and preparing for depositions and trials. Legal strategies will vary depending on the

specifics of the fraud, the jurisdiction, and the borrower's financial circumstances.

The decision to pursue criminal prosecution, while potentially more time-consuming and resource-intensive, may be warranted in cases involving egregious fraud or systemic patterns of deception. Collaboration with law enforcement agencies is crucial in such instances. This involves providing them with all relevant evidence and cooperating fully with their investigations. Successful criminal prosecution not only results in recovering losses but also acts as a deterrent to future fraudulent activity.

Furthermore, it protects the reputation of the lending institution and reinforces the importance of ethical conduct within the industry.

Beyond the immediate response to fraud, lenders must learn from past experiences to improve their preventative measures. A post-incident review is crucial, examining the weaknesses in the existing internal controls that allowed the fraud to occur. This analysis should identify specific areas for improvement, leading to the implementation of stronger preventative measures. This could involve upgrading technology, enhancing employee training, or refining the internal audit process. The goal is not simply to recover losses but to strengthen the entire system and make it more resilient to future fraudulent activity. This continuous improvement cycle, informed by lessons learned from past experiences, is vital for maintaining the long-term financial health and stability of the lending institution. The successful management of fraud and financial misrepresentation demands a proactive, multi-faceted approach that encompasses strong preventative measures, robust investigative techniques, and decisive legal action, all supported by a culture of ethical conduct and continuous improvement. The ultimate aim is not only to mitigate losses but also to safeguard the reputation and integrity of the institution. The cost of neglecting this responsibility far outweighs the investment required in establishing and

Maintaining robust fraud detection and prevention programs. The financial consequences of fraud can be devastating, but the reputational damage can be even more far-reaching and long-lasting, affecting relationships with borrowers,

investors, and regulators alike.

Managing Operational Risks and Cybersecurity Threats

Operational risks, encompassing a wide range of potential disruptions to lending operations, represent a significant challenge for financial institutions. These risks extend

beyond fraud and encompass issues such as technology failures, human error, process inefficiencies, and regulatory non-compliance. A robust risk management framework is crucial for identifying, assessing, and mitigating these

threats. This framework should incorporate a comprehensive risk assessment, regularly updated to reflect changing

circumstances and emerging technologies. This assessment should consider both the likelihood and potential impact of various operational risks, enabling the prioritization of

mitigation efforts.

A crucial element of operational risk management is the development of clear and concise procedures for all key business processes. These procedures should be meticulously documented, readily accessible to staff, and regularly

reviewed and updated to ensure they remain relevant and effective. Regular staff training on these procedures, coupled with ongoing monitoring and auditing, is essential to ensure consistent adherence and the prompt identification of any deviations. This training should include practical exercises and simulations to prepare staff for potential disruptions and emergencies.

Technology plays a vital role in modern lending operations, but it also introduces its own set of risks. System failures, data breaches, and cyberattacks can all have significant consequences. Robust IT infrastructure, including redundant systems and disaster recovery plans, is essential for

Maintaining business continuity in the event of a

technological disruption. Regular system backups, securely stored off-site, are crucial for data recovery. This involves not only the technical aspects but also a comprehensive understanding of the organization's data protection policies, including regular security audits and vulnerability

assessments. Strong password policies, multi-factor

authentication, and regular security awareness training for staff are critical components of a comprehensive

cybersecurity strategy.

Cybersecurity threats pose a particularly significant

challenge in the current digital landscape. The sophistication and frequency of cyberattacks are continually increasing, demanding a proactive and multi-layered approach to

security. This approach necessitates a strong emphasis on prevention, early detection, and swift response. Robust firewalls, intrusion detection systems, and antivirus software are fundamental elements of a comprehensive cybersecurity strategy. Regular penetration testing and security audits are critical for identifying vulnerabilities and weaknesses in the organization's security posture before they can be exploited by malicious actors.

Protecting sensitive customer and financial data is

paramount. Compliance with relevant data privacy

regulations, such as GDPR or CCPA, is not just a legal

requirement, but also a crucial aspect of maintaining

customer trust and confidence. Data encryption, both in transit and at rest, is vital for protecting sensitive information from unauthorized access. Access controls should be

implemented to restrict access to sensitive data based on the principle of least privilege, ensuring that only authorized personnel have access to the information they need to

perform their jobs. The importance of thorough staff

background checks and security clearances cannot be

Overstated, ensuring the trustworthiness and reliability of those handling sensitive information.

Incident response planning is crucial for minimizing the impact of operational disruptions and cybersecurity threats.

This plan should outline clear procedures for identifying, containing, and resolving incidents. Regular testing and drills are vital for ensuring the effectiveness of the plan and preparing staff for real-world scenarios. These drills should simulate various types of incidents, including technology failures, data breaches, and cyberattacks. They should involve different teams within the organization, ensuring coordinated response and effective communication during a crisis. The plan should also include procedures for

communicating with regulators, customers, and other

stakeholders during and after an incident.

In addition to technology and procedures, human factors play a crucial role in operational risk management.

Employee training, awareness, and adherence to established procedures are essential for preventing errors and mitigating risks. A strong organizational culture of risk awareness and accountability is vital for fostering a proactive approach to risk management. Employees at all levels should be

empowered to report potential risks or concerns without fear of retribution. Regular performance reviews should

incorporate an assessment of risk management practices, ensuring that individual performance is aligned with

organizational risk objectives.

Effective communication is crucial throughout the risk management process. Open communication channels between different departments and teams are essential for ensuring that potential risks are identified and addressed promptly. Regular reporting on key risk indicators should provide management with a clear picture of the

Organization's risk profile, allowing for proactive decision-making and resource allocation. The communication strategy should also extend to external stakeholders, such as

regulators, customers, and investors, ensuring transparency and maintaining confidence.

The management of operational risks and cybersecurity threats is an ongoing process, requiring continuous

improvement and adaptation. Regular reviews of the risk management framework, procedures, and technologies are essential for ensuring their effectiveness in the face of

evolving risks. This review should include assessments of emerging threats and technologies, incorporating best

practices and lessons learned from industry incidents. The investment in robust risk management programs is not just a cost, but a strategic imperative for maintaining the long-term financial health and stability of the lending institution. The cost of inaction far outweighs the investment in proactive risk mitigation strategies.

Furthermore, collaboration and information sharing within the industry can significantly enhance the collective ability to manage operational risks and cybersecurity threats. Participating in industry forums, sharing best practices, and cooperating on threat intelligence can provide valuable insights and enhance the effectiveness of individual risk management programs. This collaboration is particularly important in the face of sophisticated and evolving threats, where sharing information can help prevent others from falling victim to the same attacks. Regulatory cooperation and information sharing with law enforcement are also crucial aspects of a comprehensive approach to threat

management, enabling timely response and effective

prosecution of malicious actors.

In conclusion, effectively managing operational risks and cybersecurity threats in commercial and asset-based lending requires a multifaceted approach encompassing robust risk assessment, comprehensive mitigation strategies, and

thorough incident response planning. This includes investing in secure IT infrastructure, implementing stringent data protection measures, and fostering a strong culture of risk awareness and accountability. Continuous improvement, informed by regular reviews and lessons learned, is essential for maintaining the resilience of the lending institution

against ever-evolving threats. Ultimately, a proactive and comprehensive approach to risk management is not just about minimizing losses but also about safeguarding the reputation and long-term sustainability of the organization.

The investment in robust risk management is not simply a cost, but a crucial investment in the future security and stability of the lending institution. Ignoring these risks is simply not an option in today's dynamic and increasingly complex financial landscape.

Responding to Regulatory Scrutiny and Enforcement Actions

Responding to regulatory scrutiny is a critical aspect of operating within the financial sector. The consequences of non-compliance can be severe, ranging from hefty financial penalties to reputational damage and even criminal charges. A proactive approach to compliance, therefore, is not merely advisable but essential for the long-term sustainability of any lending institution. This involves a deep understanding of applicable regulations, the implementation of robust compliance programs, and the development of a culture of compliance throughout the organization. This extends beyond mere legal adherence; it's about cultivating a mindset where compliance is viewed not as a burden but as an integral part of responsible and ethical business practices.

The first line of defense against regulatory scrutiny is a robust and comprehensive compliance program. This program should encompass all aspects of the lending operation, from loan origination and underwriting to collections and reporting. It should include clearly defined policies and procedures, regularly updated to reflect changes in regulations and best practices. These policies should be readily accessible to all staff, with regular training and awareness programs ensuring understanding and adherence. The program must also include mechanisms for identifying and reporting potential compliance issues, with clear channels for escalation to senior management. Regular internal audits, conducted by independent parties, are crucial for identifying weaknesses and ensuring the effectiveness of the program.

When regulatory scrutiny does arise, whether in the form of an audit, investigation, or enforcement action, the response must be swift, decisive, and fully cooperative. Delaying or obstructing the regulatory process will only exacerbate the situation and potentially lead to more severe penalties. Full transparency and open communication with the regulators are paramount. This includes providing all requested

information promptly and accurately, even if it reveals areas of weakness or non-compliance. Concealing information or attempting to mislead regulators will almost certainly result in more severe consequences.

Effective communication also extends internally within the institution. A clear chain of command should be established to handle regulatory inquiries, ensuring that all relevant personnel are informed and coordinated. This includes legal counsel, compliance officers, and relevant operational staff.

Internal communication should be clear, concise, and

consistent, avoiding any ambiguity that could lead to

misunderstandings or misinterpretations. A dedicated crisis management team can be instrumental in navigating these situations, ensuring a coordinated and effective response. This team should have clear roles and responsibilities, and should be regularly trained on crisis management protocols.

One of the most crucial aspects of responding to regulatory scrutiny is the preservation of evidence. This involves

maintaining comprehensive and accurate records of all

relevant transactions, communications, and activities. This documentation should be readily accessible and easily

retrievable, allowing for a swift and efficient response to any regulatory requests. The secure storage and protection of this information are paramount, particularly given the increasing prevalence of cyberattacks and data breaches. This often involves implementing robust IT infrastructure, including data encryption, access controls, and regular backups. The

Destruction or alteration of evidence, even unintentionally, can have serious legal repercussions.

Case studies illustrate the importance of proactive compliance and effective response to regulatory action.

Consider a scenario where a bank failed to adequately

monitor its loan portfolio for compliance with fair lending laws. A subsequent regulatory audit reveals significant

disparities in loan approvals based on protected

characteristics. The bank's failure to have a robust

monitoring system and appropriate internal controls resulted in substantial fines, reputational damage, and a lengthy

corrective action plan. In contrast, another institution, with a proactive compliance program and thorough internal audits, uncovered a similar issue internally before a regulatory audit. By self-reporting the issue and proactively

implementing corrective measures, they mitigated the impact and avoided significant penalties. The difference underscores the critical role of proactive compliance and early

intervention.

Another critical example involves a financial institution that experienced a data breach, resulting in the unauthorized access of sensitive customer information. The institution's delayed response and lack of transparency with regulators significantly worsened the situation. This led to substantial fines, legal action from affected customers, and severe reputational damage. In comparison, another institution, upon discovering a data breach, immediately notified

regulators, cooperated fully with the investigation, and implemented comprehensive remediation measures. While the breach still incurred costs and reputational challenges, the institution's swift, transparent, and cooperative response minimized the overall impact, showcasing the value of proactive measures and transparency. The cost of inaction in

Both instances significantly outweighed the costs associated with proactive compliance and efficient incident response.

These examples highlight the significant financial and reputational risks associated with regulatory non-

compliance. The potential penalties can be substantial, including monetary fines, civil penalties, and even criminal prosecution for individuals and the institution. Beyond the immediate financial ramifications, regulatory enforcement actions can severely damage an institution's reputation, impacting its ability to attract and retain customers and business partners. This reputational damage can be long-lasting, affecting the institution's access to capital markets and overall financial stability.

Beyond financial penalties and reputational harm, regulatory enforcement actions can lead to operational disruptions. The need to implement corrective measures and undergo

extensive audits can divert resources and disrupt normal business operations. This can negatively impact productivity, profitability, and employee morale. Moreover, regulatory actions can lead to increased scrutiny from other

stakeholders, including investors, credit rating agencies, and insurance providers, further impacting the institution's

financial stability and market position.

The importance of collaboration with regulators cannot be overstated. A cooperative approach, marked by transparency and open communication, can significantly mitigate the negative consequences of regulatory scrutiny. This approach demonstrates a commitment to compliance and a willingness to address any identified issues. In turn, regulators are more likely to consider mitigating factors and adopt a less punitive approach when assessing penalties. Conversely, an

adversarial or uncooperative approach can intensify the

Regulatory response, leading to more stringent penalties and heightened scrutiny.

Furthermore, engaging experienced legal counsel specializing in financial regulatory matters is critical. Legal expertise is vital in navigating the complexities of regulatory investigations and enforcement actions. Legal counsel can provide guidance on legal obligations, assist in preparing responses to regulatory inquiries, and represent the institution in any formal proceedings. Their experience in handling similar cases can be invaluable in mitigating risks and achieving the best possible outcome. Early engagement of legal counsel can prevent costly mistakes and ensure a comprehensive and effective response.

In conclusion, navigating regulatory scrutiny and enforcement actions within the financial sector requires a multifaceted strategy encompassing proactive compliance, a swift and cooperative response, open communication, and expert legal counsel. A robust compliance program, regular internal audits, and a culture of compliance are essential for mitigating risk and avoiding regulatory issues. When regulatory scrutiny does occur, a timely, transparent, and cooperative response minimizes negative consequences.

Proactive compliance and effective crisis management are not merely cost-saving measures but critical investments in the long-term stability and success of any lending institution. The cost of inaction far outweighs the investment in robust compliance and effective response strategies.

Leveraging Technology for Enhanced Credit Analysis

The preceding discussion emphasized the paramount importance of regulatory compliance in the lending industry.

However, maintaining compliance is only one facet of successful lending operations. Equally crucial is the efficiency and accuracy of the credit analysis process itself.

This is where technological innovation, particularly the application of artificial intelligence (AI) and machine learning (ML), comes into play, offering transformative potential for enhancing credit risk assessment and streamlining lending workflows.

Traditional credit analysis methods, while established and reliable, often suffer from limitations in terms of speed, scalability, and the depth of analysis they can achieve.

Manual review of extensive datasets, involving multiple data points and often complex calculations, is time-consuming and prone to human error. This can lead to delays in loan processing, increased operational costs, and potentially inaccurate assessments of creditworthiness, impacting both the lender's profitability and the borrower's access to capital.

The integration of AI and ML offers a solution to these challenges, enabling lenders to analyze vast amounts of data far more efficiently and accurately than ever before.

AI-powered systems leverage advanced algorithms to analyze diverse data sources, including traditional credit reports, financial statements, transactional data, and even alternative data sources like social media activity and online purchasing patterns. This holistic approach goes beyond the constraints of traditional models, providing a more comprehensive view of a borrower's creditworthiness. The

Algorithms can identify patterns and correlations that might be overlooked by human analysts, leading to more nuanced and accurate risk assessments. For instance, an AI system might detect subtle shifts in a company's cash flow or subtle changes in its online reputation that would signal potential financial distress. This predictive capacity can assist in identifying potential risks early on, facilitating more

informed lending decisions and mitigating potential losses.

Machine learning, a subset of AI, plays a crucial role in refining the accuracy of credit analysis. ML algorithms are trained on large datasets of historical loan performance, enabling them to learn and identify factors that are strongly correlated with loan defaults or repayment success. This continuous learning process allows the algorithms to adapt to evolving market conditions and borrower behavior,

enhancing the precision of their predictions. The more data the system processes, the more accurate and reliable its predictions become, providing a powerful advantage in credit risk management.

Specific technologies are instrumental in this transformation.

Natural Language Processing (NLP) allows AI systems to analyze textual data from loan applications, financial reports, and other documents, extracting key insights that might be missed in a manual review. This ability is particularly

valuable in evaluating qualitative factors, such as the

management team's experience or the overall strength of a business plan. Optical Character Recognition (OCR)

technology further enhances automation by enabling the seamless digitization of physical documents, streamlining the data ingestion process and reducing manual data entry.

Another powerful tool is robotic process automation (RPA). RPA utilizes software robots to automate repetitive tasks, such as data entry, document verification, and loan

Application processing. This frees up human analysts to focus on more complex tasks, such as evaluating qualitative data and interacting with borrowers, leading to improved efficiency and productivity. The combination of NLP, OCR, and RPA creates a powerful synergy, significantly

accelerating the credit analysis process and reducing

operational costs.

The benefits of leveraging technology in credit analysis extend beyond enhanced efficiency and accuracy. It also allows lenders to expand their lending capabilities to

previously underserved market segments. Traditional lending methods often struggled to assess the creditworthiness of borrowers with limited credit histories or those operating in unconventional business models. However, AI-powered systems can analyze alternative data sources, providing insights into the creditworthiness of these borrowers,

fostering financial inclusion and expanding access to credit.

This ability to assess risk more comprehensively leads to a more inclusive and equitable financial system.

However, the implementation of AI and ML in credit

analysis is not without its challenges. Data quality remains a crucial factor, as the accuracy of AI-driven predictions

depends heavily on the quality of the data used to train the algorithms. Incomplete, inaccurate, or biased data can lead to flawed predictions, potentially resulting in unfair or

discriminatory lending practices. Therefore, robust data governance processes are essential to ensure the integrity and reliability of the data used in credit analysis.

Furthermore, the "black box" nature of some AI algorithms can pose challenges in terms of interpretability and

explainability. Understanding how an AI system arrives at a specific credit assessment is crucial for ensuring fairness and transparency. Regulators are increasingly demanding

Explainable AI (XAI) to ensure that lending decisions are not based on discriminatory or arbitrary factors. The

development and adoption of XAI techniques are therefore essential to address these concerns and maintain regulatory compliance.

Another important concern is the potential for bias in AI algorithms. If the training data reflects existing societal biases, the algorithm may perpetuate and even amplify those biases in its predictions. This can lead to discriminatory lending practices, negatively impacting certain demographic groups. Mitigating bias in AI algorithms requires careful attention to data selection, algorithm design, and ongoing monitoring of the system's performance to ensure fairness and equity.

The ongoing evolution of AI and ML also presents both opportunities and challenges. Keeping pace with

technological advancements requires continuous investment in infrastructure, training, and talent acquisition. Lenders must invest in skilled data scientists, AI engineers, and compliance professionals to ensure that they can effectively implement and manage these advanced technologies.

Moreover, adapting to new regulations and guidelines related to AI in lending is also crucial for maintaining compliance.

In conclusion, while the integration of AI and ML into credit analysis presents challenges, the potential benefits in terms of efficiency, accuracy, and inclusivity are compelling. By addressing concerns related to data quality, bias,

explainability, and regulatory compliance, lenders can

harness the transformative power of technology to improve their credit analysis processes, mitigate risk, and foster a more inclusive and equitable financial system. The proactive adoption of these technologies will be a significant factor in determining the success and sustainability of lending

Institutions in the years to come. It is not simply a matter of adopting new tools, but of fundamentally reshaping the credit analysis process to maximize the potential of these advanced technologies while minimizing their inherent risks. This strategic investment in technological advancement is a key differentiator for lenders seeking to thrive in an

increasingly competitive and data-driven landscape.

Digital Transformation in assetbased Lending

The preceding discussion highlighted the transformative potential of AI and machine learning in enhancing credit analysis. However, the benefits of technological innovation extend far beyond the realm of credit scoring. Digital

transformation is fundamentally reshaping the landscape of asset-based lending (ABL), impacting every stage of the lending process, from origination to collection. This

revolution is characterized by automation, improved data management, and enhanced borrower communication, leading to greater efficiency, reduced risk, and improved customer experience.

One of the most significant impacts of digital transformation in ABL is the automation of previously manual processes.

Tasks like document review, data entry, and collateral

valuation, once performed laboriously by human analysts, are now increasingly automated through the use of

sophisticated software and AI-powered tools. Optical

Character Recognition (OCR) technology plays a pivotal role, automatically extracting data from various documents, including invoices, financial statements, and legal

agreements. This eliminates the need for manual data entry, reducing errors, accelerating the processing time, and freeing up human resources for more strategic tasks. Robotic

Process Automation (RPA) further enhances automation by taking on repetitive tasks like data validation and

transferring data between different systems, streamlining the entire workflow.

The improved data management capabilities enabled by digital transformation are equally transformative. ABL lending relies heavily on the accurate and timely collection

Of data from diverse sources. Digital platforms provide a centralized repository for all relevant data, allowing lenders to access a comprehensive view of the borrower's financial position in real-time. This improved visibility helps lenders to make more informed decisions, monitor the performance of loans more effectively, and proactively identify potential risks. Furthermore, data analytics tools provide the ability to analyze vast datasets, identifying trends and patterns that might be overlooked in a manual review, enabling more accurate risk assessments and more tailored lending

strategies. Data visualization tools transform complex

financial information into easily understandable dashboards and reports, enhancing decision-making and communication with both internal teams and borrowers.

Digital transformation also fosters improved communication with borrowers. Online portals and mobile applications provide borrowers with convenient access to their loan information, allowing them to monitor their account

balances, make payments, and communicate with their lenders directly. This improved transparency and

accessibility strengthens the lender-borrower relationship, building trust and facilitating a smoother loan process.

Automated communication tools can streamline the delivery of important notifications and reminders, ensuring that borrowers are kept informed throughout the loan lifecycle. This reduces the risk of missed payments and minimizes the need for manual interventions, improving overall efficiency and reducing operational costs.

The implementation of digital tools has significantly

impacted various aspects of the ABL process. For instance, in the origination stage, online applications and digital

onboarding processes dramatically reduce the time and effort required to initiate a loan. Borrowers can submit their

applications electronically, providing necessary

Documentation through secure portals. Automated credit scoring systems accelerate the underwriting process,

allowing lenders to make quicker decisions and offer faster turnaround times. Furthermore, advanced analytics can help lenders identify potential borrowers who might be

overlooked using traditional methods, expanding access to credit for businesses in underserved markets.

In the monitoring and management phase, digital tools offer real-time insights into the performance of loans. Automated monitoring systems track key performance indicators (kpis), such as borrowing base utilization and debt service coverage ratios, enabling lenders to identify potential problems early on and take proactive measures to mitigate risk. Automated reporting systems provide timely and accurate information to both lenders and borrowers, ensuring transparency and

facilitating efficient communication. Predictive analytics can anticipate potential payment defaults, enabling lenders to take proactive measures such as renegotiating terms or

offering support services.

During the liquidation process, digital tools streamline the sale or disposal of collateral. Online auction platforms and digital marketplaces provide access to a wider range of

potential buyers, maximizing the recovery value of the

collateral. Automated valuation models enable more accurate and timely assessments of collateral value, minimizing

disputes and accelerating the liquidation process.

The adoption of blockchain technology presents another exciting frontier in ABL. Blockchain's inherent transparency and security can improve the efficiency and security of collateral management, reducing the risk of fraud and

disputes. Smart contracts can automate loan agreements and payment processes, further streamlining operations. While the integration of blockchain in ABL is still in its early

Stages, it holds the potential to revolutionize the industry, increasing trust and transparency.

However, the transition to a digitally-driven ABL environment is not without its challenges. Cybersecurity threats remain a significant concern, necessitating robust security measures to protect sensitive borrower data. The need for significant investments in technology infrastructure and employee training can also present a barrier to entry for smaller lenders. Moreover, regulatory compliance continues to evolve, requiring lenders to adapt their systems and practices to meet changing requirements. The potential for data bias in AI-powered systems also needs careful consideration, ensuring fairness and equity in lending practices.

The success of digital transformation in ABL relies not just on technological advancements but also on the ability of lenders to adapt their organizational structures, processes, and employee skillsets. This requires a strong commitment to change management, including comprehensive employee training programs and the adoption of agile methodologies that facilitate continuous improvement. Furthermore, effective collaboration between technology providers, lenders, and regulators is essential to establish best practices and address potential challenges.

In conclusion, digital transformation is fundamentally reshaping the asset-based lending landscape. By embracing automation, enhancing data management, and fostering improved borrower communication, lenders can significantly improve efficiency, reduce risk, and enhance the customer experience. While challenges remain, the potential rewards of digital adoption are substantial, paving the way for a more efficient, transparent, and inclusive ABL industry. The ongoing evolution of technology, particularly in areas like

AI, machine learning, and blockchain, presents exciting opportunities for further innovation, driving further

improvements in efficiency, risk management, and customer service. Lenders who actively embrace these changes will be well-positioned to thrive in the competitive environment of the modern financial sector. The proactive and strategic implementation of these technological advancements will be crucial for not just survival, but for achieving sustainable growth and market leadership in the evolving ABL arena.

This is a transformation that is not merely about updating existing processes, but fundamentally reimagining the core functions of asset-based lending to meet the demands of the twenty-first-century financial landscape.

Using Data Analytics for Risk Management

The integration of data analytics represents a quantum leap forward in risk management within the lending sector.

Moving beyond rudimentary credit scoring, sophisticated analytical techniques now allow lenders to delve deep into borrower behavior, market trends, and economic indicators, providing a far more nuanced and predictive understanding of risk. This proactive approach enables the development of robust early warning systems, allowing for timely

intervention and mitigation of potential losses.

One crucial application of data analytics is in the identification of early warning signals of loan default.

Traditional methods often relied on lagging indicators, such as missed payments, which often came too late for effective intervention. Modern data analytics, however, can leverage a wide range of leading indicators to predict potential

problems before they manifest. For instance, analyzing a borrower's cash flow patterns, coupled with macroeconomic data like industry-specific economic forecasts and changes in interest rates, can reveal early signs of financial distress.

Machine learning algorithms can identify subtle anomalies and patterns in transaction data that might otherwise go unnoticed, providing valuable insights into a borrower's evolving financial health.

This predictive capability allows lenders to proactively engage with borrowers experiencing difficulties, offering tailored support and exploring restructuring options. This proactive engagement can significantly reduce the likelihood of default, preserving both the lender's investment and the borrower's business. Early intervention strategies might include renegotiating loan terms, providing access to

Financial advisory services, or offering temporary

forbearance periods. This proactive approach is significantly more cost-effective than managing defaults, minimizing losses and preserving lender-borrower relationships.

Furthermore, data analytics enables lenders to refine their risk assessment models, moving beyond simple credit scores to encompass a broader range of factors. This holistic

approach considers not only the borrower's financial history, but also industry trends, macroeconomic conditions, and even qualitative factors such as management quality and operational efficiency. By incorporating alternative data sources, such as social media sentiment analysis, satellite imagery of borrower facilities, and geolocation data, lenders can obtain a richer and more comprehensive picture of the borrower's creditworthiness. This multifaceted assessment helps to reduce bias, making lending decisions more

objective and accurate.

The development of sophisticated risk scoring models is another key benefit of data analytics. These models go beyond simple linear regressions, employing advanced machine learning techniques such as neural networks and decision trees to capture complex relationships between variables and predict default probabilities with greater accuracy. These models can be continuously updated and refined as new data becomes available, allowing lenders to adapt their risk assessments to evolving market conditions and borrower behaviors.

The implementation of data analytics also leads to a more efficient allocation of resources. By identifying higher-risk borrowers, lenders can allocate more resources to monitor these accounts closely, while lower-risk borrowers may require less intensive monitoring. This targeted approach optimizes resource allocation, freeing up resources that can

Be redeployed to other areas, increasing overall operational efficiency. Furthermore, data analytics can help lenders to optimize their pricing strategies, adjusting interest rates and fees based on the assessed level of risk, ensuring profitability while maintaining competitive pricing.

The effectiveness of data analytics in risk management is not limited to the credit decision process. It also plays a crucial role in portfolio management, enabling lenders to identify and manage concentrations of risk within their loan

portfolios. For instance, by analyzing the geographic

distribution of their loans and the exposure to specific

industries, lenders can assess their overall risk profile and diversify their portfolio accordingly to mitigate potential losses. Similarly, analysis of the correlations between

different loans in the portfolio can highlight potential

systemic risks, enabling lenders to take proactive steps to reduce their exposure.

However, the effective implementation of data analytics in risk management requires a robust technological

infrastructure and skilled personnel. Lenders need to invest in powerful computing resources and sophisticated data management systems to process and analyze the vast

amounts of data required. Furthermore, they need to recruit and retain skilled data scientists and analysts who can develop and maintain sophisticated analytical models and interpret the results effectively. This requires ongoing investment in training and development programs to ensure that employees possess the necessary expertise.

Furthermore, ethical considerations are paramount. The use of data analytics raises concerns about data privacy and the potential for bias in algorithms. Lenders must ensure that they comply with all relevant data privacy regulations and that their analytical models are fair and unbiased, avoiding

Discrimination against certain borrower groups. Regular audits and monitoring are crucial to ensure the ethical and responsible use of data analytics.

In addition to the internal use of data analytics, external data sources provide an invaluable supplement to internal data. Accessing industry reports, macroeconomic forecasts, and market intelligence significantly enhances the accuracy and robustness of risk assessments. This integration enables lenders to develop a more comprehensive understanding of the broader economic environment and its impact on their borrowers.

In conclusion, data analytics is not just a supplemental tool; it is fundamentally reshaping risk management in lending.

By leveraging the power of sophisticated analytical

techniques, lenders can move from a reactive to a proactive approach, identifying and mitigating risks more effectively, optimizing resource allocation, and ultimately, improving their profitability and sustainability. The continuous

advancement of analytical tools and techniques, coupled with a commitment to ethical considerations and a robust technological infrastructure, will ensure that data analytics continues to play a crucial role in driving innovation and efficiency in the lending industry. The future of responsible and profitable lending rests, in no small part, on the

intelligent application and responsible stewardship of data.

Implementing Fintech Solutions in Lending Operations

The transformative potential of data analytics in risk management lays a strong foundation for understanding the next wave of innovation in lending: the integration of fintech solutions. These technologies are not merely supplementary tools; they represent a fundamental shift in how lending operations are conducted, promising enhanced efficiency, reduced costs, and a significantly improved customer experience. The successful implementation of fintech, however, requires a strategic approach that considers both the technological and operational aspects, as well as the crucial human element.

One of the most impactful areas where fintech is revolutionizing lending is loan origination. Traditional loan origination processes are often cumbersome, involving extensive paperwork, manual data entry, and lengthy processing times. Fintech solutions, such as automated underwriting systems, streamline this process considerably. These systems utilize sophisticated algorithms and machine learning to analyze vast amounts of data, including credit scores, financial statements, and alternative data sources, to assess creditworthiness far more quickly and efficiently than human underwriters alone. This automation significantly reduces processing times, allowing lenders to approve loans more rapidly and improve their turnaround times, enhancing customer satisfaction and potentially increasing loan volume. Furthermore, the reduced manual intervention minimizes the risk of human error, improving the accuracy and consistency of credit decisions.

Beyond automated underwriting, robotic process automation (RPA) is another game-changer in loan origination. RPA involves using software robots to automate repetitive tasks, such as data entry, document verification, and

communication with borrowers. This automation frees up human employees to focus on more complex and value-added activities, such as relationship management and client interaction. The result is a more efficient and cost-effective loan origination process, allowing lenders to handle a larger volume of applications with fewer resources. For instance, RPA can automate the process of verifying borrower

identities, ensuring compliance with Know Your Customer (KYC) and Anti-Money Laundering (AML) regulations.

This automated verification reduces the risk of fraud and streamlines the onboarding process.

The integration of fintech also extends to customer

relationship management (CRM) within lending operations.

Sophisticated CRM systems provide lenders with a

centralized platform to manage all aspects of their

interactions with borrowers. These systems track

communication, loan status updates, and customer

preferences, enabling lenders to provide personalized service and build stronger relationships with their clients. This

enhanced customer service can lead to improved customer retention and loyalty. Furthermore, CRM systems can

provide valuable insights into customer behavior, helping lenders tailor their offerings to better meet customer needs and anticipate potential problems. Features such as

automated email responses for frequently asked questions, personalized communication based on individual borrower profiles, and integrated online portals for account

management all contribute to a seamless and user-friendly customer experience.

Another critical aspect of fintech in lending is the use of blockchain technology. Blockchain offers the potential to revolutionize the security and transparency of lending processes. By creating a secure and immutable record of loan transactions, blockchain can reduce the risk of fraud and disputes. It can also streamline the process of

transferring loan documents and payments, reducing

processing times and costs. For example, the use of smart contracts can automate the disbursement of loan funds and the repayment schedule, reducing the need for manual intervention. This automation improves efficiency and reduces operational risk. While the full implementation of blockchain in lending is still evolving, its potential to transform the industry is undeniable.

The rise of open banking apis has opened up exciting new possibilities for lenders. Open banking allows third-party providers to access customer financial data with their

consent, providing lenders with a richer and more

comprehensive picture of a borrower's financial health. This data can be used to improve the accuracy of credit scoring models and personalize loan offers. However, the successful utilization of open banking requires careful consideration of data privacy and security. Lenders must ensure that they comply with all relevant regulations and protect customer data from unauthorized access. The transparent and ethical use of this data is crucial for maintaining customer trust and confidence.

The use of mobile lending platforms is another significant trend in the fintech space. Mobile lending apps offer

borrowers a convenient and accessible way to apply for loans and manage their accounts. These platforms typically provide a user-friendly interface and real-time updates on loan applications and repayments. This convenience

improves the customer experience and can increase the

Volume of loan applications. The integration of biometric authentication adds an extra layer of security, making the process more secure for both the lender and the borrower.

Moreover, these platforms often integrate seamlessly with other fintech solutions, such as mobile payment systems and digital identity verification tools, creating a truly integrated and seamless lending experience.

The implementation of these fintech solutions is not without its challenges. Lenders need to invest in the necessary

infrastructure and technology, as well as train their staff to use these new tools effectively. Moreover, cybersecurity is a paramount concern; robust security measures are essential to protect sensitive customer data from cyber threats. Effective data governance policies and procedures are critical to

ensuring compliance with regulatory requirements. Finally, managing the transition to new systems and integrating them with existing infrastructure can be a complex undertaking.

Careful planning and project management are crucial for a successful implementation.

In conclusion, the integration of fintech solutions in lending operations is transforming the industry, leading to greater efficiency, reduced costs, and improved customer

experiences. From automated underwriting and RPA to blockchain technology, open banking apis, and mobile lending platforms, fintech is offering a myriad of

opportunities for lenders to improve their operations and compete in an increasingly digital landscape. However, the successful adoption of these technologies requires a

comprehensive strategic approach that considers the

technological, operational, and human aspects. Lenders must invest in the necessary infrastructure, train their staff, and implement robust security measures to fully realize the benefits of fintech and maintain a competitive edge in the dynamic world of modern lending. The future of lending is

Inextricably linked to the intelligent and responsible adoption of these innovative technologies.

The Future of Lending and Technological Advancements

The integration of fintech into lending practices, as

discussed, marks a significant turning point. However, this is merely the prelude to an even more transformative era. The future of lending is inextricably linked to the continued evolution and adoption of emerging technologies,

particularly blockchain and distributed ledger technology (DLT). These technologies promise to reshape the lending landscape in profound ways, offering solutions to long-standing challenges while simultaneously presenting new complexities.

One of the most compelling applications of blockchain in lending lies in its potential to enhance security and

transparency. Traditional lending processes often involve multiple intermediaries, each handling different aspects of the loan lifecycle. This fragmented approach creates

inefficiencies and increases the risk of errors or fraud.

Blockchain, with its decentralized and immutable ledger, can streamline these processes significantly. By recording all loan transactions on a shared, secure, and transparent ledger, blockchain eliminates the need for intermediaries in many instances, reducing costs and enhancing efficiency.

Furthermore, the immutability of the blockchain ensures that all transactions are auditable and tamper-proof, minimizing the risk of disputes and fraud. This enhanced transparency fosters trust between lenders and borrowers, facilitating a more efficient and secure lending ecosystem.

Consider the process of loan origination. Currently, verifying a borrower's identity and creditworthiness can be a time-consuming and complex process. Blockchain can automate

And simplify this verification process through the use of smart contracts. Smart contracts are self-executing contracts with the terms of the agreement directly written into lines of code. Upon fulfillment of pre-defined conditions, such as identity verification and credit score checks, the smart

contract automatically releases the loan funds. This

automation significantly reduces processing times and

eliminates the need for manual intervention, making the loan origination process faster, more efficient, and less prone to errors.

Beyond loan origination, blockchain can also transform loan servicing and repayment. Smart contracts can automate the repayment schedule, ensuring that payments are processed automatically and on time. This automation reduces

administrative overhead for lenders and provides borrowers with greater clarity and control over their loan repayments. Furthermore, blockchain can facilitate the seamless transfer of loan documents and payments, reducing processing times and costs. By eliminating the need for intermediaries,

blockchain increases the efficiency and transparency of the entire loan lifecycle, from origination to repayment.

The potential applications of DLT extend beyond individual loans. DLT can facilitate the creation of decentralized

lending platforms, where borrowers and lenders can interact directly without the need for intermediaries. These platforms could offer greater flexibility and accessibility to borrowers, potentially disrupting the traditional banking model. Imagine a world where individuals can access loans directly from a decentralized platform, bypassing the complexities and requirements of traditional lending institutions. This

increased accessibility could be particularly beneficial for underserved populations, such as small businesses and

individuals in developing economies.

However, the integration of blockchain and DLT into the lending industry is not without its challenges. The

technology is still relatively nascent, and its scalability and regulatory implications require further investigation. The development of robust security protocols is crucial to ensure the security of the blockchain network and prevent attacks.

Furthermore, the adoption of blockchain requires a

significant shift in mindset and business processes for

lenders, and the training and support needed for successful implementation are substantial. Regulatory uncertainty poses another challenge, as many jurisdictions are still grappling with the legal and regulatory frameworks for blockchain technology. Clarification and standardization of regulations are essential for fostering wider adoption.

The future of lending will also be significantly shaped by advancements in artificial intelligence (AI) and machine learning (ML). These technologies are already transforming various aspects of the lending process, as discussed

previously, from automated underwriting to customer

service. However, their potential is far from fully realized. Future iterations of AI and ML will likely lead to even more sophisticated risk assessment models, capable of analyzing vast amounts of data to identify and mitigate potential risks with greater accuracy and efficiency. This enhanced risk assessment will potentially lead to lower loan defaults and reduced losses for lenders.

Furthermore, AI and ML can personalize the lending

experience for borrowers. By analyzing borrower data, AI systems can tailor loan offerings to individual needs and preferences. This personalized approach can lead to greater customer satisfaction and potentially higher loan approval rates. AI-powered chatbots and virtual assistants can provide 24/7 customer support, answering borrowers' questions and providing timely updates on their loan applications. This

Improved customer service can increase customer loyalty and enhance the overall lending experience.

The convergence of blockchain and AI presents particularly exciting possibilities. AI algorithms can be used to analyze data on the blockchain, providing insights into market trends and borrower behavior. This data analysis can inform lending decisions and help lenders optimize their strategies.

For example, AI could identify patterns in loan defaults or predict future market fluctuations, allowing lenders to adjust their lending practices accordingly. The synergy between these two technologies promises to drive significant innovation in the lending industry.

However, the ethical implications of deploying AI in lending must be carefully considered. Algorithmic bias, for instance, can perpetuate existing inequalities if not properly addressed. Ensuring fairness and transparency in AI-powered lending systems is crucial to preventing discrimination and promoting equal access to credit. Robust oversight mechanisms and ethical guidelines are essential to mitigate potential biases and ensure responsible use of AI in the lending industry.

Data privacy and security remain paramount concerns in the evolving landscape of lending technologies. The increasing reliance on data analytics and AI necessitates the development of strong security measures to protect sensitive customer information from unauthorized access or breaches. Compliance with relevant data protection regulations, such as GDPR, is critical. Investing in robust cybersecurity infrastructure and implementing stringent data governance policies are essential to ensuring the security and privacy of customer data. Transparency regarding data collection and usage practices is also crucial to building and maintaining customer trust.

Finally, the future of lending will require a workforce

equipped to navigate this complex technological landscape. The integration of new technologies will demand upskilling and reskilling initiatives to ensure that lending professionals possess the necessary expertise to operate and manage these advanced systems effectively. Investing in training and

development programs will be vital in bridging the skills gap and ensuring a smooth transition to a technology-driven lending environment. A focus on data literacy, cybersecurity awareness, and ethical considerations related to AI is

essential for fostering a responsible and innovative lending ecosystem.

In conclusion, the future of lending is bright, brimming with possibilities driven by technological advancements.

Blockchain, DLT, AI, and ML are poised to revolutionize the lending industry, offering solutions to long-standing

challenges and creating opportunities for greater efficiency, transparency, and accessibility. However, the successful adoption of these technologies requires careful consideration of the ethical, regulatory, and security implications. A

proactive and responsible approach to innovation, coupled with a commitment to workforce development, is essential for navigating the complexities of this rapidly evolving landscape and ensuring a future where lending is both

efficient and equitable for all. The journey is one that

requires collaboration, innovation, and a keen eye on the ever-shifting technological and societal landscape.

Case Study Responding to a Major Market Disruption

The global financial crisis of 2008 serves as a stark reminder of the fragility of even the most robust financial systems.

While the crisis originated in the US subprime mortgage market, its impact reverberated across the globe, triggering a cascade of bankruptcies, bailouts, and regulatory reforms.

This event underscored the critical need for effective crisis management protocols within financial institutions, capable of navigating unforeseen market disruptions and

safeguarding both the institution and its stakeholders. One prominent example illustrating the importance of proactive crisis management is the response of a major European bank, let's call it "Bank X," to the sudden collapse of a major

European sovereign bond market.

Bank X, a significant player in the commercial and asset-based lending sector, held a substantial portfolio of

sovereign bonds issued by a Eurozone nation experiencing a severe economic downturn. The initial signs of distress were subtle: slight widening of credit default swap (CDS) spreads, a gradual decline in bond prices, and increased volatility in the market. However, these early warning signals were

initially dismissed by many market analysts as temporary fluctuations. Bank X, however, possessed a sophisticated risk management framework that emphasized early

identification and assessment of potential threats. This

proactive approach proved critical in mitigating the impact of the subsequent crisis.

Their risk management team, comprised of experienced professionals with expertise in various aspects of credit analysis, market risk, and operational risk, began closely

Monitoring the situation. They utilized advanced

econometric models and stress-testing methodologies to assess the potential impact of various scenarios, including a complete sovereign debt default. These sophisticated tools allowed them to project potential losses with reasonable accuracy, providing valuable insights into the severity of the looming threat. Unlike many institutions that downplayed or ignored these early warnings, Bank X's leadership promptly initiated a crisis management plan.

This plan wasn't a dusty document gathering virtual cobwebs in a filing cabinet; it was a living document, regularly

reviewed and updated based on evolving market conditions and regulatory changes. It outlined specific roles and

responsibilities, establishing clear communication channels and decision-making processes. The establishment of a dedicated crisis management team, comprising senior

executives from various departments, proved invaluable.

This team worked around the clock, conducting regular briefings and coordinating responses.

Their initial strategy focused on risk mitigation. They

immediately began reducing their exposure to the troubled sovereign bonds, strategically selling a portion of their holdings to minimize potential losses. This action, although incurring short-term losses, proved a crucial move in

averting a potentially catastrophic financial blow.

Simultaneously, they engaged in active dialogue with other financial institutions and regulatory bodies to assess the overall market situation and gauge the potential for broader systemic consequences.

The communication strategy adopted by Bank X was equally critical. Transparency was a guiding principle; they

proactively informed their stakeholders – including

depositors, investors, and regulatory bodies – about the

Developing situation and the steps being taken to mitigate the risks. This open communication fostered trust and

confidence, preventing panic and minimizing the potential for a liquidity crisis. This approach contrasted sharply with other institutions that opted for secrecy, a strategy that often exacerbated the situation.

However, selling the bonds was only part of the solution. Recognizing the potential liquidity squeeze and maintaining confidence among depositors, the bank took preemptive measures to shore up their liquidity position. This involved securing additional lines of credit from central banks and other financial institutions. It also involved reducing

dividend payouts and suspending share buyback programs. These steps ensured they had sufficient funds to meet their obligations, even in the event of a severe market downturn.

The crisis management team also focused on maintaining operational stability. They implemented robust contingency plans to ensure the continuity of critical services, even under extreme pressure. This involved strengthening their IT

infrastructure, diversifying their operational processes, and ensuring business continuity across multiple locations. Their preparedness prevented a disruption of their core banking functions, preserving customer trust and confidence.

Another crucial element of Bank X's response was its focus on preserving its reputation. They worked diligently to maintain a positive image, actively communicating their actions and demonstrating a commitment to transparency and ethical practices. This focus on their reputation helped mitigate potential reputational damage, a factor that can be as devastating as financial losses.

In the aftermath of the crisis, Bank X conducted a thorough post-mortem analysis, identifying areas for improvement in

Their risk management and crisis management frameworks. This review process resulted in refinements to their risk models, strengthening their early warning systems and enhancing their ability to anticipate and respond to future crises. They also invested in additional training for their staff, ensuring they were equipped to handle similar

situations in the future.

The lessons learned from this case study are profound.

Proactive risk management, a well-defined crisis

management plan, transparent communication, and a focus on operational stability are all critical elements of a

successful response to market disruptions. Bank X's

experience serves as a model for other financial institutions, emphasizing the importance of preparedness and a holistic approach to crisis management. Ignoring early warning signs or resorting to secrecy can exacerbate the situation, leading to severe financial consequences and reputational damage. In contrast, a proactive, transparent, and well-coordinated

response can significantly mitigate the impact of even the most significant market disruptions. The meticulous

planning and swift execution of Bank X's strategy highlight the importance of continuous improvement in risk

management and crisis preparedness within the financial sector. The success of their response underscores the fact that preparedness isn't just a good practice—it's a necessity for survival in the often-turbulent world of finance. The integration of robust technological tools, advanced analytical models, and a highly trained crisis management team are key ingredients for mitigating the impact of future unforeseen market events.

Case Study Managing a largescale Loan Default

This case study analyzes the response of a major commercial bank, let's refer to it as "Bank Y," to a significant loan default by a large industrial conglomerate. The conglomerate, a previously highly rated client with a long-standing

relationship with Bank Y, experienced a sudden and sharp decline in profitability due to unforeseen geopolitical events and a subsequent contraction in global demand for its

primary product. The loan in question was a substantial asset-based lending facility, secured by the conglomerate's inventory, accounts receivable, and several key

manufacturing plants.

The initial signs of trouble were subtle. While the

conglomerate met its scheduled interest payments, the bank's internal credit risk assessment flagged a gradual

deterioration in several key financial ratios, including the current ratio and the debt-to-equity ratio. Initially, these deviations were attributed to temporary market fluctuations. However, as the geopolitical situation worsened, the bank's risk management team initiated a more thorough review.

This review utilized sophisticated quantitative models, incorporating stress tests that considered various adverse scenarios, including a complete collapse in global demand for the conglomerate's core product. The results were

alarming. The models predicted a significant increase in the probability of default, raising serious concerns about the loan's recoverability.

This situation highlighted the critical importance of

comprehensive and ongoing due diligence in asset-based lending. Bank Y's proactive risk monitoring system, coupled with its sophisticated analytical capabilities, provided early

Warning signs, which allowed the bank to react before the situation spiraled out of control. The bank's response

immediately moved from monitoring to active intervention.

A dedicated crisis management team was assembled, comprised of seasoned lending officers, legal counsel specializing in restructuring, and financial analysts with expertise in distressed asset valuations. Their primary objectives were to minimize losses, preserve the bank's reputation, and protect its financial stability.

The bank's initial strategy involved a proactive approach to negotiations with the conglomerate. Instead of issuing a formal demand for immediate repayment—a course of action that would likely have resulted in immediate bankruptcy proceedings and a costly and lengthy legal battle—Bank Y opted for a collaborative and constructive dialogue. This strategy recognized the complex interplay of factors driving the conglomerate's financial difficulties and acknowledged that a mutually beneficial solution was more likely to be achieved through negotiation rather than litigation.

The negotiations involved extensive financial modeling and scenario planning. The bank worked closely with the

conglomerate's management team to develop various

restructuring options, exploring possibilities such as debt forgiveness, extension of repayment terms, and reduction in interest rates. Crucially, Bank Y also conducted a

comprehensive valuation of the collateral, using a

combination of discounted cash flow analysis and market comparable data. This valuation provided a realistic

assessment of the recoverable value of the assets, informing the negotiation strategy and facilitating a more informed decision-making process.

Throughout the negotiation process, transparency and open communication were central. Bank Y maintained a clear and

Consistent line of communication with the conglomerate's management team and its stakeholders. This transparency fostered trust and encouraged a collaborative approach, significantly improving the chances of reaching a mutually acceptable agreement. Furthermore, maintaining open

channels of communication with regulatory bodies was vital.

Regular updates were provided to relevant banking

authorities, keeping them apprised of the situation and the steps being taken to mitigate potential risks. This approach minimized potential regulatory scrutiny and helped build confidence in the bank's handling of the situation.

The negotiations were complex and protracted, lasting several months. They involved numerous meetings, detailed financial analyses, and tough compromises from both sides.

Ultimately, an agreement was reached that involved a

combination of debt reduction, an extended repayment

schedule, and a phased release of collateral. The agreement ensured that the bank recovered a significant portion of its loan, minimizing its losses while avoiding the high costs and protracted uncertainties of bankruptcy proceedings.

Beyond the specific negotiation strategy, the bank's response highlighted the importance of post-mortem analysis.

Following the successful resolution, Bank Y conducted a thorough review of the entire process, identifying areas where its response could have been improved. This review covered aspects such as early warning systems, the

effectiveness of its credit scoring model, the efficacy of its communication protocols, and the timeliness of its

intervention. The insights gained from this post-mortem analysis were incorporated into the bank's internal

procedures, strengthening its credit risk management

framework and enhancing its ability to navigate similar situations in the future. This proactive approach to learning from past experiences underscores a crucial element of

Effective crisis management: the continuous pursuit of improvement and adaptation.

The case study of Bank Y's response to a large-scale loan default underscores several key lessons. First, proactive risk management and early identification of potential problems are critical. The bank's sophisticated risk assessment model and its diligent monitoring of client performance played a significant role in the successful resolution. Second, a

collaborative negotiation strategy, focused on finding

mutually beneficial solutions, can be significantly more effective than adversarial approaches. Bank Y's focus on communication and transparency fostered trust and

facilitated a mutually acceptable outcome. Third,

comprehensive asset valuation is essential in determining the realistic recoverability of a loan and in formulating effective negotiation strategies. Finally, a structured post-mortem analysis allows for continuous improvement in crisis

management capabilities, enhancing the resilience of the bank in the face of future challenges. Bank Y's experience serves as a valuable example of how proactive risk

management, effective negotiation, and post-crisis analysis can help minimize losses and protect the financial stability of a lending institution in the face of a significant loan default. The lessons learned from this case underscore the need for a comprehensive and adaptable approach to crisis management within the financial sector, emphasizing the importance of continuous learning and improvement. This proactive

approach, combined with sound financial modeling and risk assessment tools, is crucial for navigating the often-

unpredictable landscape of commercial lending.

Furthermore, the emphasis on transparency and open

communication reinforces the importance of trust-building and collaboration as key elements of successful crisis

resolution. The long-term value derived from such an

approach surpasses the immediate short-term gains. Building

Strong relationships and fostering trust with clients isn't just good practice; it's a vital component of effective risk

management and a cornerstone of sustained success in the highly competitive world of commercial lending.

Case Study Navigating a Reputational Crisis

This case study focuses on "Bank Z," a mid-sized regional bank with a strong reputation for community involvement and conservative lending practices. Their crisis stemmed not from a single catastrophic event, like the massive loan default in Bank Y's case, but from a series of smaller, seemingly unrelated incidents that cumulatively eroded public trust. It began with a series of critical articles in the local newspaper questioning the bank's lending practices regarding small business loans in underserved communities. The articles, citing anonymous sources, alleged that Bank Z had unfairly rejected loan applications from minority-owned businesses, suggesting a bias in their credit scoring algorithms and a lack of commitment to diversity and inclusion. While the bank vehemently denied these allegations, the articles sparked a wave of negative social media commentary, fueled by existing anxieties about economic inequality and banking practices.

The initial response from Bank Z was reactive and somewhat disorganized. Press releases denying the allegations lacked specific data to refute the claims. Attempts to engage with online critics were often perceived as dismissive or unconvincing, further inflaming public sentiment. This lack of a cohesive and proactive communication strategy exacerbated the crisis. The absence of a designated spokesperson and a clear messaging framework only compounded the problem, creating a vacuum filled with speculation and misinformation. The bank's internal communications were equally inadequate. Staff felt uninformed and unprepared to handle inquiries from customers and the media, leading to inconsistent messaging and further damaging the bank's reputation.

The crisis intensified when a prominent community activist organized a protest outside the bank's headquarters. The protest, while relatively small, received considerable media attention, further amplifying negative perceptions of the bank. This visible demonstration of public discontent served as a stark reminder of the urgency of the situation and the need for a more comprehensive and strategic response. The initial damage control efforts failed to address the core issue: the perception of a lack of transparency and fairness in the bank's lending practices. The bank's attempts to simply deny the accusations without providing concrete evidence to support their claims were ultimately unconvincing. The public, especially those who had been directly impacted by the bank's loan decisions, were skeptical of the bank's

denials, leading to a significant decline in customer trust and confidence.

Recognizing the inadequacy of their initial response, Bank Z's leadership assembled a crisis management team

composed of senior executives, public relations

professionals, and legal counsel. Their first step was to conduct a thorough internal review of the bank's lending practices. This review wasn't merely a cursory investigation but a detailed examination of their loan application

processes, credit scoring algorithms, and documentation procedures. The goal was to identify any potential biases or inconsistencies in their approach. The team also reviewed and updated the bank's diversity and inclusion policies, aiming to demonstrate a genuine commitment to equitable lending practices.

The findings of the internal review were significant. While the accusations of systematic discrimination were

unfounded, the review did reveal several areas where improvements could be made. For example, the credit

Scoring algorithm was found to disproportionately penalize applicants with lower credit scores, a demographic that often included individuals from underserved communities.

Additionally, the bank's loan application process lacked sufficient transparency, leading to confusion and frustration among potential borrowers. These findings, while not

validating the original allegations of bias, demonstrated a need for internal reform.

Having identified these weaknesses, Bank Z developed a comprehensive action plan aimed at rebuilding trust and improving its reputation. This plan encompassed several key elements: firstly, a complete overhaul of the bank's credit scoring algorithm to mitigate potential biases and improve fairness. Secondly, a commitment to increase transparency in the loan application process, providing clear and accessible information to applicants and simplifying the process.

Thirdly, a robust diversity and inclusion training program for all bank employees to promote awareness and understanding of potential biases. Fourthly, a public awareness campaign aimed at directly addressing the concerns raised by the initial critical articles and demonstrating the bank's commitment to equitable lending practices. This involved a series of town hall meetings, community outreach initiatives, and an

updated website with detailed information about the bank's lending policies and performance metrics.

The bank's communication strategy also underwent a

significant transformation. A dedicated spokesperson was appointed, tasked with delivering consistent and transparent messaging across all platforms. Open and honest

communication was prioritized, both internally with

employees and externally with the public. This involved regular updates on the progress of the action plan,

acknowledging the bank's shortcomings while highlighting their commitment to change. The bank also established

Proactive engagement with social media, actively responding to criticisms and concerns. This more transparent and

responsive approach fostered a sense of accountability and demonstrated a genuine willingness to address the issues raised by the public.

Furthermore, Bank Z partnered with several community organizations to demonstrate its commitment to serving underserved communities. This included providing financial literacy workshops, offering microloans to small businesses, and investing in local community development projects.

These initiatives aimed not only to rebuild trust but also to demonstrate the bank's commitment to positive social

impact. The bank also commissioned an independent audit of their lending practices to further reinforce their commitment to transparency and accountability. The results of the audit, publicly released, further validated the bank's claims of improved fairness and transparency in their lending

procedures.

The crisis management strategy employed by Bank Z

differed significantly from the approach adopted by Bank Y.

While Bank Y dealt with a single, major event requiring focused negotiation and financial restructuring, Bank Z faced a multifaceted reputational crisis requiring a sustained and multifaceted response focused on rebuilding trust and transparency. Bank Y's success relied on shrewd negotiation and financial analysis, whereas Bank Z's success hinged on effective communication, demonstrating a commitment to internal reform, and rebuilding public confidence. Both cases, however, underscore the critical importance of

proactive risk management, well-defined crisis management protocols, and consistent communication.

The long-term impact of Bank Z's crisis was significant. While the initial reputational damage was substantial, the

Bank's proactive and transparent response, coupled with demonstrable changes in its lending practices, ultimately led to a gradual restoration of public trust. The bank's

willingness to acknowledge its shortcomings, coupled with its commitment to meaningful reform, proved more effective than simply denying the allegations. This case study

demonstrates that even in the face of intense public scrutiny, a well-executed crisis management strategy can mitigate reputational damage and lead to a stronger, more resilient organization. The key lessons are that swift, transparent responses, coupled with genuine efforts towards reform and demonstrable commitment to improved practices, are crucial to rebuilding trust after a reputational crisis. Ignoring the situation, offering weak justifications, or displaying a lack of transparency will only serve to exacerbate the problem and ultimately harm the long-term viability of the institution. The ability to learn from mistakes, adapt swiftly, and demonstrate genuine remorse and commitment to change is what truly distinguishes effective crisis management. This, more than anything else, is the key takeaway from both Bank Y and Bank Z's experiences.

Case Study Addressing Regulatory Enforcement Actions

This case study focuses on "First National Bank" (FNB), a large national bank facing scrutiny from multiple regulatory bodies, including the Office of the Comptroller of the Currency (OCC), the Federal Reserve (Fed), and the Consumer Financial Protection Bureau (CFPB). The investigation stemmed from allegations of widespread violations of the Bank Secrecy Act (BSA) and anti-money laundering (AML) regulations. These allegations, initially brought to light by an internal whistleblower, suggested systemic failures within FNB's compliance program, specifically in its customer due diligence (CDD) processes, transaction monitoring systems, and suspicious activity reporting (SAR) procedures. The initial findings suggested a pattern of insufficient scrutiny of high-risk customers, resulting in potential money laundering and other illicit financial activities.

The bank's initial response was characterized by a defensive posture. They initially downplayed the severity of the allegations, claiming that the identified shortcomings were isolated incidents rather than systemic issues. This approach, however, proved counterproductive. The regulators, armed with evidence gathered from the whistleblower's testimony and their own independent investigations, pressed forward with their enforcement actions. FNB's attempts to minimize the situation only served to escalate the regulators' concerns, leading to a more extensive and intrusive investigation.

Internal communication within FNB was also severely lacking. Employees were unsure of the situation's gravity and lacked guidance on how to respond to inquiries from regulators or the media, causing inconsistent and often

Conflicting information to be relayed. This internal confusion further hampered the bank's ability to present a unified and coherent defense.

The situation deteriorated further when the OCC issued a cease-and-desist order, outlining specific areas of non-compliance and demanding immediate corrective action.

This formal regulatory action put immense pressure on FNB's management and board of directors. The cease-and-desist order was not only a public rebuke but also carried significant financial implications, including potential fines and restrictions on the bank's operations. The order

specifically highlighted failures in FNB's AML program including deficiencies in the onboarding of high-risk

customers, the monitoring of suspicious transactions, and a high percentage of incomplete SAR filings.

Recognizing the severity of the situation and the inadequacy of their initial response, FNB's leadership immediately

assembled a crisis management team composed of seasoned legal counsel, experienced compliance officers, and senior executives specializing in risk management. This team

adopted a fundamentally different approach, prioritizing full cooperation with regulatory authorities and a complete

overhaul of its compliance program. The team's initial task was to conduct a comprehensive independent review of FNB's BSA/AML compliance program. This review was not limited to the specific allegations but involved a rigorous assessment of all aspects of the program, encompassing procedures, technology, personnel training, and overall effectiveness.

The independent review uncovered significant shortcomings. It revealed not only weaknesses in the processes highlighted by the regulators and the whistleblower but also broader deficiencies in the bank's overall risk management

Framework. The review pinpointed systemic weaknesses in data analysis, inadequate training for staff responsible for AML compliance, insufficient resources allocated to the compliance department, and a lack of robust oversight mechanisms. These issues went beyond simple procedural errors; they represented fundamental flaws in the bank's approach to managing financial crime risks.

Based on the findings of the independent review, FNB

developed a comprehensive remediation plan. This plan encompassed a multitude of initiatives designed to address each identified deficiency. First, the bank invested heavily in upgrading its transaction monitoring systems, incorporating advanced analytics and machine learning algorithms to enhance its ability to detect suspicious activity. This

involved not just purchasing new technology but also

retraining staff on how to effectively utilize the new systems and interpret the data generated. Second, FNB implemented a comprehensive employee training program covering all aspects of BSA/AML compliance. This training program went beyond simple compliance checklists and included interactive scenarios, case studies, and regular refresher courses to ensure ongoing adherence to best practices.

Third, the bank substantially increased the resources

allocated to its compliance department, hiring experienced AML specialists and strengthening its leadership. This reorganization established a clear chain of command and improved communication within the compliance team, fostering a culture of accountability and proactive risk management. Fourth, FNB implemented a robust internal audit program specifically focused on AML compliance. This program included regular independent assessments of the bank's compliance procedures, technology, and

personnel, providing ongoing monitoring and ensuring the effectiveness of implemented improvements.

FNB's cooperation with the regulatory authorities was a pivotal element of its crisis management strategy. The bank provided regulators with unfettered access to its systems and personnel, openly sharing information and actively assisting in their investigations. This transparent and collaborative approach fostered a constructive relationship with the

regulators, reducing adversarial tensions and facilitating a smoother resolution to the enforcement actions. This

proactive approach, in contrast to the bank's initial defensive stance, was crucial in mitigating the severity of potential penalties.

The cooperation extended beyond simply providing

information. FNB actively collaborated with the regulators in the development of its remediation plan, ensuring that the proposed changes met their expectations and aligned with best practices. This collaborative approach fostered trust and demonstrated a genuine commitment to resolving the issues and preventing future violations.

The outcome of the regulatory enforcement actions was more favorable than initially anticipated. While FNB

incurred significant financial penalties, including substantial fines and remediation costs, the penalties were significantly less severe than could have been expected given the initial scope of the alleged violations. The regulators recognized and acknowledged FNB's demonstrable commitment to improving its BSA/AML compliance program, as evidenced by the comprehensive remediation plan, its proactive

cooperation, and the significant investment made in

upgrading its systems and training its staff. The regulators also lauded the bank's commitment to transparency and the thoroughness of its self-assessment process. This case study underscores the critical importance of a proactive,

transparent, and cooperative approach when facing

Regulatory enforcement actions. A defensive posture only serves to escalate the situation, resulting in more severe penalties and lasting reputational damage. Conversely, a proactive approach focused on cooperation, remediation, and a genuine commitment to compliance can significantly

mitigate negative outcomes and demonstrate to regulators and the public that the institution has learned from its

mistakes and is committed to future compliance. The long-term success of FNB's response showcases the importance of a strong, well-resourced, and independent compliance function, and the necessity of ongoing training and robust oversight mechanisms within a robust risk management framework. The lesson is clear: investing in compliance is not a cost but a crucial strategic imperative for financial institutions aiming for long-term sustainability and stability.

Case Study A Successful Workout Strategy

This case study examines the successful workout strategy implemented by a regional commercial bank, which we will refer to as "Regional Bank X," to recover losses from a distressed loan portfolio associated with a mid-sized

manufacturing company, "Acme Manufacturing." Acme Manufacturing, a long-standing client of Regional Bank X, had secured a significant loan facility to finance its

expansion into a new product line. The facility, initially structured as a revolving credit facility with a term loan component, consisted of a mix of asset-based lending and traditional commercial lending. The collateral included inventory, accounts receivable, and fixed assets.

The initial loan terms reflected a positive outlook for Acme Manufacturing, with projected growth based on market analysis and the company's track record. However,

unforeseen economic downturns, coupled with aggressive pricing strategies from competitors, caused a sharp decline in Acme's sales. The company's cash flow rapidly deteriorated, resulting in missed loan payments and a significant decline in the value of its collateral. The inventory, once considered a strong asset, became obsolete due to shifts in consumer demand. Accounts receivable, though initially robust,

showed a trend of increasing delinquency, negatively

impacting the bank's ability to recover funds through

receivables financing. The fixed assets, primarily specialized manufacturing equipment, lost significant value in the

secondary market due to decreased demand and

technological advancements.

Regional Bank X's initial response was to engage in close communication with Acme Manufacturing's management.

This early intervention proved crucial in gathering accurate financial information and understanding the root causes of the company's financial distress. The bank's credit analysts conducted a thorough reassessment of Acme's financial situation, analyzing the company's financial statements, projections, and market conditions. This analysis formed the basis of the workout strategy.

Unlike the reactive and defensive approach exhibited by First National Bank in the previous case study, Regional Bank X adopted a proactive and collaborative approach. Recognizing that forcing immediate liquidation would likely result in significant losses for both the bank and the

borrower, the bank prioritized finding a viable solution that would maximize recovery while minimizing the overall impact. This involved open communication, transparency, and a willingness to explore various restructuring options.

This contrasted sharply with a more adversarial approach, which might have led to costly and protracted legal battles.

The bank's workout strategy focused on three key areas: negotiation, restructuring, and asset management. The

negotiation phase involved extensive discussions with Acme Manufacturing's management and owners. The bank worked to understand the company's operational challenges and explore potential solutions. This collaborative approach involved identifying areas where efficiency could be

improved and cost reductions implemented. A crucial

element of the negotiations was the establishment of realistic financial projections and targets. The bank worked closely with Acme's management team to develop a comprehensive business plan that outlined steps to improve profitability and cash flow. This included reviewing production processes, exploring alternative sourcing strategies, and improving sales and marketing efforts. This collaboration fostered trust

And a sense of shared responsibility between the bank and the borrower.

The restructuring phase involved modifying the existing loan facility to provide Acme Manufacturing with additional financial breathing room. This involved extending the loan maturity, adjusting the interest rate based on the prevailing economic conditions, and adjusting amortization schedules to align with the revised financial projections. The bank also considered converting a portion of the debt into equity,

providing Acme with additional working capital while

mitigating the bank's risk. This innovative restructuring solution prevented the complete collapse of the company and allowed for a gradual recovery. Such a strategy also avoids the significant costs and uncertainties associated with forced liquidation.

Concurrent with the negotiations and restructuring, Regional Bank X implemented a proactive asset management strategy. This involved actively monitoring the collateral, assessing its market value, and taking steps to protect and preserve its worth. For instance, the bank worked with Acme

Manufacturing to liquidate obsolete inventory in a controlled manner, minimizing potential losses. Furthermore, the bank implemented measures to improve the collection of accounts receivable. They also explored options for the sale or lease of some of Acme's fixed assets to generate cash flow and reduce debt burden. This active asset management strategy aimed at maximizing the value of the collateral, ensuring that the bank could recover as much as possible from the loan facility.

The ultimate outcome of Regional Bank X's workout

strategy was far more successful than a liquidation-based approach would have yielded. While the bank incurred some losses, they were significantly less than what would have

Been incurred through immediate foreclosure and asset

seizure. The bank recovered a substantial portion of the outstanding loan principal, and Acme Manufacturing was able to reorganize and regain its financial footing. The case study highlights the benefits of a strategic, collaborative, and proactive approach to workout situations. It demonstrates that a well-structured workout strategy, combining effective negotiation, creative restructuring, and diligent asset

management, can significantly improve the chances of

recovery while preserving the borrower's viability and

reputation.

Several best practices emerge from Regional Bank X's

successful workout strategy. First, early intervention and proactive communication with the borrower were

instrumental in gathering essential information and fostering a collaborative relationship. Second, a thorough assessment of the borrower's financial situation, including a realistic appraisal of its assets and liabilities, is crucial for

formulating a sound workout plan. Third, the ability to creatively restructure the loan facility, adapting to the

changing circumstances of the borrower and the market, demonstrated flexibility and a willingness to compromise.

Fourth, active asset management, which prioritized

preserving and maximizing the value of the collateral, was vital in ensuring a higher recovery rate. Finally, the bank's commitment to open communication and transparency built trust, facilitating a more efficient and collaborative workout process.

This case study serves as a compelling example of how a well-executed workout strategy can lead to a positive outcome for both the lender and the borrower. It contrasts significantly with scenarios where a more confrontational approach may lead to protracted legal battles and greater financial losses. The success hinges upon a proactive

Approach centered on thorough due diligence, open communication, and a willingness to adapt and restructure to mitigate losses. In the financial sector, particularly in asset-based lending, a proactive and flexible approach often proves more effective and less expensive than aggressive litigation. The ability to navigate complex financial situations with a nuanced understanding of both the borrower's circumstances and the lender's interests is paramount in mitigating financial distress and promoting long-term sustainable relationships. The approach taken by Regional Bank X underscores the importance of incorporating a flexible workout strategy into comprehensive risk management frameworks. Such a strategy can provide valuable tools to manage and minimize losses when faced with distressed loans and economic uncertainty. In essence, the long-term success of this approach depends on viewing the workout process not merely as a cost of doing business, but as a crucial aspect of prudent risk management and a key factor in maintaining client relationships and business stability.

Understanding International Lending Regulations

The intricacies of international lending extend far beyond the complexities of domestic transactions. Navigating the global financial landscape requires a deep understanding of diverse regulatory frameworks, each with its own nuances and

potential pitfalls. These regulations, designed to protect borrowers, lenders, and the overall stability of the financial system, often differ significantly across jurisdictions,

creating a challenging environment for cross-border

transactions. A key difference lies in the approach to due diligence and risk assessment. While domestic lending often relies on established relationships and readily available information, international lending demands a more

comprehensive approach. Borrowers' financial statements may be prepared under different accounting standards,

requiring careful interpretation and reconciliation.

Furthermore, obtaining reliable credit information on international borrowers can be more challenging,

necessitating reliance on specialized credit reporting agencies and potentially more in-depth investigations into the borrower's business operations and financial standing.

One critical aspect is the determination of applicable law. In cross-border transactions, the governing law might be

subject to negotiation between the lender and the borrower, often influenced by the location of assets, the borrower's residence, or the place where the loan agreement is signed.

This choice of law has significant implications for the

enforcement of contracts, the resolution of disputes, and the interpretation of legal provisions. Furthermore, the

governing law might affect the validity and enforceability of security interests, significantly impacting the lender's ability to recover its losses in case of default. Understanding these

Legal intricacies is crucial for structuring secure loan

agreements that minimize legal and financial risks. In many jurisdictions, legal opinions are frequently sought to ensure compliance with local laws and to reduce uncertainty.

Another significant area is the treatment of collateral. The availability and enforceability of security interests vary dramatically across different countries. Some jurisdictions may recognize and enforce security interests over specific types of assets more readily than others. For example, the enforceability of security interests over intellectual property or real estate can vary greatly depending on the country's legal system and registration requirements. This disparity highlights the need for careful structuring of security

arrangements to ensure that the lender's position is

adequately protected in the event of a borrower's default. A thorough understanding of the applicable laws and

registration procedures is critical to safeguard the lender's collateral and facilitate efficient recovery processes.

Regulatory compliance in international lending also involves navigating a web of anti-money laundering (AML) and know-your-customer (KYC) regulations. These regulations, implemented to combat financial crime and terrorism

financing, impose stringent due diligence requirements on financial institutions. International lenders are obligated to identify and verify the identity of their borrowers and to scrutinize the source of their funds. Failure to adhere to these requirements can result in significant penalties, including substantial fines and reputational damage. Compliance

programs typically involve thorough background checks, ongoing monitoring of transactions, and robust reporting procedures. These measures are essential in mitigating risks associated with international lending and maintaining the integrity of the financial system.

The Basel Accords play a crucial role in shaping the regulatory environment for international lending. These internationally recognized banking regulations establish minimum capital requirements for banks, designed to ensure their solvency and ability to absorb potential losses.

International lending often involves higher risk profiles due to currency fluctuations, political uncertainties, and potential legal complexities. Therefore, banks are typically required to hold more capital against international loans compared to domestic ones. Understanding these capital requirements is vital for banks to manage their regulatory capital efficiently and comply with international standards. Failure to comply can lead to significant penalties and reputational damage.

In addition to the Basel Accords, other international regulations and guidelines influence the international lending landscape. For example, the Organisation for Economic Co-operation and Development (OECD) guidelines on corporate governance influence the expectations regarding transparency and accountability in corporate borrowers involved in international transactions. These guidelines highlight the importance of robust corporate governance structures to minimize risks and enhance the reliability of financial information provided to lenders. Further complicating the matter is the existence of regional regulatory frameworks. The European Union, for instance, has developed comprehensive regulations for banking and finance within its member states, creating a unified regulatory space but requiring specialized expertise to navigate effectively. Similarly, other regional blocs may have their own regulatory standards impacting cross-border lending activities within their territories.

International lending often involves different currencies, introducing additional risks associated with currency fluctuations. Regulations regarding hedging strategies and

Foreign exchange risk management are often important considerations. The impact of currency movements on loan repayments and overall profitability must be factored into the risk assessment and pricing of the loan. Effective

currency risk management strategies are critical for lenders to protect themselves from losses caused by fluctuations in exchange rates.

Another key consideration in international lending is the differing levels of legal and political risk across jurisdictions.

Lenders must assess the political stability and legal

framework of the countries where their borrowers operate.

Countries with weak legal systems or unstable political environments may pose higher risks of loan defaults or difficulties in enforcing contracts. A comprehensive political risk assessment is therefore essential for effective risk

management in international lending. This assessment

typically includes an evaluation of the country's political system, economic stability, and legal framework, as well as the presence of any political, social or economic factors that might impact the borrower's ability to repay the loan.

In conclusion, the regulatory landscape of international lending is a complex and dynamic environment.

Successfully navigating this landscape requires a thorough understanding of diverse regulatory frameworks, legal systems, and compliance requirements. Banks and other financial institutions must develop robust risk management strategies, incorporating comprehensive due diligence procedures, appropriate legal structuring, and effective compliance programs. A collaborative approach, engaging legal counsel specializing in international transactions, and continuous monitoring of regulatory changes is critical to minimizing risks and ensuring successful international lending ventures. Ignoring these intricacies can lead to significant financial losses, legal disputes, and reputational

Damage. The proactive approach showcased by Regional Bank X in their domestic workout strategy must be extended and adapted to the complexities of the global financial

landscape, demanding continuous learning and adaptation to the evolving regulatory environment.

Managing Currency Risk and Exchange Rate Fluctuations

The preceding discussion highlighted the multifaceted challenges inherent in international lending, encompassing regulatory complexities, legal intricacies, and the crucial role of thorough due diligence. However, a critical element often overlooked in the initial stages of planning is the pervasive influence of currency risk and the unpredictable nature of exchange rate fluctuations. These fluctuations can significantly impact the profitability and even the viability of international lending ventures. Failing to adequately address currency risk can transform a seemingly sound investment into a substantial loss, underlining the importance of proactive and sophisticated risk management strategies.

Currency risk, in the context of international lending, refers to the potential for losses arising from changes in exchange rates between the lender's currency and the borrower's currency. This risk is particularly acute in transactions involving multiple currencies, where the value of loan repayments can fluctuate significantly depending on market dynamics. For example, a loan denominated in Euros extended to a borrower repaying in US dollars faces considerable risk if the Euro appreciates against the dollar during the loan's tenure. The lender would receive fewer Euros than initially anticipated, potentially impacting the profitability of the transaction. Conversely, if the Euro depreciates, the lender benefits, receiving more Euros than projected. This inherent uncertainty necessitates a robust risk management framework.

Several factors influence exchange rate movements.

Macroeconomic indicators, such as inflation rates, interest

Rate differentials, and economic growth, play a pivotal role.

Government policies, including monetary and fiscal

measures, can also impact exchange rates. Geopolitical events, such as political instability or international conflicts, often introduce significant volatility. Market sentiment and speculative trading further contribute to the inherent

unpredictability of currency markets. Understanding these driving forces is crucial for effective currency risk

management.

One of the most common strategies for mitigating currency risk is hedging. Hedging involves using financial

instruments to offset potential losses arising from exchange rate fluctuations. Various hedging techniques are available, each with its own advantages and disadvantages. Forward contracts, for instance, lock in a specific exchange rate for a future transaction, eliminating the uncertainty associated with fluctuating exchange rates. This provides certainty regarding the amount of the lender's currency received upon repayment. However, forward contracts require commitment to a specific exchange rate, potentially missing out on

favorable exchange rate movements.

Another popular hedging technique is the use of currency options. Options give the lender the right, but not the

obligation, to buy or sell a currency at a predetermined price on or before a specific date. This flexibility allows the lender to benefit from favorable exchange rate movements while protecting against unfavorable ones. The cost of an option is the premium paid to acquire the right. This premium

represents the cost of insurance against potential losses. The choice between a forward contract and an option depends on the lender's risk appetite and the level of certainty desired.

Currency swaps are another valuable hedging tool. A currency swap involves exchanging principal and interest

Payments in one currency for those in another currency. This is particularly useful for long-term loans where the lender seeks to reduce exposure to exchange rate fluctuations over an extended period. The complexity of currency swaps necessitates expertise in financial engineering and a deep understanding of derivative instruments. Misuse of these instruments can exacerbate risks instead of mitigating them.

Beyond these primary hedging techniques, several other strategies can contribute to a comprehensive currency risk management plan. Diversification of loan portfolios across different currencies can reduce overall exposure to any

single currency's fluctuations. Careful selection of borrowers whose business operations are less sensitive to exchange rate movements can also lessen the impact of currency risk.

Furthermore, the structure of the loan agreement itself can influence the exposure to currency risk. For example, a loan denominated in the borrower's currency might shift some exchange rate risk to the borrower. However, this approach must be carefully considered, balancing the sharing of risk with the potential impact on the borrower's willingness to secure the loan.

The importance of robust internal controls and risk

assessment frameworks cannot be overstated. Financial institutions should establish clear policies and procedures for managing currency risk, including regular monitoring of exchange rate movements and periodic reviews of hedging strategies. The involvement of specialized personnel with expertise in foreign exchange risk management is crucial. These experts should assess the institution's overall currency risk exposure and recommend appropriate hedging strategies based on the institution's risk tolerance and investment

objectives. Sophisticated quantitative models can support this process by providing forecasts of exchange rate

Movements and measuring the impact of various hedging scenarios.

Beyond the quantitative aspects, qualitative factors play a critical role in managing currency risk. A thorough

understanding of the borrower's business model and its susceptibility to currency fluctuations is essential. The

borrower's ability to manage its own currency risk, through hedging or other strategies, can influence the lender's

assessment of the overall credit risk. Qualitative assessments incorporate considerations beyond pure financial metrics.

The interaction between currency risk and other aspects of international lending cannot be ignored. Currency risk is intricately linked to the overall credit risk associated with the borrower. Unfavorable exchange rate movements can

exacerbate the financial distress of a borrower, increasing the likelihood of default. Similarly, legal and regulatory

complexities in international transactions can impact the lender's ability to recover losses resulting from currency fluctuations. The effective management of currency risk thus necessitates a holistic approach, integrating it into the

broader risk management framework for international

lending.

Effective communication between the lender and the

borrower regarding currency risk is vital. Transparency about the lender's risk management strategies and the

potential impact of exchange rate fluctuations on loan

repayments helps to establish a constructive working

relationship. A shared understanding of the risks involved fosters trust and mutual accountability. This collaboration should extend to the negotiation of the loan agreement itself, ensuring clear and unambiguous clauses addressing currency risk management.

Finally, ongoing monitoring and adaptation are critical for effective currency risk management. Exchange rate

movements are influenced by a complex interplay of factors that can change rapidly. Regular reviews of hedging

strategies, considering economic indicators and evolving market conditions, are essential to ensure that the lender maintains an optimal level of protection. This necessitates a flexible approach, ready to adjust strategies as necessary to meet changing market dynamics and mitigate unforeseen risks. Continuous learning and adaptation to new hedging techniques and risk management methodologies are crucial for success in the dynamic world of international lending.

The failure to adequately address currency risk can

undermine even the most meticulously planned international lending ventures. A proactive and comprehensive approach, combining sophisticated hedging strategies with rigorous risk assessment and ongoing monitoring, is essential for navigating the complexities of international finance and securing profitable and sustainable cross-border transactions.

Crossborder Loan Documentation and Enforcement

The preceding sections have emphasized the significant challenges inherent in international lending, from navigating regulatory hurdles and conducting thorough due diligence to mitigating the considerable risks associated with currency fluctuations. However, the success of any international lending venture ultimately hinges on the meticulous

preparation and execution of the loan documentation and the robust mechanisms in place for enforcement. This is where the complexities of cross-border transactions truly come into sharp focus. Simply put, a flawlessly structured loan,

meticulously underwritten and hedged against currency risk, can still fail if the underlying documentation is deficient or unenforceable in the relevant jurisdictions.

Cross-border loan documentation requires a level of

precision and foresight far exceeding that of domestic

lending. The legal frameworks governing contracts, debt recovery, and insolvency differ significantly across

countries. What constitutes a legally binding agreement in one jurisdiction might be wholly ineffective in another. This necessitates a deep understanding of the relevant legal systems involved, often requiring the expertise of multiple legal counsel specializing in different national laws and international commercial arbitration.

One critical aspect is the choice of governing law. This clause dictates which legal system will interpret and govern the loan agreement in case of disputes. Carefully selecting the governing law is crucial. A lender might choose the law of its own jurisdiction, providing a degree of familiarity and predictability. However, this choice might not be favorably

Received by the borrower and may not be easily enforceable in the borrower's jurisdiction. Conversely, selecting the

borrower's jurisdiction's law might appear more equitable but could expose the lender to potentially less favorable legal protections. Often, a compromise is sought, sometimes

involving a neutral jurisdiction with a reputation for robust legal systems and efficient dispute resolution mechanisms. The choice of governing law should be carefully negotiated and documented, ideally with expert legal counsel guiding the process.

Jurisdictional clauses specifying the court or forum where disputes will be resolved are equally important. This clause helps to prevent future disputes regarding the appropriate venue for litigation. Clearly defining the jurisdiction

minimizes the potential for protracted legal battles over which court has authority. Again, the choice must carefully balance the lender's interests with the practical realities of enforcement and the borrower's acceptance of the terms. The possibility of international arbitration, a process conducted under the auspices of established international arbitral

institutions, provides an alternative dispute resolution

mechanism that can be significantly more efficient and less costly than litigation in national courts. International

arbitration often allows for a neutral forum, governed by established rules and procedures, which can be preferable to navigating the complexities of multiple national legal

systems.

Beyond the governing law and jurisdiction clauses, the loan agreement itself needs meticulous drafting to address

specific cross-border issues. The definition of key terms, such as events of default and remedies available to the

lender, must be unambiguous and aligned with the applicable legal frameworks. For example, specifying the process for enforcing security interests, such as collateral, varies

Significantly across jurisdictions. A loan agreement must clearly articulate the lender's rights to seize and liquidate the collateral in the event of default, recognizing the potential complexities and legal requirements in different locations.

This may involve navigating different legal regimes on secured transactions, potentially requiring specific

registration or perfection procedures to ensure the lender's priority claim on the assets.

The issue of enforcement is paramount. Obtaining a

judgment in one jurisdiction doesn't automatically guarantee enforcement in another. The lender must understand the specific rules and processes for enforcing foreign judgments in the borrower's jurisdiction, which can involve significant legal hurdles and delays. Reciprocal recognition of

judgments varies considerably across jurisdictions.

Understanding these limitations from the outset and

incorporating appropriate protective measures within the loan agreement is vital for minimizing the risks of non-enforcement. For instance, ensuring the loan agreement includes provisions for effective attachment of assets within the borrower's jurisdiction can help ensure swift recovery in the event of default.

Furthermore, the loan agreement should account for

potential differences in accounting standards and financial reporting practices. The financial information provided by the borrower must be consistently and clearly presented, aligned with the requirements of the governing law and readily understandable to the lender. Inconsistencies or ambiguity in the financial reporting can complicate the assessment of the borrower's financial health and ultimately impede the lender's ability to make informed decisions, including the enforcement of the loan agreement.

Another critical element is the documentation related to any collateral or security provided by the borrower. The nature of collateral and the processes for its perfection must be

carefully examined and meticulously documented. For

example, real estate security may require registration in land registries, subject to local laws and procedures which vary greatly from one country to the next. Similarly, intellectual property rights or other intangible assets may necessitate compliance with specific registration requirements and

processes, varying by country and type of asset. Failing to properly document and register the security interest can result in significant challenges in enforcing the lender's security interest.

The complexity of cross-border lending necessitates a proactive, multi-faceted approach to documentation and enforcement. This starts with selecting legal counsel with extensive experience in international commercial law and a profound understanding of the relevant legal systems.

Detailed due diligence, extending beyond the borrower's financials to encompass the legal and regulatory

environment, is essential. The drafting of the loan agreement requires meticulous attention to detail, ensuring that each clause addresses potential contingencies and anticipates possible disputes. The use of clear, unambiguous language, consistent with international standards, helps to avoid future misunderstandings.

International lending presents unique risks and challenges, but with careful planning, thorough documentation, and a robust enforcement strategy, these risks can be managed effectively. The upfront investment in legal expertise and meticulous documentation is far outweighed by the potential costs and complications of attempting to enforce a poorly structured agreement. Moreover, a well-drafted agreement can significantly improve the likelihood of amicable

Resolution of disputes, even when unforeseen circumstances arise. The ultimate goal is not only to secure a loan but also to establish a transparent and enforceable framework that protects the interests of both the lender and the borrower. The importance of clear communication and a collaborative approach throughout the process cannot be overstated. A strong working relationship fosters trust and mutual

understanding, making it more likely that any issues that arise will be resolved effectively and efficiently, mitigating the risks inherent in cross-border transactions. Proactive risk management, encompassing all aspects of the transaction from initial due diligence to enforcement strategy, remains the cornerstone of success in international lending.

Due Diligence and Risk Assessment in International Lending

The complexities inherent in international lending necessitate a far more rigorous approach to due diligence and risk assessment than domestic transactions. While financial statements and credit history remain crucial, international lending demands a deeper dive into political, economic, and legal landscapes of the borrower's jurisdiction. This expanded scope encompasses a broader range of potential risks, requiring a more sophisticated risk mitigation strategy.

Political risk assessment is paramount. This involves analyzing the stability of the borrower's government, the potential for political upheaval, changes in regulatory frameworks, and the enforcement of contracts. Countries with a history of political instability, frequent changes in government, or a weak rule of law present a higher risk.

Lenders need to assess the likelihood of government intervention, expropriation of assets, or changes in regulations that could negatively impact the borrower's ability to repay the loan. Factors such as corruption levels, the independence of the judiciary, and the presence of strong regulatory bodies all contribute to the overall political risk profile. Information sources for this assessment include reports from international organizations like the World Bank and the International Monetary Fund (IMF), political risk rating agencies, and geopolitical analysts. Furthermore, conducting on-the-ground investigations, using local consultants who possess in-depth knowledge of the political climate, can prove invaluable. This ground-level intelligence can uncover nuanced details and subtle shifts in the political landscape often overlooked in broader reports.

Economic risk assessment is equally critical. This goes

beyond a simple analysis of macroeconomic indicators such as GDP growth, inflation, and unemployment rates. It

requires a more in-depth examination of the specific industry in which the borrower operates, its competitiveness, and the overall health of the economy in relation to the borrower's sector. A robust assessment considers factors like exchange rate volatility, the potential for currency devaluation, and the availability of foreign exchange. Countries with volatile exchange rates or significant currency risks require careful hedging strategies to mitigate the potential for losses.

Economic sanctions imposed on the borrower's country or disruptions to global trade flows can also have significant implications. Understanding the country's reliance on

exports, its vulnerability to global economic shocks, and the resilience of its domestic market are all vital considerations. Economic forecasts from reputable sources and projections from industry analysts offer valuable insights.

Legal and regulatory risk assessment forms another crucial component of the due diligence process. This aspect delves into the legal framework governing contracts, debt recovery, and insolvency procedures in the borrower's jurisdiction. Variations in legal systems, the enforceability of contracts, and the efficiency of the judicial system can significantly impact the lender's ability to recover its loan in the event of default. A thorough assessment examines the legal

protections afforded to lenders, the processes for enforcing security interests in collateral, and the potential for delays or complications in legal proceedings. Accessing legal counsel with expertise in the relevant jurisdiction is paramount.

These specialists can provide critical insights into legal nuances, potential pitfalls, and best practices for structuring loan agreements to minimize legal risks. A comprehensive review of relevant laws and regulations, including those

Pertaining to foreign investment, tax, and banking, is essential to ensure compliance and reduce regulatory risks.

Beyond the macro-level assessment, a thorough micro-level due diligence is essential. This involves a detailed

examination of the borrower's financial health, including the quality of their management team, their track record, the nature of their business operations, and their capacity to manage risks effectively. Detailed financial analysis includes not only a review of financial statements but also a

comprehensive assessment of the borrower's liquidity

position, cash flow projections, and debt-to-equity ratio.

Understanding the borrower's industry dynamics, its

competitive landscape, and its strategic planning is crucial.

An in-depth analysis of the borrower's business model, its resilience to market fluctuations, and its ability to adapt to changing economic conditions are crucial factors in

evaluating creditworthiness. This involves gathering

information from multiple sources, including the borrower's financial records, industry reports, and market analysis, complemented by face-to-face meetings with management to ascertain their business acumen, expertise, and honesty.

Risk mitigation strategies are crucial in international lending.

These strategies aim to minimize the impact of potential negative events. The choice of governing law and the

selection of a suitable jurisdiction for dispute resolution are critical elements. As discussed previously, carefully

selecting the governing law and jurisdiction requires a

delicate balance between the lender's interests and the

practical realities of enforcement. The inclusion of well-defined events of default and comprehensive remedies in the loan agreement safeguards the lender's interests. These

clauses specify the circumstances under which the borrower is considered to be in default and outline the legal recourse available to the lender in such cases. Clearly specifying these

Parameters upfront helps to mitigate future disputes and ensures the lender's ability to enforce its rights swiftly and decisively.

Another effective risk mitigation strategy is the use of appropriate hedging mechanisms to mitigate currency risks.

Currency fluctuations can significantly impact the value of loan repayments, and hedging strategies, such as forward contracts or currency swaps, protect against these risks.

Careful consideration of the borrower's sector, its

operational characteristics, and its susceptibility to financial and regulatory changes, is necessary to determine the

optimal hedging strategies. Similarly, ensuring that the loan agreement includes provisions for effective asset attachment within the borrower's jurisdiction can substantially improve the lender's ability to recover its loan in case of default. These provisions facilitate the prompt seizure and liquidation of assets pledged as collateral in the event of non-payment.

Furthermore, credit insurance or political risk insurance can provide an additional layer of protection. These insurance policies compensate lenders for losses incurred due to events such as political instability, currency devaluation, or the borrower's failure to repay the loan. These policies can be particularly crucial in high-risk environments, offering

significant reassurance to the lender and reducing the overall risk profile of the transaction. However, the lender should thoroughly review the terms and conditions of such policies before committing, paying attention to the specifics of

coverage and any exclusion clauses.

In conclusion, international lending requires a meticulous and multifaceted approach to due diligence and risk

assessment. It demands a thorough understanding of not only the borrower's financial health but also the political,

economic, and legal environment of the borrower's

Jurisdiction. The incorporation of robust risk mitigation strategies, ranging from careful contract drafting to the

utilization of appropriate hedging mechanisms and insurance policies, is essential to managing the unique challenges and complexities inherent in international lending transactions. A proactive and well-informed approach, combining detailed analysis with effective risk management strategies,

significantly enhances the probability of a successful

outcome. The commitment to thorough due diligence and risk mitigation is not merely a matter of prudence; it is a fundamental requirement for responsible and profitable international lending.

Case Studies in International Lending

The theoretical framework established in the previous sections finds its practical application in real-world scenarios. This section delves into specific case studies of international lending transactions, showcasing both successful and unsuccessful endeavors. These examples illuminate the critical role of thorough due diligence, robust risk mitigation strategies, and the importance of adapting to the unique circumstances of each transaction. A detailed examination of these cases will reveal crucial lessons applicable to any lender considering participation in the international lending market.

Our first case study involves a German manufacturing company, seeking financing to expand its operations into Brazil. The company, a well-established player in its domestic market with a strong track record, presented compelling financial statements and a robust business plan. However, a cursory review of the Brazilian market failed to fully appreciate the complexities of operating in a developing economy. While macroeconomic indicators seemed favorable at the outset, a deeper dive into the specific industry revealed intense competition and a volatile regulatory environment. The lender, initially confident based on the borrower's strong financials, overlooked the political risks associated with Brazil's fluctuating government policies concerning foreign investment and the potential for currency devaluation. The loan, structured with inadequate hedging mechanisms, ultimately suffered significant losses due to both currency fluctuations and unexpected regulatory changes impacting the borrower's operating environment. This situation underscores the necessity of a comprehensive risk assessment that transcends simple financial analysis and

Incorporates a nuanced understanding of the political and economic realities of the target market. A detailed evaluation of industry specifics, including the competitive landscape, and a thorough review of the regulatory environment would have been crucial. This oversight resulted in the lender experiencing substantial losses. Furthermore, the absence of political risk insurance exacerbated the financial repercussions.

In stark contrast, our second case study showcases the success of a well-managed international lending transaction. A US-based bank financed a large-scale infrastructure project in South Korea. Recognizing the inherent risks associated with such an undertaking in a foreign jurisdiction, the bank employed a multi-layered due diligence process.

This included not only rigorous financial analysis of the borrower, a well-established Korean conglomerate, but also an extensive political and economic risk assessment conducted by specialized consultants with extensive experience in the region. They carefully analyzed the South Korean government's commitment to the project, assessed the political stability of the country, and evaluated the macroeconomic factors influencing the project's viability.

The loan agreement incorporated comprehensive risk mitigation strategies, including robust hedging mechanisms to offset currency fluctuations, clearly defined events of default, and provisions for effective asset attachment in the event of default. Furthermore, the bank secured political risk insurance to mitigate against unforeseen political disruptions. The project proved highly successful, underscoring the significance of proactive risk management and the utilization of multiple risk mitigation techniques. The detailed due diligence process, coupled with the use of political risk insurance, provided a safety net against unforeseen challenges, which demonstrated the crucial role of comprehensive risk management. The bank's success

Exemplifies the strategic advantages of collaborating with experienced local consultants who understand the cultural and legal nuances of the specific business and legal context, particularly during the due diligence phase.

The third case study highlights the importance of thorough legal due diligence. A European bank extended a loan to a company in Russia, failing to fully understand the intricacies of the Russian legal system. While the borrower's financial standing appeared strong initially, the loan agreement lacked sufficient protection against unforeseen legal challenges.

Specifically, the contract lacked explicit provisions

governing dispute resolution and asset recovery. When

economic sanctions were imposed on Russia, leading to significant operational challenges for the borrower, the

lender encountered considerable difficulty in enforcing its rights. The inefficiencies in the Russian legal system,

coupled with the lack of clear contractual remedies,

prolonged the legal battles and reduced the likelihood of full recovery. This situation emphasizes the critical need for legal counsel specializing in the specific jurisdiction, ensuring that the loan agreement is drafted to effectively protect the

lender's interests within the local legal framework. The use of local legal expertise would have significantly mitigated the lender's exposure. This case highlights the critical

importance of securing legal advice from specialists

experienced in international transactions and familiar with the specific jurisdiction's legal framework. A robust legal framework protects lender rights in case of unforeseen

events.

A fourth case study illustrates the complexities of cross-border mergers and acquisitions financing. A US private equity firm sought financing for the acquisition of a

technology company based in India. The due diligence process focused not only on the target company's financials

And management but also considered regulatory hurdles, including foreign direct investment regulations and potential anti-trust issues. The complexity of the transaction required specialized expertise in both the US and Indian legal

systems, including tax implications and compliance

requirements. The financing structure had to accommodate the regulatory nuances of both countries. This case

demonstrates that in complex cross-border transactions, the lenders need to engage a multidisciplinary team with

expertise in various aspects, including legal, accounting, and tax matters, in both the domestic and foreign jurisdiction. This comprehensive approach is vital to effectively navigate potential regulatory obstacles and ensure compliance.

These case studies collectively highlight the critical success factors in international lending. They reinforce the necessity of a comprehensive due diligence process extending beyond financial analysis, encompassing political, economic, and legal risk assessments. The crucial role of risk mitigation strategies, from hedging and insurance to well-drafted

contracts, is further emphasized. The lessons learned

highlight the importance of a proactive approach, combining thorough research, local expertise, and effective risk

management to mitigate the inherent complexities and

uncertainties of international lending transactions. The

consistent theme is the need for a holistic approach,

anticipating potential challenges and deploying appropriate strategies to navigate the complexities of operating in

foreign markets. Effective communication and collaboration with local partners and legal advisors are vital elements for successful outcomes in these challenging transactions. The selection of appropriate financial instruments to hedge

against currency fluctuations and other risks is also a critical component of effective risk management in the international arena. Finally, these case studies underscore the need for lenders to continually adapt their strategies to evolving

Political, economic, and regulatory environments in the global market. The dynamic nature of international

commerce requires flexibility and a willingness to refine approaches based on lessons learned from past experiences.

Integrating ESG Factors into Credit Risk Assessments

The preceding case studies vividly illustrate the multifaceted challenges inherent in international lending, emphasizing the need for a comprehensive and nuanced approach to risk assessment. However, the landscape of responsible lending is evolving, with a growing recognition of Environmental, Social, and Governance (ESG) factors as critical

determinants of creditworthiness. Simply analyzing financial statements is no longer sufficient; a holistic assessment incorporating ESG considerations is becoming paramount for prudent lending practices. This shift reflects a broader societal awareness of the interconnectedness of

environmental sustainability, social equity, and good

governance with long-term financial stability.

Integrating ESG factors into credit risk assessments requires a fundamental shift in the traditional lending paradigm. While financial ratios and historical performance remain important, lenders must now incorporate qualitative data related to a borrower's environmental impact, social

responsibility, and governance structures. This involves a more comprehensive due diligence process, extending

beyond purely financial analysis to include a detailed

examination of a borrower's ESG performance and its

potential impact on the credit risk.

The evaluation of a borrower's environmental performance begins with assessing its carbon footprint. This involves scrutinizing its energy consumption, greenhouse gas

emissions, and waste generation. Lenders may consider a company's commitment to renewable energy sources, its efforts to reduce its carbon emissions, and the presence of

Carbon offsetting initiatives. Beyond direct emissions, a thorough assessment should also evaluate the company's supply chain's environmental impact. For instance, a manufacturer sourcing raw materials from suppliers with poor environmental practices might face higher environmental risks and, consequently, higher credit risk.

The use of sustainable materials, the efficient management of water resources, and the implementation of robust waste management programs are all positive indicators. Companies that fail to address environmental concerns may face regulatory penalties, reputational damage, and increased operational costs, all of which translate into heightened credit risk. The assessment must also incorporate potential risks from climate change, such as extreme weather events, sea-level rise, and resource scarcity. A company's vulnerability to these factors should be rigorously evaluated.

For instance, a coastal refinery faces a greater risk from hurricanes than an inland facility, and a company highly reliant on water-intensive processes in an arid region faces increased water scarcity risk. Understanding and assessing these risks is essential for a comprehensive credit assessment.

The social dimension of ESG focuses on a company's impact on its employees, customers, communities, and wider society. This involves evaluating factors such as labor practices, human rights, product safety, and community engagement. A company with a history of labor disputes, poor working conditions, or human rights violations will likely face higher credit risk due to potential reputational damage, legal liabilities, and operational disruptions.

Similarly, a company involved in the production of unsafe products faces significant legal and financial risks.

Conversely, a company with a strong record of employee engagement, community investment, and ethical business practices will likely be viewed as a lower credit risk. The

Assessment should delve into the company's diversity and inclusion policies, its commitment to fair wages and benefits, and its efforts to support local communities.

Lenders should also consider the company's supply chain's social responsibility, particularly in industries with high risks of human rights abuses or unethical labor practices. A

detailed analysis of the company's policies, practices, and performance across these areas is crucial for a

comprehensive ESG assessment. Transparency and

accountability in social performance are also critical

indicators of a company's creditworthiness. Companies that actively report on their social performance, including

through independent audits, demonstrate a commitment to transparency and accountability. This transparency can

significantly reduce credit risk for lenders.

The governance aspect of ESG focuses on the company's management structure, internal controls, and ethical

behavior. This includes evaluating the board's composition, the independence of its directors, the company's executive compensation policies, and the effectiveness of its risk

management systems. A company with a weak corporate governance structure faces a higher credit risk due to

increased susceptibility to fraud, mismanagement, and

regulatory penalties. Conversely, a company with strong governance structures will be perceived as a lower credit risk. This also incorporates assessing the company's

transparency in its financial reporting, the independence of its audit committee, and the strength of its internal controls. Lenders should examine the company's adherence to ethical business practices and its compliance with relevant laws and regulations. The presence of robust anti-corruption

measures, data privacy protocols, and whistleblower

protection mechanisms are all significant positive indicators. A company's history of regulatory infractions or significant legal actions is a critical red flag that increases credit risk.

The assessment should also investigate whether the company has established a dedicated ESG committee or function and the resources allocated to ESG initiatives. Robust

governance structures can mitigate risks and improve financial stability, contributing to a company's creditworthiness.

Specific ESG metrics can be used to quantify and analyze the different aspects of a borrower's ESG performance.

These metrics can vary depending on the industry and the specific risk factors involved, but some common examples include carbon emissions intensity, water consumption per unit of output, employee turnover rates, the number of safety incidents, and the percentage of women in leadership

positions. The selection of appropriate metrics is crucial for providing a comprehensive and accurate assessment of the borrower's ESG profile. These metrics provide a quantitative framework for assessing ESG performance, enabling a more objective and data-driven evaluation. However, quantitative metrics must be considered in conjunction with qualitative assessments, incorporating the company's overall ESG strategy and the effectiveness of its implementation.

Integrating ESG factors into credit risk assessments is not a simple process; it requires a multi-disciplinary approach involving specialists in finance, environmental science, social impact, and governance. Lenders must develop robust methodologies for collecting, analyzing, and interpreting ESG data. This requires a deep understanding of the

industry-specific ESG challenges and opportunities.

Collaboration with ESG rating agencies and other specialized consultants can also be invaluable.

Furthermore, the financial industry itself is facing increasing pressure from regulators and investors to incorporate ESG considerations into their lending practices. Mandatory ESG

Disclosures are becoming more prevalent globally, and lenders that fail to adequately assess and manage ESG risks may face regulatory penalties and reputational damage. The integration of ESG considerations is not merely an ethical imperative but also a prudent risk management strategy. By incorporating ESG factors into credit risk assessments, lenders can enhance their ability to identify and mitigate potential risks, improve their portfolio performance, and contribute to a more sustainable and equitable financial system. This approach strengthens the long-term viability of businesses and the financial system as a whole. Ignoring these factors increasingly carries substantial financial and reputational consequences.

ESG Due Diligence and Reporting

The increasing integration of Environmental, Social, and Governance (ESG) factors into lending practices necessitates a robust due diligence process and transparent reporting mechanisms. Lenders are no longer solely focused on traditional financial metrics; they are increasingly scrutinizing a borrower's environmental impact, social responsibility, and governance structures to gauge long-term creditworthiness and mitigate potential risks. This shift reflects a convergence of ethical concerns, regulatory pressures, and a growing recognition that ESG performance is intrinsically linked to financial performance.

ESG due diligence goes beyond a simple checklist. It demands a comprehensive, multi-faceted approach that incorporates both quantitative and qualitative data.

Quantitative data might include metrics such as carbon emissions intensity, water consumption rates, employee turnover, and safety incident frequency. These metrics offer a standardized framework for comparison across different companies and industries. However, these numbers, alone, tell only part of the story. A thorough due diligence process also requires a deep dive into the qualitative aspects of a borrower's ESG performance. This includes reviewing the company's ESG policies, assessing its commitment to sustainability initiatives, and evaluating the effectiveness of its implementation strategies. For example, a company might boast impressive quantitative data related to waste reduction but fail to disclose its reliance on unsustainable sourcing practices within its supply chain. Such a discrepancy highlights the limitations of relying solely on numerical metrics. A comprehensive assessment requires a holistic view, which includes an examination of the company's

Overall ESG strategy, its alignment with international

standards, and its commitment to continuous improvement.

Several globally recognized frameworks and standards provide a foundation for evaluating and reporting ESG performance. The Global Reporting Initiative (GRI)

Standards, for instance, are widely used by companies to report on their economic, environmental, and social

performance. The Sustainability Accounting Standards Board (SASB) standards offer industry-specific metrics for material ESG issues, ensuring that the assessment is relevant to the nature of the business. The Task Force on Climate-related Financial Disclosures (TCFD) provides a framework for companies to disclose climate-related risks and

opportunities. These standards and frameworks provide a common language for ESG reporting, enhancing

comparability and transparency across different companies and industries. Using these established frameworks ensures consistency and reduces the risk of "greenwashing"—the practice of making misleading or unsubstantiated claims about a company's environmental performance. Lenders increasingly require borrowers to adhere to at least one of these widely accepted frameworks, demonstrating a credible commitment to ESG principles.

The process of ESG due diligence requires expertise across various disciplines. Lenders often assemble multidisciplinary teams comprising finance professionals, environmental scientists, social impact experts, and legal counsel. Such a holistic approach ensures that all material ESG risks are identified and assessed. The team will review a borrower's ESG policies, analyze its environmental footprint,

investigate its social impact, and scrutinize its governance structures. External resources, such as ESG rating agencies, sustainability consultants, and specialist environmental and social auditors, can provide valuable insights and

Independent verification of a company's reported

performance. The cost of conducting thorough ESG due diligence can be significant, especially for complex

multinational corporations, but it is a necessary investment to mitigate potential financial and reputational risks.

Reporting requirements for ESG performance are becoming increasingly stringent and standardized. Regulators

worldwide are mandating greater transparency, demanding that companies disclose their ESG performance in a clear, consistent, and comparable manner. The aim is to provide investors and lenders with reliable information to inform their decision-making. For instance, the European Union's Corporate Sustainability Reporting Directive (CSRD)

mandates extensive ESG reporting for a wide range of

companies, setting a high bar for transparency and

accountability. Similar regulations are emerging in other jurisdictions, reflecting a global trend toward greater ESG disclosure. Non-compliance can result in significant

financial penalties and reputational damage. Therefore, companies must develop robust ESG reporting systems and processes that meet or exceed these evolving regulatory requirements. Effective ESG reporting involves not only the compilation of data but also the interpretation and

communication of that data in a transparent and

understandable manner. This often involves creating a

narrative alongside the quantitative data, explaining the company's approach to ESG, its performance against targets, and its future strategy.

The integration of ESG considerations into lending is not merely a matter of compliance; it represents a fundamental shift in the way credit risk is assessed. By incorporating ESG factors, lenders can gain a deeper understanding of a

borrower's long-term resilience and sustainability. This

enables a more holistic and nuanced evaluation of

Creditworthiness, going beyond traditional financial metrics to consider the broader societal and environmental context.

Companies with strong ESG profiles often demonstrate better risk management practices, leading to reduced operational costs and enhanced financial stability.

Conversely, companies that fail to address ESG issues may face higher credit risk due to increased exposure to

regulatory penalties, reputational damage, and operational disruptions.

Furthermore, the integration of ESG into lending practices has significant societal benefits. By prioritizing responsible lending, financial institutions can encourage companies to adopt more sustainable and equitable business models,

contributing to a more environmentally responsible and socially just world. This, in turn, fosters greater investor confidence and contributes to the long-term stability and resilience of the financial system. The financial industry is recognizing that ESG performance is not just a 'nice to have'; it's a critical determinant of long-term value creation and a key factor in mitigating financial risks. Investing in ESG due diligence and reporting is therefore not merely an exercise in compliance; it's a strategic imperative for responsible and sustainable lending. Ignoring ESG factors increasingly

carries substantial financial and reputational risks for lenders and borrowers alike. The future of lending is inextricably linked to its capacity to understand, measure, and effectively manage ESG-related risks and opportunities. The transition to this new paradigm is underway, driven by a confluence of regulatory pressure, investor demand, and an increasing recognition that sustainability and profitability are not

mutually exclusive but, rather, intrinsically linked.

Esglinked Lending and Green Finance

The integration of Environmental, Social, and Governance (ESG) factors into traditional lending practices is rapidly evolving into a mainstream approach, significantly altering the landscape of commercial and asset-based lending. This shift is fueled by a confluence of factors: heightened

awareness of climate change and its financial implications; increasing pressure from investors and stakeholders

demanding greater corporate social responsibility; and the emergence of robust regulatory frameworks promoting transparency and accountability in ESG performance. This subsection explores the burgeoning field of ESG-linked lending and green finance, examining its mechanisms, benefits, and challenges.

ESG-linked lending involves structuring loan agreements where the interest rate or other loan terms are directly tied to a borrower's performance against pre-defined ESG targets. This creates a powerful incentive for businesses to improve their ESG profile, fostering a virtuous cycle of sustainable development and financial performance. For instance, a company seeking a loan might agree to a lower interest rate if it meets specific targets related to carbon emissions

reduction, waste management, or diversity and inclusion within its workforce. Failure to achieve these targets could result in higher interest rates or even loan covenant breaches. This mechanism effectively aligns the interests of the lender and the borrower, fostering collaboration towards shared sustainability goals.

The design of an effective ESG-linked loan requires careful consideration of several key factors. First, the selection of appropriate ESG Key Performance Indicators (kpis) is

Crucial. These kpis should be material to the borrower's business, measurable, and verifiable. Generic, easily

manipulated metrics should be avoided. Instead, kpis should be tailored to the specific industry and the borrower's unique operational characteristics. For example, a manufacturing company's kpis might focus on energy efficiency and waste reduction, while a technology company might prioritize data privacy and employee well-being. Furthermore, the kpis should be aligned with internationally recognized standards and frameworks, such as the GRI Standards, SASB

Standards, or TCFD recommendations, ensuring consistency and transparency.

Second, the establishment of clear and measurable targets is essential. These targets should be ambitious yet achievable, setting a challenging yet realistic path for the borrower's ESG improvement. The targets should be defined in

collaboration with the borrower, ensuring that they are integrated into the borrower's overall business strategy and operational plans. The process of target-setting should be transparent and documented, with regular progress reporting and review mechanisms built into the loan agreement. The chosen targets must be specific, measurable, achievable, relevant, and time-bound (SMART) to ensure effectiveness and accountability.

Third, the development of robust monitoring and verification mechanisms is vital. The lender needs a reliable system for tracking the borrower's progress towards its ESG targets.

This might involve regular reporting from the borrower, supplemented by independent third-party verification. Verification can be accomplished through various methods, including audits, self-reporting, and data analysis from publicly available sources. The selection of the appropriate verification method depends on the complexity of the kpis and the resources available to the lender. Thorough

Monitoring ensures that the ESG-linked loan remains aligned with its intended objectives.

Green finance, a closely related concept, encompasses various financial instruments and practices that support environmentally sustainable projects and activities. This includes green bonds, green loans, and other financial products designed to fund environmentally friendly initiatives such as renewable energy projects, energy efficiency improvements, and sustainable transportation. Green finance plays a pivotal role in transitioning to a low-carbon economy, directing capital towards projects that contribute to environmental sustainability.

The incentives for lenders to embrace ESG-linked lending and green finance are multifaceted. Beyond the ethical imperative, there are significant financial and reputational benefits. First, ESG-linked lending can enhance credit risk management. By incorporating ESG factors into their credit assessment, lenders gain a deeper understanding of a borrower's long-term sustainability and resilience, mitigating potential risks associated with environmental and social issues. Companies with strong ESG profiles often demonstrate better risk management practices, leading to reduced operational costs and enhanced financial stability.

Second, ESG-linked lending can attract new investment and improve a lender's reputation. Investors are increasingly seeking opportunities to align their portfolios with their ESG values. By incorporating ESG considerations into their lending practices, financial institutions can attract socially responsible investors who are willing to pay a premium for sustainable investments. Furthermore, a strong commitment to ESG can enhance a lender's reputation among stakeholders, building trust and improving brand value.

Third, ESG-linked lending can generate new business opportunities. The growing demand for green finance presents significant opportunities for lenders to develop innovative products and services tailored to the needs of environmentally conscious businesses. This can lead to increased market share and profitability. The market for green finance is expanding rapidly, creating lucrative opportunities for lenders willing to invest in this sector.

However, challenges remain in the widespread adoption of ESG-linked lending and green finance. One of the most significant challenges is the lack of standardized ESG

metrics and reporting frameworks. While various standards exist, the absence of a universally accepted framework can make it difficult to compare the ESG performance of

different companies across different sectors. This lack of standardization creates challenges for lenders in assessing and comparing ESG risks, leading to inconsistent application of ESG criteria in lending decisions.

Another challenge is the difficulty in accurately measuring and verifying the ESG impact of projects. Some ESG

impacts are difficult to quantify precisely, making it

challenging to create robust ESG kpis and targets. This can lead to disputes between lenders and borrowers regarding the accuracy of reported ESG data. Third-party verification can help address this issue, providing independent assurance of the accuracy and completeness of ESG data. However, the cost of third-party verification can be significant, especially for smaller borrowers.

Furthermore, the limited availability of data on ESG

performance can hinder the adoption of ESG-linked lending.

Many companies do not publicly disclose their ESG data, making it difficult for lenders to assess their ESG risks. This lack of data hinders the development of robust ESG kpis

And targets. Increased transparency and disclosure

requirements from regulatory bodies are slowly addressing this issue. However, better data collection and management practices are required from both lenders and borrowers.

Despite these challenges, the rise of ESG-linked lending and green finance represents a significant shift in the financial industry. By integrating ESG considerations into their

lending practices, financial institutions can create a more sustainable and equitable future, while also improving their risk management and enhancing their reputation. While the transition is not without its hurdles, the long-term benefits of embracing ESG in lending outweigh the challenges, and the future of the finance sector is increasingly interwoven with the principles of environmental and social responsibility. The ongoing evolution of robust frameworks, better data

availability, and a growing understanding of the complex interplay between ESG factors and financial performance will ensure the continued growth and sophistication of this vital sector.

ESG Risk Management and Disclosure

The integration of ESG factors into lending decisions necessitates a robust risk management framework. Failing to adequately assess and mitigate ESG risks can lead to significant financial losses, reputational damage, and regulatory penalties. A comprehensive ESG risk management strategy should encompass identification, assessment, mitigation, monitoring, and reporting of ESG-related risks across the lending lifecycle.

The identification phase involves systematically reviewing a borrower's ESG performance across environmental, social, and governance dimensions. This entails analyzing publicly available data, conducting due diligence, and engaging in direct communication with the borrower to gain a comprehensive understanding of their ESG profile. For example, in the case of a manufacturing company, a lender might examine its carbon footprint, waste management practices, and adherence to environmental regulations. For a technology company, data privacy practices, employee well-being, and supply chain ethics would be crucial aspects to investigate. In the financial services sector itself, lenders must scrutinize their own ESG performance, including their impact on climate change through financing activities, and the diversity and inclusion within their workforce.

Assessing the identified risks involves evaluating their likelihood and potential impact on the loan. This requires a qualitative and quantitative approach, incorporating both financial and non-financial data. Sophisticated risk scoring models can be employed to quantify the relative significance of different ESG risks. For instance, the likelihood of a natural disaster impacting a borrower's operations, based on

Its geographical location and vulnerability to specific climate-related events, should be carefully considered.

Similarly, the potential impact of a reputational crisis

resulting from unethical labor practices or environmental damage should be evaluated. Sensitivity analysis can be used to gauge the impact of various scenarios on the borrower's financial performance and the lender's exposure to potential losses.

Once risks have been identified and assessed, mitigation strategies should be developed and implemented. These strategies could range from adjusting loan terms and

conditions to requiring the borrower to implement specific ESG improvements. For instance, a lender might incorporate ESG performance into loan covenants, linking interest rates or other loan terms to the borrower's progress towards pre-defined ESG targets. They might also require the borrower to undertake environmental audits, improve their governance structures, or adopt specific risk management policies.

Collateral valuation may also need to incorporate climate change risks, for example, evaluating the impact of rising sea levels on the value of coastal properties used as collateral.

Ongoing monitoring of the borrower's ESG performance is crucial. This involves regularly collecting and analyzing data on the borrower's ESG performance, tracking progress

towards agreed-upon targets, and identifying any emerging ESG risks. The frequency and methods of monitoring should be tailored to the specific risks and the borrower's industry.

For instance, regular reporting requirements might be

imposed on borrowers, with independent verification

employed to ensure accuracy and transparency. Regular communication between the lender and the borrower is also vital to fostering collaboration and early identification of potential issues. This necessitates building a strong working relationship based on trust and mutual understanding.

Finally, appropriate disclosure of ESG-related risks is vital. This involves transparently communicating the lender's ESG risk management practices to stakeholders, including

investors, regulators, and the public. Disclosure should be comprehensive and consistent with relevant regulatory

requirements and internationally recognized standards, such as the Task Force on Climate-related Financial Disclosures (TCFD) recommendations. The disclosure should include a description of the lender's ESG risk assessment

methodology, the identified ESG risks, the implemented mitigation strategies, and the outcomes of monitoring efforts.

Transparency in this aspect builds trust and confidence amongst stakeholders.

Effective ESG risk management requires collaboration and coordination across different departments within the lending institution. The risk management department, the credit underwriting team, and the legal and compliance functions should all be involved in the process. Furthermore,

establishing a clear chain of accountability for ESG risk management is essential. Senior management should be responsible for overseeing the implementation and

effectiveness of the ESG risk management framework.

Regular reviews of the framework are also necessary to ensure it remains effective and adapts to evolving ESG considerations and regulatory developments.

The increasing regulatory scrutiny of ESG risks is driving the adoption of more rigorous risk management practices.

Regulators are increasingly mandating the disclosure of ESG-related information and imposing stricter penalties for failures in ESG risk management. This creates a powerful incentive for lenders to integrate ESG considerations into their operations. Compliance with these regulations is

paramount, not only to avoid penalties but also to enhance a

Lender's reputation and build trust with stakeholders. Failing to adhere to regulatory frameworks can result in severe consequences, including financial penalties, reputational damage, and even legal action.

Beyond regulatory compliance, there are significant business benefits to effective ESG risk management. Integrating ESG factors into lending decisions can improve credit risk

assessment, leading to a reduction in loan defaults. Strong ESG performance is often associated with better financial performance and enhanced operational efficiency.

Companies with robust ESG practices tend to have lower operational costs, improved employee morale, and better access to capital. This translates into reduced risk for lenders, and stronger financial outcomes for borrowers.

Furthermore, effective ESG risk management can enhance a lender's reputation and attract investors who value

sustainable investments. Investors are increasingly

prioritizing ESG factors in their investment decisions,

seeking opportunities to align their portfolios with their values. Lenders with a strong track record in ESG risk management are better positioned to attract this type of investor, enjoying improved access to capital and enhanced financial performance. This virtuous cycle demonstrates the strong synergy between ESG principles and financial

success.

However, challenges remain in the effective management of ESG risks. The lack of standardized metrics and reporting frameworks can make it difficult to compare the ESG

performance of different companies across different sectors. The difficulty in accurately measuring and verifying the ESG impact of certain activities remains a hurdle. Limited data availability can hinder the development of robust ESG kpis and targets. Overcoming these challenges requires

Collaborative efforts from lenders, borrowers, regulators, and standard-setting bodies to develop universally accepted standards and reporting frameworks that facilitate robust and reliable ESG risk assessments. The continuous development of technology and data analytics solutions will play a crucial role in advancing this space.

In conclusion, ESG risk management and disclosure are integral components of modern lending practices. By

implementing robust risk management frameworks, lenders can identify, assess, mitigate, and monitor ESG risks, while also ensuring appropriate disclosure to stakeholders. This not only mitigates financial risks but also enhances the lender's reputation, attracts socially responsible investments, and contributes to a more sustainable and equitable financial system. The ongoing evolution of ESG standards, data

availability, and regulatory oversight will continue to shape the development of best practices in this crucial field.

Proactive and forward-thinking institutions will find

themselves better prepared to navigate the complexities of the evolving ESG landscape and capitalize on the

opportunities presented.

The Future of ESG in Lending and Finance

The evolving landscape of Environmental, Social, and

Governance (ESG) factors presents both challenges and opportunities for the future of lending and finance. The increasing integration of ESG considerations into lending decisions is not simply a matter of compliance; it represents a fundamental shift in how financial institutions assess risk and value opportunities. This shift is driven by several

powerful forces, including escalating regulatory scrutiny, the growing influence of socially responsible investors, and the undeniable reality of climate change and its attendant risks.

One of the most significant trends shaping the future of ESG in lending is the rapid expansion of regulatory frameworks.

Governments worldwide are enacting legislation and

implementing policies aimed at promoting sustainable

finance and holding financial institutions accountable for their ESG performance. These regulations encompass a wide range of areas, from mandatory ESG disclosures and

climate-related risk assessments to restrictions on financing activities deemed environmentally harmful. For example, the European Union's Sustainable Finance Disclosure

Regulation (SFDR) and the Taxonomy Regulation are setting global standards for transparency and accountability,

prompting financial institutions to align their practices with the broader goals of the European Green Deal. Similar

initiatives are emerging in other jurisdictions, creating a progressively more unified and demanding regulatory

environment. The lack of harmonization between various jurisdictions, however, remains a challenge for globally active financial institutions, requiring careful navigation of diverse regulatory landscapes. This necessitates a robust legal and compliance function within lending institutions,

Capable of interpreting and adapting to constantly evolving regulatory frameworks.

The increasing pressure from investors is another crucial driver of the ESG evolution in lending. Investors, both

institutional and individual, are increasingly incorporating ESG factors into their investment decisions. This is driven by a growing awareness of the financial risks associated with unsustainable practices and a desire to align investments with personal values. Investors are scrutinizing not only the ESG performance of the companies they invest in but also the ESG policies and practices of the financial institutions managing their assets. This necessitates greater transparency and accountability from lenders, requiring them to

demonstrate their commitment to ESG principles through comprehensive reporting and robust risk management

frameworks. This increased investor scrutiny encourages a more rigorous approach to ESG integration, driving

competition amongst lenders to showcase their sustainability leadership and attract ethical investment. This also motivates the development of innovative financing instruments

designed to support sustainable initiatives, encouraging investment in renewable energy, green technologies, and socially responsible projects.

The integration of technology is crucial to the advancement of ESG in lending. Technological advancements are enabling lenders to collect, analyze, and interpret ESG data more efficiently and effectively. Advanced data analytics, machine learning, and artificial intelligence (AI) are improving the ability to assess ESG risks, identify sustainability leaders, and develop customized ESG scoring models. The use of satellite imagery, for instance, allows for the real-time

monitoring of deforestation and other environmental

impacts, while social media analytics can offer insights into a company's social performance and reputational risks.

However, the ethical considerations of employing AI and data analytics in ESG assessments must be carefully addressed. Bias in algorithms and data privacy concerns require careful management. The accuracy and reliability of data sources must be meticulously validated to avoid misleading or inaccurate ESG ratings.

Furthermore, the future of ESG in lending is likely to see an increased focus on specific environmental and social issues. Climate change is undeniably at the forefront, with lenders increasingly focusing on the physical and transition risks associated with climate change. The physical risks, such as the impact of extreme weather events on borrowers' operations, are becoming increasingly apparent and necessitate more sophisticated risk assessment models. The transition risks, associated with the shift towards a low-carbon economy, also require careful consideration. The growing awareness of biodiversity loss and its financial implications is another important trend. Lenders are beginning to incorporate biodiversity considerations into their risk assessments, particularly in sectors heavily reliant on natural resources. Social issues, such as labor standards, human rights, and supply chain ethics, are also gaining prominence, driven by heightened consumer awareness and regulatory scrutiny. The development of robust ESG frameworks and data-driven insights will continue to shape the integration of these crucial elements into the lending process.

The development of standardized ESG reporting frameworks is essential for the future of ESG in lending. The lack of consistent and comparable ESG data remains a major challenge. The development of universally accepted standards, such as those proposed by the Sustainability Accounting Standards Board (SASB) and the Global Reporting Initiative (GRI), is crucial to enhance

Transparency and facilitate informed decision-making. The alignment of reporting frameworks with existing financial reporting standards will also streamline the process and ensure greater comparability between companies across different sectors. This harmonization is pivotal in removing ambiguity and creating a standardized method of assessing ESG performance. Harmonization, however, faces

challenges regarding jurisdictional differences and the diversity of sectors, which makes achieving a universal standard a complex task that necessitates international collaboration.

The future of ESG in lending also hinges on innovation in financial products and services. The growing demand for sustainable finance initiatives is creating opportunities for lenders to develop innovative financial products designed to support sustainable projects and businesses. Green bonds, sustainability-linked loans, and other impact investing

instruments are gaining traction, providing financial

institutions with new avenues for growth and demonstrating a commitment to sustainability. The development of these products, however, necessitates sophisticated knowledge and experience in financial structuring, risk management, and sustainable development. Careful assessment of the

environmental and social impacts of these projects is crucial, requiring thorough due diligence and independent

verification. The development of novel financial structures, like green securitizations, is also crucial in efficiently

channeling capital toward sustainable ventures and

encouraging greater participation from a wider range of investors.

Finally, fostering collaboration and knowledge sharing is key to the successful integration of ESG considerations in

lending. Lenders need to collaborate with borrowers,

regulators, investors, and other stakeholders to develop

Robust ESG standards and frameworks. Sharing best practices and lessons learned is crucial in accelerating progress and ensuring a consistent approach. Industry associations and governmental bodies can play a crucial role in facilitating collaboration, establishing common standards, and ensuring the accuracy and reliability of ESG data.

International collaboration is paramount in harmonizing standards and creating a global approach to responsible lending. This collaborative approach is essential in navigating the complexities of ESG and fostering a sustainable financial system that benefits all stakeholders. The future success of ESG integration relies on the collective efforts of all players involved, emphasizing cooperation over competition to create a resilient and sustainable financial landscape.

Building highperforming Lending Teams

Building a high-performing lending team is paramount to success in any financial institution, particularly during

periods of economic uncertainty or crisis. A strong team, characterized by expertise, collaboration, and resilience, is the cornerstone of effective lending practices and adept crisis management. This necessitates a multifaceted approach encompassing strategic talent acquisition, comprehensive training and development programs, and the cultivation of a positive and productive team dynamic.

The first critical element lies in the strategic acquisition of talent. Attracting and retaining top-tier lending professionals requires a well-defined recruitment strategy focused on identifying individuals possessing not only technical skills but also possessing crucial soft skills essential for navigating the complexities of the lending landscape. This includes a deep understanding of financial markets, regulatory

compliance, risk assessment, and credit analysis. Beyond these technical competencies, qualities such as strong

communication skills, problem-solving abilities, and a

collaborative spirit are equally vital. These individuals need to be able to effectively communicate with borrowers, build strong relationships, and work collaboratively within the team to reach effective solutions. The recruitment process should involve rigorous assessment techniques, including behavioral interviews and scenario-based assessments, to gauge the candidates' ability to handle pressure, make sound judgments under uncertainty, and work effectively under tight deadlines. Furthermore, a competitive compensation and benefits package is essential to attract and retain the best talent, ensuring that the institution remains competitive in the market.

Once a strong team is assembled, a comprehensive training and development program is crucial for maintaining high performance and ensuring continued professional growth. This necessitates a structured approach that addresses both technical and soft skills. Technical training should

encompass up-to-date knowledge of lending regulations, credit analysis techniques, and risk management

methodologies. It is vital to stay current with the evolving legal and regulatory framework, ensuring compliance with all relevant laws and guidelines. Regular updates on lending policies, procedures, and best practices are also necessary.

Moreover, technological advancements in the lending

industry demand continuous training on new software, data analytics tools, and other technologies that streamline

processes and improve efficiency. For instance, training on advanced credit scoring models, automated underwriting systems, and fraud detection software can significantly enhance the team's performance. Specialized training in areas such as asset-based lending, commercial real estate financing, or other niche lending products should also be available to deepen the team's expertise and broaden its capabilities. Furthermore, advanced training in financial modeling, stress testing, and scenario planning is especially critical for equipping the team to effectively navigate

economic downturns and crisis situations.

Beyond technical skills, cultivating crucial soft skills

through training is equally important. Effective

communication is vital for navigating complex transactions, managing client relationships, and fostering internal

collaboration. Negotiation skills are essential for securing favorable terms for both the lender and the borrower.

Problem-solving training enables the team to effectively address unforeseen challenges and make sound judgments under pressure. Training programs should also focus on

Conflict resolution and teamwork skills, fostering a

collaborative environment where team members can work together efficiently and effectively. Workshops and

simulations that mirror real-world lending situations can provide invaluable practice in developing these soft skills. Regular team-building exercises, both formal and informal, can further improve cohesion and communication within the team. This could range from professional development conferences to social events that encourage camaraderie and build trust among team members.

Furthermore, a robust performance management system is essential to maintain high standards and drive continuous improvement. Clear performance expectations should be established from the outset, and regular performance reviews should provide constructive feedback and identify areas for growth. A performance management system that

incorporates both quantitative and qualitative measures is essential, taking into account both individual and team

contributions. Key performance indicators (kpis) should be established to track team performance and identify areas for improvement. This can include metrics such as loan

origination volume, loan quality, delinquency rates, and customer satisfaction. Regular performance reviews provide an opportunity for constructive feedback and coaching, enabling team members to enhance their skills and achieve their full potential. Moreover, it's crucial to recognize and reward exceptional performance, fostering a culture of high achievement and motivating team members to strive for excellence. This could include bonuses, promotions, or other forms of recognition that demonstrate the institution's

appreciation for their hard work and dedication.

Leadership plays a crucial role in fostering a high-performing lending team. Effective leaders create a supportive, collaborative, and challenging environment

Where team members feel empowered, motivated, and

valued. This includes providing clear direction and guidance, setting realistic expectations, and providing regular

feedback. Leaders should foster open communication,

encouraging team members to share their ideas and concerns openly. A strong leader creates a culture of trust and respect, where team members feel comfortable expressing their

opinions and seeking assistance when needed. Active

listening, empathy, and a willingness to help team members overcome challenges are vital characteristics of effective leadership. Furthermore, effective leaders possess a strong ethical compass, ensuring that all team members adhere to the highest standards of integrity and compliance. This

includes promoting a culture of ethical lending practices and ensuring that all transactions comply with relevant

regulations. During periods of crisis, strong leadership is particularly crucial. A skilled leader can calm anxieties, facilitate effective decision-making, and maintain morale during challenging times.

In addition to these individual aspects, careful consideration of team dynamics is vital. A high-performing lending team relies heavily on effective collaboration and communication.

This requires the right mix of personalities and skill sets to ensure all areas are covered. Team members should be

encouraged to share their expertise, provide constructive feedback, and support each other during demanding

situations. Regular team meetings should be held to discuss progress, address challenges, and ensure that everyone is working towards common goals. Conflict is inevitable in any team, but it's how the team navigates and resolves conflict that determines its overall performance. Training in conflict resolution techniques and team-building exercises can help mitigate this. Open communication, mutual respect, and a willingness to compromise are crucial in resolving conflicts effectively and maintaining a productive working

Environment. Furthermore, creating a diverse and inclusive team enriches the perspectives and experiences brought to the table, which can contribute to a more creative and effective approach to problem-solving. A diverse team is better equipped to understand the needs of a wider range of clients, reflecting the diverse communities they serve.

Finally, maintaining a strong focus on risk management is essential for building a high-performing lending team. This involves establishing robust risk assessment procedures, implementing effective controls, and regularly monitoring the team's performance to identify potential risks and

prevent problems before they escalate. Regular risk

assessments should be undertaken to evaluate the potential risks associated with specific loans and transactions. The use of advanced technology, such as machine learning and

artificial intelligence (AI), can greatly assist in the

assessment and management of risk. Implementing effective controls helps ensure that all lending decisions are made in accordance with established policies and procedures. These controls can involve multiple checks and balances to avoid errors, fraud, and other potential problems. Ongoing

monitoring of the team's performance is crucial to identify potential problems promptly and address them before they escalate. This can involve regular reporting on key

performance indicators (kpis), such as loan defaults,

delinquency rates, and customer complaints.

In conclusion, building a high-performing lending team is a continuous process that requires ongoing effort and

commitment. By focusing on strategic talent acquisition, comprehensive training and development, fostering effective team dynamics, promoting strong leadership, and prioritizing risk management, financial institutions can create a team capable of delivering exceptional results even under the most challenging circumstances. This ensures not only short-term

Success but also the long-term sustainability and resilience of the organization, enhancing its ability to weather economic storms and emerge stronger from periods of crisis. The

investment in human capital is not merely an expense; it is a strategic investment that yields substantial returns in terms of performance, stability, and the overall success of the

financial institution.

Cultivating a Culture of Risk Awareness

Cultivating a pervasive culture of risk awareness is not merely a compliance exercise; it's the lifeblood of a successful and sustainable lending operation. It's a continuous process, demanding consistent effort and a commitment from every level of the organization, from the boardroom to the loan officer on the front lines. This goes beyond simply adhering to regulatory requirements; it necessitates a fundamental shift in mindset, where risk assessment and mitigation become integral to every decision, every interaction, and every process.

Effective training programs form the bedrock of any successful risk awareness initiative. These programs cannot be a one-size-fits-all approach. They must be tailored to the specific roles and responsibilities of each employee, acknowledging the differing levels of risk exposure inherent in various positions. For example, a junior loan officer will require a comprehensive foundational understanding of credit analysis, risk assessment methodologies, and regulatory compliance, focusing on practical applications and real-world scenarios. Their training should emphasize identifying red flags, understanding the implications of loan defaults, and adhering to internal policies and procedures. This might involve interactive workshops, case studies, and simulated lending scenarios to provide hands-on experience and reinforce learning.

Senior loan officers and managers, conversely, require training that delves into more strategic risk management.

Their programs should focus on advanced risk assessment techniques, stress testing, and scenario planning. They need to understand how macroeconomic factors, market volatility,

And geopolitical events can impact loan portfolios and the overall health of the institution. Training might incorporate financial modeling, advanced statistical analysis, and risk mitigation strategies for navigating complex situations.

Furthermore, their training should emphasize leadership skills, enabling them to effectively communicate risk

assessments to their teams and make well-informed

decisions under pressure. They should be adept at identifying and managing systemic risks across the entire loan portfolio.

This might involve participation in industry conferences, specialized workshops, and mentorship programs with seasoned professionals.

Beyond role-specific training, a comprehensive risk

awareness program should also address common pitfalls and vulnerabilities. This includes dedicated sessions on fraud detection and prevention, encompassing everything from identifying sophisticated schemes to implementing robust internal controls. For example, training might cover various forms of identity theft, fraudulent documentation, and the use of advanced technologies to perpetrate fraud. This

necessitates practical exercises, simulations, and discussions of real-world fraud cases to equip employees with the skills to identify and respond to such threats.

Another crucial element is training on regulatory

compliance. The financial landscape is constantly evolving, with new regulations and guidelines frequently emerging. Ongoing training ensures that all employees remain up-to-date on the latest legal and regulatory requirements,

minimizing the risk of non-compliance. This needs to be a dynamic process, incorporating regular updates, workshops, and compliance audits to ensure that everyone understands their responsibilities and adheres to the institution's internal policies and external regulations. This might involve

quizzes, interactive online modules, and scenario-based

Simulations to test employees' knowledge and ensure retention.

Effective communication strategies are equally crucial in building a culture of risk awareness. The dissemination of information about risk management practices should not be a one-way street. It requires a continuous, open dialogue

involving all levels of the organization. Regular internal newsletters, seminars, and town hall meetings can be

effective mechanisms for communicating important

information, sharing best practices, and encouraging open discussion about risk-related issues. This could cover topics such as recent regulatory changes, emerging risks within the financial sector, and internal successes or failures in risk management.

Moreover, establishing a robust system for reporting and addressing risk-related concerns is essential. A clear and accessible channel for employees to voice their concerns without fear of retribution is paramount. This could involve an anonymous reporting system, regular feedback sessions, and open-door policies for raising issues. The institution must demonstrate a genuine commitment to addressing these concerns promptly and transparently. Ignoring or dismissing concerns can significantly erode trust and damage the overall effectiveness of the risk awareness program. The feedback received should be used to identify areas for improvement in policies, procedures, and training.

Furthermore, the institution's leadership plays a pivotal role in shaping the culture of risk awareness. Senior management needs to actively champion risk management initiatives, leading by example and consistently emphasizing the

importance of risk awareness at all levels of the organization.

This requires a visible commitment, including regular communication about the institution's risk appetite, the

Importance of responsible lending, and the consequences of neglecting risk management. Regular updates to the board on risk management practices, including metrics, incident

reports, and remediation plans, underscore the institution's commitment to transparency and accountability.

Incentivizing responsible lending behaviors is equally

important. The compensation and rewards system should reflect the institution's commitment to risk awareness. This means rewarding employees who consistently demonstrate responsible lending practices, actively identify and mitigate risks, and comply with regulatory requirements. This could involve bonuses, promotions, or public recognition of

employees who have made significant contributions to risk management. In contrast, disciplinary action should be taken against employees who consistently ignore or disregard risk management policies and procedures. This establishes a clear link between behavior and reward, reinforcing the importance of risk awareness throughout the organization.

Finally, fostering a blame-free environment for reporting errors or near-misses is essential. A culture where employees feel comfortable reporting mistakes without fear of

punishment encourages proactive risk identification and helps improve overall risk management practices. Near-misses, while not resulting in immediate losses, can serve as valuable lessons, providing opportunities to identify and address potential vulnerabilities before they escalate into larger problems. Regular reviews of near-miss reports should be conducted, identifying common causes of errors,

developing corrective actions, and implementing

preventative measures to avoid similar incidents in the

future. This should be coupled with ongoing training and education to mitigate identified weaknesses.

In conclusion, creating a culture of risk awareness within a financial institution is a multifaceted endeavor, requiring a concerted effort across all levels of the organization.

Through comprehensive training programs, transparent communication strategies, strong leadership support,

appropriate incentives, and a commitment to reporting and learning from mistakes, institutions can foster an

environment where risk management is not simply an add-on but an ingrained part of the corporate DNA. This not only ensures compliance but also enhances operational efficiency, protects the institution from financial losses, and contributes significantly to long-term sustainability and success. The proactive management of risk is not a cost; it's a strategic investment in the future stability and resilience of the

organization.

Developing Strong Communication and Collaboration Skills

Effective communication and collaboration are not merely desirable traits in the lending and crisis management arenas; they are absolute necessities. The complexity of modern financial transactions, the interconnectedness of global markets, and the ever-evolving regulatory landscape demand a high degree of coordination, transparency, and shared understanding. Without these, even the most meticulously crafted risk management strategies can falter, leaving institutions vulnerable to financial losses and reputational damage.

The foundation of effective communication rests on clarity and precision. Loan officers, credit analysts, and risk managers must be able to articulate complex financial information concisely and accurately. This involves not only a strong grasp of financial terminology but also the ability to tailor communication to the audience's level of understanding. A detailed credit report, for instance, needs to be summarized effectively for a senior manager who may not have time for in-depth analysis, while a more nuanced explanation might be required for a junior colleague.

Beyond individual proficiency in communication, the ability to foster collaborative relationships across departments is critical. The lending process itself involves numerous stakeholders, including loan officers, underwriters, legal counsel, compliance officers, and senior management. Each plays a vital role, and their effective interaction is essential for efficient and responsible lending. For example, effective collaboration between loan officers and credit analysts ensures that all relevant information is considered during the

Loan application process, mitigating potential risks. Strong communication between the legal team and loan officers minimizes potential legal pitfalls, ensuring that all loan agreements comply with applicable regulations. Moreover, regular communication between compliance officers and loan officers prevents violations and maintains the

institution's regulatory standing.

In crisis management, the importance of effective

communication and collaboration intensifies exponentially. During periods of market volatility, economic downturn, or unexpected events, the ability to rapidly disseminate

information, coordinate responses, and maintain a unified front is paramount. Effective communication channels, both internal and external, are essential for disseminating vital information to stakeholders, such as clients, investors, and regulatory bodies. Internal communication needs to be swift, accurate, and consistent, ensuring that all team members are aware of the situation, their roles, and the institution's

response strategy. This might involve crisis management teams, regular briefings, and designated communication channels. External communication, on the other hand, needs to be measured, transparent, and reassuring, maintaining confidence in the institution's ability to weather the storm.

Building strong communication and collaboration skills requires a multifaceted approach. Training programs should incorporate workshops focusing on active listening, clear articulation, and persuasive communication techniques.

Role-playing exercises simulating real-world lending scenarios and crisis situations can help develop practical skills in communicating under pressure. Additionally, training should emphasize the importance of nonverbal communication, recognizing that body language and tone significantly impact the effectiveness of any message.

Moreover, developing empathy and emotional intelligence is crucial. Understanding and responding to the perspectives and emotions of colleagues, clients, and other stakeholders builds trust and promotes collaboration. For example, a loan officer exhibiting empathy toward a struggling business owner can foster a more constructive dialogue, potentially leading to mutually agreeable solutions. Similarly, managers with strong emotional intelligence can better understand and address the concerns of their teams during times of stress, helping to maintain morale and productivity. These skills, often overlooked, can play a significant role in crisis

resolution and building resilience.

Investing in technology that facilitates communication and collaboration is another important element. Intranets,

collaboration platforms, and secure communication systems can significantly enhance information sharing and team coordination. For instance, a shared platform where all relevant documents and updates are centrally stored and accessible ensures everyone has the same information, eliminating potential misunderstandings and delays. Regular updates and training on the efficient use of these tools are necessary to maximize their benefit. The use of these

technologies also needs to comply with strict data privacy regulations to mitigate potential risks.

The institution's culture also plays a crucial role in shaping communication and collaboration. A culture that values open communication, encourages feedback, and rewards

teamwork creates an environment where employees feel comfortable sharing ideas, raising concerns, and

collaborating effectively. This involves leadership actively modeling these behaviors, fostering an environment where constructive criticism is welcomed, and celebrating

successful collaborations. Regular team-building activities can also foster stronger relationships and improve

Communication flows within the teams. For instance, regular meetings focusing on project updates and addressing

challenges can enhance communication and prevent

misunderstandings.

Beyond internal communication and collaboration, external relations are equally critical. Maintaining strong

relationships with clients, suppliers, and regulatory bodies is essential for both day-to-day operations and effective crisis management. This necessitates clear, consistent, and

transparent communication with all stakeholders,

maintaining their trust and confidence. This could include regular client meetings, transparent reporting to regulatory bodies, and active engagement with industry associations. A well-managed crisis involves proactive communication with all these groups, maintaining a transparent dialogue and responding promptly to their inquiries.

Furthermore, the institution should establish formal

processes for communication and collaboration. Clear

protocols for handling loan applications, managing risk, and responding to crises minimize the potential for confusion and miscommunication. These processes need to be

documented, regularly reviewed, and updated to reflect evolving needs and best practices. The implementation of consistent procedures ensures that all members of the

organization are aware of their roles and responsibilities during both normal operations and emergency situations.

Finally, the institution should regularly assess the

effectiveness of its communication and collaboration

strategies. This could involve employee surveys, feedback sessions, and post-incident reviews. By identifying areas for improvement and implementing corrective actions, the institution can continuously enhance its communication and collaboration capabilities, strengthening its resilience and

Ensuring its long-term success. This ongoing evaluation ensures that the institution is not just reacting to events but proactively anticipating and preparing for potential

challenges. The proactive nature of this approach is key to effective risk management and crisis preparedness. This ongoing cycle of improvement strengthens the organization's response capability, fostering an environment of continuous learning and improvement.

Employee Training and Development in Crisis Management

The preceding discussion highlighted the paramount importance of effective communication and collaboration within a lending institution, particularly during periods of crisis. However, these crucial skills are not innate; they require deliberate cultivation through comprehensive employee training and development programs. A robust crisis management training program isn't a luxury; it's a necessity for the survival and continued success of any financial institution navigating the complexities of the modern lending landscape. The absence of such a program leaves the institution vulnerable, exposing it to significant financial losses, reputational damage, and regulatory penalties.

A well-structured training program should be multifaceted, addressing a range of skills and scenarios. It should go beyond simply disseminating information; it should actively engage employees, fostering practical application and critical thinking. The core elements of such a program should include:

Scenario-Based Training:

The most effective method for preparing employees for crisis situations is through realistic simulations. These simulations should encompass a variety of potential crises, from sudden market downturns and

cybersecurity breaches to natural disasters and regulatory investigations. Participants should be presented with realistic challenges, requiring them to apply their knowledge and problem-solving skills under pressure. For example, a

simulation could involve a sudden surge in loan defaults, forcing participants to devise strategies for managing the

Situation, communicating with affected clients, and

mitigating further losses. The use of case studies from actual past events, appropriately anonymized to protect sensitive information, can greatly enhance the realism and impact of these exercises. Debriefing sessions following each

simulation are crucial, providing opportunities for

participants to analyze their actions, identify areas for

improvement, and learn from their experiences.

Risk Identification and Assessment:

A key component of crisis management is the ability to identify and assess potential risks proactively. Training should equip employees with the tools and techniques to effectively analyze their respective areas of responsibility, identifying vulnerabilities and potential threats. This includes understanding various types of risks, such as credit risk, market risk, operational risk, and reputational risk. Training programs should incorporate techniques like SWOT analysis, scenario planning, and stress testing to improve risk assessment skills. Regular updates to risk assessment methodologies and training materials are crucial as regulatory environments and market dynamics evolve. This would include regular review and updating of crisis management plans, incorporating lessons learned from actual crises and evolving best practices.

Communication Protocols:

Crises often amplify the need for clear and consistent communication, both internally and externally. Training should establish standardized

communication protocols, ensuring that information flows efficiently and accurately. This includes defining roles and responsibilities for communication during a crisis,

designating spokespersons, and establishing clear channels for disseminating information to employees, clients,

investors, and regulatory bodies. Training could include role-playing exercises focusing on managing communication

During high-pressure situations, with scenarios ranging from addressing concerned clients to interacting with media representatives. The program should emphasize the ethical and legal obligations associated with communication during a crisis, especially in relation to disclosure and transparency requirements.

Decision-Making Under Pressure:

Crises often require quick, decisive actions. Training should help employees develop their decision-making skills under pressure. This includes fostering critical thinking, encouraging the

consideration of alternative solutions, and establishing a culture of reasoned risk-taking. The training might involve cognitive skills exercises focused on mental agility and quick problem-solving, enabling employees to handle the fast-paced nature of crisis situations efficiently and

effectively. Decision-making frameworks and processes should be clearly articulated to aid quick responses and limit the potential for paralysis. This includes defining clear decision-making authority and escalation procedures for handling situations that exceed individual employee

responsibilities.

Technological Proficiency:

In the modern financial

landscape, technological tools play a crucial role in crisis management. Training should ensure that employees are proficient in using relevant technologies for communication, data analysis, and risk assessment. This may include training on specific software or platforms used for internal

communication, data visualization tools for quickly

analyzing market trends, and cybersecurity protocols.

Regular updates to these skills are paramount due to the rapid evolution of technology. It's imperative that training incorporates the security and ethical considerations involved in using these technologies and handling sensitive data.

Teamwork and Collaboration:

Effective crisis

management demands seamless teamwork and collaboration.

Training programs should emphasize the importance of cross-functional cooperation, developing skills in active listening, conflict resolution, and collaborative problem-solving. Team-building exercises can help foster a sense of camaraderie and mutual trust, critical during periods of stress. It also means training for leaders on how to support their teams effectively during a crisis; this includes strategies for maintaining morale, providing emotional support, and fostering a cohesive and supportive team environment.

Ethical Considerations:

Ethical decision-making is paramount in crisis management. Training should include modules that address ethical dilemmas and conflicts of interest that may arise during a crisis. This involves familiarizing employees with relevant laws, regulations, and ethical guidelines. It must include creating a strong culture of ethical conduct that is reinforced throughout all levels of the organization, promoting integrity and accountability in decision-making, especially under duress.

Assessment methods should be varied and incorporate both theoretical knowledge and practical application. Written exams can assess understanding of theoretical concepts, while simulations and role-playing exercises can evaluate practical skills. Regular assessments should be incorporated as part of continuous learning and development to reflect evolving regulatory environments and technological advancements. Furthermore, ongoing feedback, both formal and informal, should be encouraged to create an environment for continuous improvement. Post-incident reviews and debriefings after actual crises (or simulations) are essential for extracting valuable lessons and improving future crisis response capabilities.

The effectiveness of the training program is not merely a function of its content but also its delivery. The use of

interactive methods such as group discussions, case studies, and simulations enhances employee engagement and

knowledge retention. Regular refresher training should be integrated to ensure ongoing competency, especially in areas such as regulatory updates and technological advancements.

The training should also be tailored to different roles and responsibilities within the institution. For example, senior management's training might focus on strategic decision-making and communication with external stakeholders, while frontline staff might receive more focused training on handling client inquiries and managing specific operational aspects during a crisis.

Furthermore, the success of any crisis management training program relies on top-down support and commitment from senior leadership. Leaders must not only champion the

program but also actively participate in training,

demonstrating their commitment to a culture of preparedness and resilience. By investing in comprehensive employee training and development, lending institutions can

significantly enhance their ability to navigate crises

effectively, safeguarding their financial stability and

reputation. A proactive approach to crisis management is not merely a cost; it is a crucial investment that secures the institution's long-term success. The ultimate aim should be to create a highly skilled and adaptable workforce that is capable of responding effectively to any eventuality,

minimizing disruptions and ensuring business continuity.

The Importance of Diversity and Inclusion in Lending

The preceding sections emphasized the critical role of robust training and development in building a resilient lending institution capable of navigating crises effectively. However, the effectiveness of any training program, and indeed the overall success of the institution, hinges significantly on the composition of its human capital. This brings us to a critical aspect often overlooked in discussions of crisis management and lending practices: the paramount importance of diversity and inclusion. A diverse and inclusive workforce is not merely a matter of social responsibility; it is a strategic imperative that directly contributes to improved decision-making, enhanced risk management, and ultimately, greater resilience in the face of financial turmoil.

The benefits of diversity in lending extend beyond simple representation. A diverse team, encompassing individuals from various backgrounds, experiences, and perspectives, brings a richer and more nuanced understanding to the lending process. Consider the assessment of loan applications. A homogeneous team, comprised of individuals sharing similar backgrounds and experiences, might inadvertently overlook critical risks or fail to identify promising opportunities. For example, a team lacking cultural understanding might misinterpret financial data from certain demographic groups or overlook the unique challenges faced by small businesses in underserved communities. In contrast, a diverse team, with members possessing varied cultural awareness and socioeconomic understanding, can provide a more comprehensive and objective assessment, identifying both potential risks and opportunities that might otherwise be missed.

This improved risk assessment translates into a lower

incidence of loan defaults and reduced financial losses for the institution. The ability to accurately assess

creditworthiness across diverse borrower profiles directly contributes to the overall financial health and stability of the lending institution. Furthermore, a more accurate assessment ensures fairer lending practices, fostering trust and positive relationships with a broader range of clients. This increased client base, particularly within previously underserved

communities, presents a significant opportunity for growth and market expansion.

Beyond risk assessment, diversity enhances the decision-making process itself. Studies consistently demonstrate that diverse teams outperform homogeneous teams in terms of creativity, problem-solving, and innovation. Different

perspectives challenge assumptions, leading to more robust and well-rounded decisions. The collaborative environment fostered by diversity encourages open communication and debate, leading to more thorough examination of various options and more informed decisions. This is particularly crucial during crisis situations, when quick and effective decision-making is paramount. The ability to consider multiple perspectives and anticipate unforeseen

consequences is essential in mitigating the impact of

unexpected events.

Inclusive practices are equally crucial. Diversity without inclusion is merely tokenism. Creating a truly inclusive work environment requires a commitment to fostering a culture of respect, belonging, and psychological safety. This involves implementing policies and practices that actively promote equity and fairness, ensuring that all employees feel valued, respected, and empowered to contribute their full potential.

An inclusive workplace attracts and retains top talent,

Leading to a more skilled and experienced workforce. This increased talent pool enhances the institution's capacity to manage risk effectively and navigate crisis situations successfully.

The impact of inclusion extends beyond the immediate workforce. An inclusive lending institution is better

positioned to serve a diverse client base, fostering trust and building stronger relationships with borrowers from all backgrounds. This broadened client base translates directly to increased business opportunities and enhanced

profitability. Moreover, an inclusive approach contributes to the institution's reputation and brand image, drawing

positive attention from investors, regulators, and customers alike. In an increasingly socially conscious world, a

commitment to diversity and inclusion is a powerful

differentiator, enhancing brand reputation and attracting talent.

Implementing a diversity and inclusion strategy within a lending institution requires a multi-pronged approach. It should not be a one-time initiative but an ongoing process requiring continuous effort and commitment. Key aspects include:

Recruitment and Hiring Practices:

Reviewing and

revising recruitment practices to actively seek out and attract candidates from diverse backgrounds. This involves

implementing blind resume screening to mitigate

unconscious bias and partnering with organizations that support underrepresented groups. Setting clear diversity goals and targets and regularly monitoring progress towards achieving them are crucial to ensure accountability.

Training and Development:

Developing tailored training programs that educate employees about unconscious bias,

Inclusive leadership, and cultural awareness. These programs should be designed to foster empathy, understanding, and respect for all team members. Regular workshops and

seminars can reinforce these principles and promote ongoing learning and development.

Mentorship and Sponsorship Programs:

Providing opportunities for employees from underrepresented groups to receive mentorship and sponsorship from senior leaders within the organization. This support network provides valuable guidance and access to opportunities, promoting career advancement and leadership development.

Flexible Work Arrangements:

Offering flexible work arrangements such as telecommuting and flexible hours to accommodate the diverse needs of employees, enabling work-life balance and increased employee retention.

Employee Resource Groups (ergs):

Establishing
employee resource groups that provide a supportive community for employees from underrepresented backgrounds. These groups can serve as a platform for networking, mentorship, and advocacy, strengthening a sense of belonging.

Performance Management and Compensation:

Implementing performance management and compensation systems that are fair and equitable, ensuring that all

employees are evaluated based on merit and not on the basis of their background or identity. Regular audits of

compensation to identify and address potential gender or ethnic pay gaps are also essential.

Data Collection and Analysis:

Collecting data on diversity metrics throughout the organization, including recruitment, promotion, and compensation. Analyzing this data regularly

Can highlight areas for improvement and track progress over time. This data-driven approach allows for strategic

decision-making based on evidence and allows for course correction if progress is not meeting targets.

Leadership Commitment:

Top-down commitment from leadership is crucial for the successful implementation of any diversity and inclusion initiative. Senior leaders must actively champion these efforts, setting the tone for

inclusivity and modeling inclusive behaviors throughout the organization. The message must be clear: diversity and inclusion are not merely compliance measures, but core values that drive organizational success.

Failure to prioritize diversity and inclusion exposes lending institutions to significant risks. Beyond the ethical

implications, the lack of diverse perspectives leads to poorer decision-making, increased risk of loan defaults, and

diminished opportunities for growth. In the competitive landscape of the financial industry, fostering a diverse and inclusive environment is not optional; it's a necessity for long-term success and sustainability. The institutions that embrace diversity and inclusion will be better positioned to navigate the complexities of the modern financial world, attract top talent, and serve a broader client base, ultimately ensuring greater financial resilience and stability. The

investment in creating a truly diverse and inclusive culture is not simply a cost; it's an investment in the future of the organization and a commitment to equitable and sustainable growth.

Developing Financial Models for Credit Analysis

Building upon the foundation of a diverse and inclusive workforce, the next crucial step in fortifying a lending institution's resilience lies in the sophisticated application of financial modeling for credit analysis. The accuracy and reliability of these models directly influence the institution's ability to assess risk, make informed lending decisions, and ultimately, navigate financial crises effectively. This process moves beyond rudimentary assessments and delves into the intricacies of predictive analytics, leveraging both traditional financial statements and advanced statistical techniques.

The cornerstone of any robust financial model is the comprehensive gathering and meticulous analysis of financial data. This involves scrutinizing a borrower's historical financial performance, projected cash flows, and key financial ratios. Traditional sources such as balance sheets, income statements, and cash flow statements provide the raw material for these analyses. However, the depth and breadth of the analysis goes beyond simply reviewing these statements; it requires a thorough understanding of the underlying trends, seasonality, and potential cyclical influences that can impact the borrower's financial health.

For instance, a company operating in a highly seasonal industry, such as agriculture or tourism, will require a more nuanced analysis than one with consistent year-round revenue streams. Understanding these cyclical patterns is critical in accurately predicting future performance and assessing creditworthiness.

Effective financial models incorporate several key financial ratios, each providing a distinct perspective on the borrower's financial health. Liquidity ratios, such as the

Current ratio and quick ratio, provide insights into the borrower's ability to meet its short-term obligations.

Solvency ratios, including the debt-to-equity ratio and times interest earned ratio, assess the borrower's long-term

financial stability and ability to service its debt. Profitability ratios, such as gross profit margin, net profit margin, and return on equity, offer a measure of the borrower's efficiency and overall profitability. Analyzing these ratios in

conjunction with each other, and over several periods, allows for a comprehensive assessment of the borrower's financial health and any potential weaknesses. A decline in several key ratios, particularly over several consecutive periods, may signal a deteriorating financial situation warranting further investigation.

Beyond traditional financial statement analysis, modern credit analysis leverages sophisticated statistical methods and predictive modeling techniques. Regression analysis, for example, can identify the relationships between various financial variables and the probability of loan default. This allows lenders to quantify the impact of specific factors, such as debt levels, profitability, and industry trends, on the likelihood of default. Such models can be calibrated using historical data from a vast number of loan applications, incorporating both defaults and successful repayments. The larger and more comprehensive the dataset, the more robust and accurate the model will likely be. This statistical

approach moves beyond subjective assessment and provides a more objective, data-driven evaluation of creditworthiness.

The advent of readily available financial software has

significantly enhanced the development and application of financial models. Spreadsheet software, such as Microsoft Excel, provides a user-friendly interface for constructing and manipulating financial data. While basic spreadsheet models can be effective for simpler analyses, more complex models,

Especially those incorporating advanced statistical

techniques, are best developed using specialized financial modeling software packages. These dedicated platforms provide a wealth of pre-built functions and tools,

accelerating the modeling process and minimizing the risk of errors associated with manual calculations. Furthermore, these platforms often integrate with various data sources, facilitating the efficient collection and analysis of large datasets.

Regardless of the software used, the rigor and thoroughness of model validation are paramount. A well-validated model is not merely a collection of formulas and data; it is a

reliable tool for decision-making, capable of providing

accurate and consistent predictions. The process of model validation typically involves a comprehensive examination of the model's inputs, outputs, and underlying assumptions. This includes verifying the accuracy and completeness of the data used, assessing the reasonableness of the model's

assumptions, and testing the model's performance against historical data. Backtesting, where the model's predictions are compared to actual outcomes from past loan applications, is a crucial step in model validation. This process helps determine whether the model accurately predicted past

outcomes and can be reasonably expected to perform well in the future. Any significant discrepancies between the

model's predictions and actual results should be carefully investigated and addressed, possibly requiring modifications to the model's structure or assumptions.

Furthermore, sensitivity analysis is a vital component of model validation. This involves systematically altering the model's inputs to assess the impact on the model's outputs. For example, we can vary assumptions about future revenue growth, interest rates, or operating expenses to determine how these changes affect the borrower's creditworthiness

Score or predicted probability of default. This helps identify critical assumptions that strongly influence the model's predictions and highlight areas where greater precision in data collection or refinement of assumptions are needed. A model which is highly sensitive to small changes in input parameters may warrant increased caution, requiring further investigation and potentially more conservative lending decisions.

Another critical aspect of model validation is stress testing. This involves subjecting the model to extreme, but plausible, scenarios, such as a significant economic downturn or a sudden increase in interest rates. This helps to gauge the model's robustness and assess its ability to withstand

unexpected events. Stress testing helps to identify potential weaknesses in the model and ensure that the model's

predictions remain reliable even under adverse conditions.

The results of stress testing can inform risk mitigation

strategies and ensure that the institution is adequately

prepared for a wide range of potential economic shocks. This is crucial in the context of crisis management, allowing the institution to anticipate and effectively respond to potential financial turmoil.

The development of accurate and reliable financial models is an iterative process. Continuous monitoring, refinement, and validation are essential to ensure that the models remain effective and relevant over time. As market conditions

change, new data become available, and lending practices evolve, the models must be updated to reflect these shifts.

Regular reviews of the models' performance, including

regular updates to the underlying dataset and recalibration of the statistical techniques, are essential to ensure the ongoing accuracy and reliability of the predictive power. This cyclical nature of model development is not simply a regulatory requirement but a strategic imperative for maintaining the

Institution's financial health and fostering its long-term resilience. The institution must be prepared to adapt to changing market conditions and incorporate new information into its models to maintain their effectiveness and accuracy.

The use of financial models in credit analysis is not merely a technical exercise; it is a critical component of effective risk management. By providing a quantitative and objective assessment of creditworthiness, these models allow lending institutions to make informed decisions, allocate capital efficiently, and minimize the risk of loan defaults. The rigorous development and validation of these models, coupled with a strong emphasis on diversity and inclusion in the workforce, enhance the overall resilience of the lending institution and contribute to its ability to effectively navigate financial crises. The integration of these approaches creates a robust and adaptable framework for successful and sustainable lending practices in an ever-evolving financial landscape. Ultimately, this holistic approach strengthens the financial institution, not only protecting it during periods of economic uncertainty but also enabling it to thrive and capitalize on emerging opportunities.

Forecasting Financial Performance of Borrowers

Forecasting the financial performance of borrowers is a crucial element of responsible lending. It's a process that goes far beyond simply extrapolating past performance; it requires a deep understanding of the borrower's business, its industry, and the broader economic environment. Accurate forecasting allows lenders to make informed decisions, minimizing risk and maximizing the potential for successful loan repayment. Several methodologies can be employed, each with its strengths and limitations.

One fundamental approach involves analyzing historical financial statements. This includes a detailed examination of balance sheets, income statements, and cash flow statements over several years, ideally spanning a full economic cycle to account for seasonal and cyclical fluctuations. Trends in key metrics such as revenue growth, profitability, and debt levels are carefully identified and analyzed. Anomalies or

significant deviations from established patterns warrant further investigation. For example, a sudden drop in

profitability could signal underlying operational problems, while a consistent increase in debt may indicate

unsustainable growth or poor financial management. The analysis isn't limited to simple numerical observation; it requires a qualitative assessment of the underlying reasons for these trends. A lender might need to explore external factors, such as changes in regulation or competition, or internal factors, like changes in management or production processes.

Beyond historical data, forecasting incorporates future projections. This often involves collaborating closely with the borrower to understand their business plans and

Strategies. The lender needs to review the borrower's

business plan, analyzing its assumptions and assessing their reasonableness. For example, projected revenue growth should align with market forecasts and industry trends.

Similarly, projected cost structures should reflect realistic operating expenses, taking into account potential inflationary pressures or efficiency improvements. The lender must

critically evaluate the borrower's management team's

experience and expertise. A highly experienced and capable management team is more likely to execute their business plan successfully, while a less experienced team may require more stringent monitoring and potentially higher risk

premiums. This qualitative assessment of management's capabilities is a critical component of the forecasting

process, often complementing the quantitative data analysis.

Quantitative forecasting methods include various techniques, ranging from simple extrapolations to sophisticated

econometric models. Simple trend analysis might involve projecting future performance based on the historical growth rate of key financial metrics. This approach is useful for stable businesses with predictable growth patterns. However, it's crucial to recognize its limitations; it doesn't account for potential disruptions or changes in market conditions. More advanced techniques, such as regression analysis, can

incorporate multiple variables to create more accurate

forecasts. These models can account for factors such as economic conditions, industry trends, and competitor

activity. For instance, a regression model might predict a company's revenue based on factors such as GDP growth, industry sales growth, and the company's market share. The model's parameters should be robustly estimated and tested. In particular, lenders should focus on both the in-sample and out-of-sample model accuracy in order to ensure its

predictive power.

Econometric modeling provides a sophisticated approach to forecasting. It involves using statistical methods to analyze the relationships between economic variables and a

borrower's financial performance. These models can be complex, requiring specialized expertise to develop and interpret. However, they can provide more accurate forecasts than simpler methods, particularly for businesses operating in dynamic or uncertain environments. Such models should be validated against historical data and subjected to various stress tests. The forecasting model should be able to handle various scenarios and unexpected economic events.

Cash flow forecasting is particularly critical in assessing a borrower's ability to repay a loan. This involves projecting the borrower's future cash inflows and outflows, determining their ability to meet debt obligations. A detailed cash flow forecast should include all sources of cash inflow, such as sales, investments, and financing activities, and all sources of cash outflow, such as operating expenses, capital

expenditures, and debt repayments. A lender must scrutinize the assumptions underlying these projections, comparing them to historical data and evaluating their reasonableness.

Sensitivity analysis, varying key assumptions, is crucial to assess the forecast's robustness and identify potential vulnerabilities.

Industry analysis is another important element of

forecasting. Understanding the borrower's industry, its

competitive dynamics, and its future prospects is vital. This involves researching industry trends, analyzing market share data, and evaluating the impact of technological

advancements or regulatory changes. For example, a lender financing a company in a rapidly evolving technology sector needs to account for the potential for rapid obsolescence and disruptive innovation. This might necessitate more stringent creditworthiness assessment criteria or a shorter loan term.

Industry-specific benchmarks can be helpful in comparing the borrower's financial performance to its peers and evaluating its relative competitive position.

Qualitative factors, while harder to quantify, significantly influence forecasting accuracy. These include the borrower's management team, their strategic plans, and their overall operating efficiency. Lenders should consider factors such as the management team's experience and expertise, their track record, and their ability to adapt to change. They should also assess the borrower's competitive advantages, its market position, and its ability to innovate and adapt to changing market conditions. The overall operational efficiency of the business is also crucial and should be examined. This

involves analyzing metrics such as inventory turnover, days sales outstanding, and asset utilization ratios. Inefficiencies may lead to underperformance and increased risk, affecting the accuracy of future performance projections.

Finally, the broader macroeconomic environment influences the forecast. Economic growth, interest rates, inflation, and unemployment rates all impact borrowers' financial

performance. A lender needs to incorporate macroeconomic forecasts into their analysis and assess the potential impact on the borrower's financial health. This involves considering how economic cycles will affect industry conditions and demand for the borrower's goods or services. For example, during an economic downturn, demand may decline

significantly for discretionary goods, reducing profitability. The macroeconomic context also impacts the availability of financing. High interest rates can make debt servicing more difficult and lead to a reduced borrowing capacity.

In conclusion, forecasting a borrower's financial

performance involves a multi-faceted approach, combining quantitative and qualitative analysis. It is a dynamic process

Demanding continuous monitoring and refinement.

Integrating historical data analysis, future projections, cash flow forecasting, industry analysis, qualitative assessment, and macroeconomic context creates a robust framework for informed lending decisions. The ultimate goal is to provide a reasonably accurate picture of the borrower's future

performance and ensure the lender's confidence in the loan's ultimate success. The accuracy and reliability of these

forecasts underpin effective risk management in lending, influencing the sustainability of both the lender and the borrower.

Sensitivity Analysis and Stress Testing

Sensitivity analysis and stress testing are indispensable components of robust financial modeling for lending. While forecasting provides a point estimate of future performance, it's crucial to understand the uncertainty surrounding that estimate. Sensitivity analysis explores the impact of changes in key assumptions on the forecast, while stress testing evaluates the model's resilience under extreme or adverse conditions. Both techniques are critical for assessing the borrower's creditworthiness and managing the lender's risk exposure.

Sensitivity analysis involves systematically varying the inputs of the financial model to observe their impact on the output variables, such as net income, cash flow, and debt service coverage ratio. This process identifies the key drivers of the forecast and helps to quantify the uncertainty

associated with each assumption. For example, in a cash flow projection for a manufacturing company, the lender might vary the assumptions about sales growth, raw material costs, and production efficiency. By changing each variable independently and observing the resulting changes in the projected cash flow, the lender can identify which

assumptions are most critical to the forecast's overall

accuracy. A high sensitivity to a particular input implies that even small deviations from the assumed value can

significantly impact the projected performance, potentially leading to loan default. This highlights the need for more in-depth investigation into that specific input and possibly the development of contingency plans.

Consider a retail business with projected sales growth of 5% annually. A sensitivity analysis might explore the impact of

Varying this assumption by plus or minus 2 percentage points. The model might show that a 3% growth rate results in a significantly lower cash flow, potentially jeopardizing the borrower's ability to repay the loan, while a 7% growth rate improves their financial position substantially. Such results underscore the importance of thoroughly researching the market and the company's competitive position to

determine the most realistic sales growth projection. The lender should also consider incorporating additional

scenarios, such as a recession, which might result in

significantly lower sales.

The process of sensitivity analysis typically involves

constructing multiple scenarios based on various input combinations. These scenarios can be generated

systematically, utilizing techniques such as Monte Carlo simulation, which uses random sampling to create a

distribution of possible outcomes. This allows the lender to assess the probability of different financial outcomes and to quantify the uncertainty inherent in the forecast. Instead of just presenting a single point forecast, the lender can present a range of possible outcomes, providing a much more

complete and nuanced picture of the borrower's financial health. The insights derived from this analysis are

instrumental in tailoring loan terms and covenants to

mitigate risks associated with the inherent uncertainties.

Stress testing goes a step further than sensitivity analysis by evaluating the financial model's performance under extreme or adverse conditions. It assesses the borrower's resilience to significant negative shocks, such as a severe economic downturn, a sudden change in interest rates, or a major operational disruption. This testing helps determine the borrower's ability to withstand unexpected events and avoid default. Stress testing scenarios should be realistic, based on

Historical data and economic forecasts, considering the sector-specific characteristics of the borrower's industry.

A common approach to stress testing involves applying specific macroeconomic shocks to the model. For example, a lender might simulate the impact of a 20% drop in GDP on the borrower's financial statements. This could involve reducing sales revenue, increasing unemployment rates among the borrower's workforce, and affecting other

macroeconomic variables. The resulting impact on the

borrower's cash flows, profitability, and liquidity can then be evaluated to identify potential vulnerabilities. Similarly, a lender might assess the impact of a sudden increase in

interest rates on the borrower's debt servicing capacity. This analysis would help to identify the borrower's vulnerability to interest rate risk and inform the lender's decision on

appropriate loan structuring and interest rate hedging

strategies.

Sector-specific stress tests are equally important. For

instance, a lender financing a construction company should stress test the model for potential declines in the real estate market, or for increased material costs. Similarly, a bank lending to a technology company might consider stress tests involving rapid technological obsolescence or increased competition. The selection of appropriate stress test

scenarios should be informed by an in-depth understanding of the industry dynamics and the company's unique risk profile. This requires expertise in both financial modeling and industry analysis.

Beyond macroeconomic and industry-specific stress tests, it's also beneficial to consider idiosyncratic risks associated with the borrower's specific operations. For example, a manufacturing company might be vulnerable to supply chain disruptions, while a retail business might be vulnerable to

Shifts in consumer preferences. The lender should work closely with the borrower to identify these risks and

incorporate them into the stress tests. By carefully

considering all potential risks, the lender can develop a robust assessment of the borrower's creditworthiness, and ultimately, make better-informed lending decisions.

The results of both sensitivity analysis and stress testing are crucial for refining the forecast and evaluating the risk-reward profile of the loan. If the model is highly sensitive to a particular input or performs poorly under a plausible stress test, it signifies the need for further due diligence and

potentially adjustments to the loan terms or a re-evaluation of the creditworthiness of the borrower. For instance, a highly sensitive model could prompt the lender to request additional collateral, demand more stringent covenants, or increase the interest rate to compensate for the higher

perceived risk.

Furthermore, the results of these analyses can be used to develop contingency plans and risk mitigation strategies. The lender can work with the borrower to identify measures to reduce vulnerability to specific risks, such as diversifying supply chains, improving liquidity management, or

implementing robust risk management practices. These collaborative efforts strengthen the borrower's ability to withstand financial shocks and improve the overall

probability of loan repayment.

In conclusion, sensitivity analysis and stress testing are not merely technical exercises; they are integral parts of a comprehensive credit assessment process. These techniques equip lenders with the tools to critically evaluate financial models, identify potential risks, and make informed lending decisions that consider various scenarios and uncertainties.

The incorporation of both quantitative and qualitative

Insights derived from these methods enhances the overall robustness of the lending process, fostering greater stability for both the lender and the borrower. The sophistication of these techniques, coupled with rigorous application and interpretation, significantly improves risk management and contributes to a sustainable lending environment. Ultimately, thorough financial modeling, including comprehensive sensitivity and stress testing, represents a cornerstone of responsible lending practice.

Using Financial Models for Loan Structuring

Using financial models is not merely about predicting future performance; it's a crucial tool for crafting loan structures that align with both the borrower's capacity and the lender's risk tolerance. The art of loan structuring involves balancing the needs of both parties, creating a deal that's profitable for the lender while remaining manageable for the borrower. This delicate balance is significantly enhanced through the strategic application of financial modeling.

A well-constructed financial model allows lenders to tailor loan terms to the borrower's specific circumstances, going beyond a simple "yes" or "no" decision. This includes

determining the appropriate loan amount, interest rate,

repayment schedule, and inclusion of any collateral or

covenants. The model provides the quantitative underpinning for these decisions, allowing for a data-driven approach to risk assessment and mitigation. For instance, a model might reveal that while a borrower can comfortably service a loan with a longer repayment period and lower interest rate, a shorter timeframe with a higher rate might expose them to considerable financial strain. The model helps to quantify this risk, allowing the lender to structure the loan

accordingly.

Loan structuring guidelines often incorporate key financial ratios derived from financial models. These ratios, such as debt-to-equity ratio, debt service coverage ratio (DSCR), and current ratio, provide a standardized way to assess a

borrower's financial health and their ability to repay the loan.

The model's projections of these ratios under various scenarios—including those explored through sensitivity analysis and stress testing—allow lenders to determine

Appropriate loan terms and covenants. For example, a low DSCR might suggest the need for a shorter loan term, a higher interest rate, or the inclusion of additional collateral to compensate for the increased risk. Conversely, a strong financial profile reflected in robust ratios could justify a longer term or a lower interest rate.

The process begins with a thorough understanding of the borrower's business, including its industry, competitive landscape, and management team. This qualitative

assessment informs the development of the financial model, ensuring that the underlying assumptions are realistic and relevant. The model should incorporate key financial

statements such as the balance sheet, income statement, and cash flow statement, projecting these figures into the future based on historical data and reasonable forecasts. These projections serve as the basis for evaluating various loan structuring options.

Let's consider a small manufacturing business seeking a loan to expand its production capacity. A financial model would project the company's future revenue, expenses, and cash flows, considering factors such as anticipated sales growth, raw material costs, and operating expenses. The model would then calculate key financial ratios, such as the DSCR and the current ratio, under various scenarios, including optimistic, baseline, and pessimistic projections. These scenarios would inform the structuring of the loan. For instance, the pessimistic scenario might reveal a significant decline in the DSCR, indicating a heightened risk of default. In response, the lender might opt for a shorter loan term, a higher interest rate, or request additional collateral to

mitigate this risk.

Furthermore, the model can incorporate various loan structuring options, allowing for a comparison of their

Impact on the borrower's financial health. For instance, the model can compare the effects of different repayment schedules (e.g., amortization, balloon payments) or interest rate structures (e.g., fixed, floating) on the borrower's financial ratios and cash flows. This comparison allows the lender to select the structure that best balances risk and reward while optimizing the borrower's financial position.

The use of financial models in asset-based lending is

particularly important. In asset-based lending, the loan is secured by the borrower's assets, providing a safety net for the lender in case of default. However, the value of these assets can fluctuate, requiring a dynamic approach to loan structuring. Financial models play a crucial role in assessing the value of these assets and their susceptibility to market fluctuations. For example, a model might project the value of inventory or accounts receivable under various economic scenarios, informing the lender's decision on the loan-to-value ratio (LTV). A higher LTV might be acceptable if the model demonstrates that the assets retain a high value even under adverse conditions.

Beyond the quantitative aspects, financial models can

facilitate a more informed dialogue between the lender and the borrower. The transparent and data-driven approach of using a model promotes a clearer understanding of the risks and opportunities involved, fostering trust and cooperation.

The model's projections can be used to demonstrate the potential impact of different loan structures on the borrower's financial position, allowing them to make informed decisions about their financing needs.

Consider a scenario where a borrower seeks a large loan for a significant capital expenditure. A financial model can demonstrate the expected return on investment (ROI) for the proposed project, and project the subsequent impact on the

Borrower's cash flow and debt servicing capacity. This allows both the lender and the borrower to assess the viability of the project and determine if the associated risk is justifiable. It may even reveal that a smaller loan amount, or a different project timeline would be more financially prudent.

The incorporation of covenants within loan agreements is another area where financial models play a vital role.

Covenants are contractual obligations imposed on the borrower to protect the lender's interest. Financial models can identify key financial metrics that should be monitored through covenants. For example, a covenant might restrict the borrower's debt-to-equity ratio, ensuring that they maintain a healthy financial position. The model can project the borrower's ability to comply with these covenants under various scenarios, helping to determine their appropriateness and feasibility.

Moreover, financial models are increasingly used in conjunction with sophisticated risk assessment tools. These tools leverage advanced statistical techniques and machine learning algorithms to evaluate borrower risk more comprehensively. By integrating the insights from financial models with these risk assessment tools, lenders can obtain a more nuanced and comprehensive understanding of the creditworthiness of potential borrowers. This holistic approach improves the accuracy of credit risk assessment and enhances the effectiveness of loan structuring decisions. This collaborative approach between modeling and advanced analytics is essential in today's complex financial landscape.

In conclusion, the effective use of financial models in loan structuring is paramount for successful lending. They allow for a data-driven approach to risk assessment, enabling lenders to tailor loan terms to the specific circumstances of

Each borrower. By projecting key financial ratios and assessing the impact of various loan structures, financial models facilitate informed decision-making, strengthen borrower-lender relationships, and contribute to a more robust and sustainable lending environment. The

sophisticated use of financial models represents a critical evolution in responsible lending practices, moving beyond rudimentary credit scoring models to a more dynamic and holistic approach to risk management. This proactive methodology contributes not only to the success of

individual loans but also to the overall stability of the financial system.

Advanced Financial Modeling Techniques

Moving beyond the foundational principles of financial modeling in lending, we now delve into advanced techniques that significantly enhance the accuracy and robustness of credit assessments. These methods incorporate probabilistic approaches and sophisticated statistical tools, providing a more nuanced and comprehensive understanding of

borrower risk than traditional deterministic models. One of the most powerful techniques is Monte Carlo simulation.

Monte Carlo simulation is a computational technique that uses repeated random sampling to obtain numerical results for problems that are too complex to solve analytically. In the context of lending, it allows us to model the uncertainty inherent in financial projections. Instead of relying on single-point estimates for variables like revenue growth or default rates, Monte Carlo simulation allows us to input probability distributions for these variables. The model then randomly samples values from these distributions, generating

thousands or even millions of potential scenarios. Each

scenario results in a different projected financial outcome, providing a range of possible results instead of a single, potentially misleading prediction.

Consider a scenario involving a loan application from a tech startup. A traditional deterministic model might project revenue based on management's optimistic forecast.

However, the inherent uncertainty in a new venture is

substantial. Using Monte Carlo simulation, we could

incorporate probability distributions for key variables, such as market adoption rate, competition intensity, and customer acquisition costs. By running the simulation many times, we can obtain a distribution of potential outcomes, including the

Probability of the startup failing to meet its debt obligations. This distribution gives a far more realistic representation of the risk involved than a single-point estimate. The results can be visualized as a histogram showing the probability of different net present value (NPV) outcomes for the loan, allowing the lender to assess the risk-reward profile more effectively.

The value of Monte Carlo simulation lies in its ability to quantify uncertainty. It doesn't simply provide a best-case or worst-case scenario, but a comprehensive view of the full range of possible outcomes, along with their associated probabilities. This enables lenders to make more informed decisions, setting loan terms that appropriately reflect the level of risk. For example, a higher probability of default might justify a higher interest rate or stricter covenants.

Furthermore, the simulation can help to identify potential "tipping points" – levels of key variables beyond which the loan becomes significantly riskier.

Beyond Monte Carlo simulations, other probabilistic

methods are increasingly being employed in advanced financial modeling for lending. These include Bayesian methods, which incorporate prior knowledge and update beliefs as new data becomes available. Bayesian approaches are particularly valuable in situations with limited historical data, such as assessing the creditworthiness of new

businesses or in emerging markets. They allow lenders to incorporate expert judgment and industry insights into the model, enhancing the accuracy of projections.

Copula functions provide another powerful tool for modeling the dependencies between different financial variables.

Traditional models often assume independence between variables, which is rarely true in reality. For example, a decline in housing prices might be correlated with a rise in

Unemployment, both affecting a borrower's ability to repay a mortgage. Copulas allow us to model these complex

dependencies, resulting in more realistic and accurate risk assessments. By incorporating copulas, we move beyond simple correlation coefficients to capture the entire joint distribution of variables, enabling a more precise

understanding of systemic risk.

Sensitivity analysis, while not strictly a probabilistic method, plays a crucial role in augmenting the insights gained from advanced financial models. Sensitivity analysis involves systematically changing the input variables of the model to observe the impact on the output. This helps to identify the variables that have the greatest influence on the overall outcome, allowing lenders to focus their due diligence

efforts on those areas. For example, in a loan to a retail

business, sensitivity analysis might reveal that projected sales growth is the most significant driver of loan repayment ability. This would prompt a more thorough investigation into the retailer's market position, competition, and sales strategy.

Stress testing is a critical component of advanced financial modeling, designed to assess the robustness of the model under extreme conditions. This often involves subjecting the model to various economic shocks, such as a sharp recession or a significant increase in interest rates. The results of stress testing reveal the model's resilience and highlight potential vulnerabilities. This allows lenders to identify potential weaknesses in the borrower's financial position and to

incorporate appropriate safeguards into the loan agreement, such as contingency plans or stricter covenants.

The integration of these advanced modeling techniques with sophisticated data analytics further elevates the accuracy and reliability of credit assessments. Machine learning

Algorithms, for instance, can be trained on vast datasets of historical loan performance, identifying subtle patterns and relationships that might be missed by traditional methods. These algorithms can be used to predict default probabilities, identify early warning signs of financial distress, and optimize loan pricing and structuring.

The application of these advanced techniques is not without its challenges. The complexity of these models requires specialized expertise in both finance and data science. Data availability and quality are also critical factors, as the accuracy of the models relies heavily on the quality and completeness of the underlying data. Furthermore, the interpretation of the results requires careful consideration and a nuanced understanding of the model's assumptions and limitations. It's crucial to remember that even the most sophisticated model is just a tool, and its output should be combined with qualitative judgment and due diligence.

However, despite these challenges, the benefits of incorporating advanced financial modeling techniques in lending are substantial. These techniques equip lenders with a more powerful arsenal of tools to assess creditworthiness, enabling more informed and responsible lending decisions. The increased accuracy and reliability of credit assessments contribute to a more stable and efficient financial system, benefiting both lenders and borrowers. By embracing these advanced techniques, the lending industry moves towards a more data-driven, risk-aware, and ultimately, more sustainable future. The use of these advanced tools allows for a granular understanding of risk, leading to a better alignment of lending practices with the realities of the market, thereby reducing systemic vulnerabilities. This proactive approach promotes both the stability of individual borrowers and the health of the broader financial ecosystem.

The future of responsible lending lies in leveraging the power of these advanced techniques.

Understanding Fair Lending Laws and Regulations

The transition from sophisticated financial modeling to the critical realm of legal and ethical considerations in lending is not merely a shift in focus but a necessary evolution. The accuracy and robustness of our credit assessments, however advanced, are ultimately meaningless without a solid

framework of legal compliance and ethical responsibility.

This subsection delves into the intricacies of fair lending laws and regulations, highlighting their crucial role in ensuring equitable access to credit while safeguarding against discriminatory practices. The financial health of individuals and the stability of the overall financial system depend heavily on adherence to these principles.

Understanding fair lending laws requires a grasp of their historical context. These regulations emerged in response to a long history of discriminatory lending practices,

disproportionately impacting minority groups and

communities with lower socioeconomic status. Redlining, for instance, a practice where lenders deliberately avoided providing services to specific neighborhoods based on race or ethnicity, created significant inequalities in access to credit and contributed to economic segregation. The legacy of these historical injustices continues to shape the landscape of fair lending, necessitating ongoing vigilance and proactive measures to ensure equitable access to financial services.

The cornerstone of fair lending legislation in the United States is the Equal Credit Opportunity Act (ECOA). Enacted in 1974, ECOA prohibits creditors from discriminating against credit applicants based on race, color, religion,

national origin, sex, marital status, age (provided the

Applicant has the capacity to enter into a binding contract), or because all or part of the applicant's income derives from a public assistance program. This broad prohibition aims to create a level playing field where credit decisions are based solely on the applicant's creditworthiness, not on arbitrary or discriminatory factors.

ECOA's scope extends beyond the initial credit application process. It mandates that lenders provide equal treatment throughout the entire credit lifecycle, encompassing

application review, loan terms, and the overall borrowing experience. This comprehensive approach addresses subtle yet significant forms of discrimination that might occur at various stages of the lending process.

The implementation of ECOA requires lenders to establish robust internal systems and procedures to ensure

compliance. This includes comprehensive training programs for loan officers, clear and consistent application processes, and meticulous documentation of all credit decisions. The rationale behind each decision must be clearly articulated, providing a defensible record in the event of a regulatory review or legal challenge. Lenders are required to keep detailed records of applications and denials, including the reasons for each decision. Failure to maintain such

documentation can result in significant penalties.

Beyond ECOA, the Fair Housing Act (FHA) also plays a crucial role in ensuring fair lending practices. While

primarily focused on housing, the FHA's prohibitions against discrimination apply to lenders involved in mortgage

financing. The intersection of ECOA and FHA highlights the interconnectedness of fair lending with broader societal goals of equality and affordable housing. Discriminatory lending practices can exacerbate existing inequalities in housing access, leading to further economic and social

Stratification. Therefore, regulatory compliance goes beyond simply avoiding legal penalties; it is a moral and social imperative.

The Community Reinvestment Act (CRA) adds another layer to the regulatory framework. CRA encourages lenders to meet the credit needs of their entire communities,

including low- and moderate-income neighborhoods. It aims to prevent lenders from concentrating their lending activities in affluent areas while neglecting the needs of underserved communities. CRA compliance often involves targeted outreach and lending programs designed to reach

populations that might otherwise face significant barriers to accessing credit. Compliance involves not just meeting a minimum numerical standard but also demonstrating a

commitment to serving diverse communities fairly and equitably. It requires a proactive approach beyond simply responding to applications. Lenders must demonstrate a tangible effort to engage with and support the credit needs of all community members.

Enforcement of fair lending laws is overseen by several federal agencies, including the Consumer Financial

Protection Bureau (CFPB), the Department of Justice (DOJ), and various other regulatory bodies. These agencies conduct regular examinations of lenders, investigating complaints and pursuing legal action against institutions found in

violation of these laws. The penalties for non-compliance can be substantial, ranging from monetary fines and civil penalties to reputational damage and even criminal charges.

The risk of legal repercussions is a significant factor motivating lenders to prioritize compliance. But more importantly, the ethical implications of discriminatory lending practices should be the ultimate guiding factor in promoting responsible lending.

The complexities of fair lending laws often necessitate the expertise of legal counsel and compliance professionals.

They provide critical guidance to ensure that lending

practices align with the letter and spirit of the regulations. Maintaining a robust compliance program requires a multi-faceted approach involving thorough training,

comprehensive documentation, and ongoing monitoring. This is not just a legal necessity; it is a crucial component of responsible corporate governance. Institutions that actively cultivate a culture of compliance are better positioned to avoid legal challenges, build trust with their customers, and contribute to a more equitable financial system.

Furthermore, fair lending goes beyond mere legal

compliance. It demands a commitment to ethical practices that promote fairness and inclusion. This entails a critical self-assessment of lending procedures to identify potential biases, both conscious and unconscious. Regular review of lending data can help detect patterns that might indicate discriminatory practices. Moreover, fostering a diverse workforce within the lending institution can contribute to more equitable decision-making processes. A more diverse team brings a broader range of perspectives, lessening the likelihood of inadvertently overlooking or perpetuating harmful biases. This focus on diversity and inclusivity is not only an ethical imperative, but it also enhances the business acumen of lending organizations.

The evolution of fair lending laws reflects a growing societal understanding of the importance of equal access to credit. These laws are not static; they adapt and evolve in response to new forms of discrimination and changing societal norms.

Staying abreast of these changes and proactively adapting lending practices to align with evolving standards is essential for lenders seeking to maintain legal compliance and operate ethically. Proactive adaptation can also present opportunities

For lenders to innovate and develop products and services that cater to underserved communities, creating both social and financial benefits.

In conclusion, understanding and adhering to fair lending laws and regulations is paramount for every lending institution. It is a critical component of responsible lending, ensuring equitable access to credit while upholding ethical business practices. Beyond legal compliance, fair lending necessitates a profound commitment to social responsibility and the creation of a more just and equitable financial system. The financial industry's role in promoting inclusivity and social justice should not be underestimated; a well-functioning financial system is a key pillar in creating a thriving and equitable society. This commitment to fair lending is not simply about avoiding penalties; it is about building a more sustainable and just financial future for all.

Contract Law and Loan Agreements

The bedrock of any lending transaction rests firmly upon the principles of contract law. Loan agreements, the formal documents outlining the terms and conditions of a loan, are legally binding contracts. Understanding the intricacies of contract law is therefore crucial for both lenders and

borrowers. A poorly drafted or negotiated loan agreement can lead to costly disputes, protracted litigation, and

irreparable damage to business relationships. This section delves into the essential elements of contract law within the context of loan agreements, highlighting best practices and potential pitfalls.

A valid contract, including a loan agreement, requires

several key elements. First, there must be an offer and acceptance. The lender extends an offer of credit with

specific terms, and the borrower accepts those terms,

creating a mutual agreement. This agreement must be

supported by consideration, which typically involves the borrower's promise to repay the loan and the lender's

promise to provide the funds. Both parties must possess the legal capacity to enter into a contract; they must be of legal age and possess the mental capacity to understand the terms and conditions of the agreement. Minors, individuals under the influence of incapacitating substances, or those deemed legally incompetent generally lack the capacity to enter into binding contracts. Any loan agreement involving such parties would be legally questionable.

The terms of the loan agreement must be clear,

unambiguous, and readily understandable. Vague or ambiguous language can lead to disputes over the

interpretation of the contract. Courts generally interpret

Contracts against the party that drafted them, so lenders should exercise extreme caution in ensuring the clarity and precision of the language used. The principle of "contra proferentem" places the burden of clear drafting squarely on the lender. Ambiguity will be resolved in favor of the

borrower, potentially leading to unfavorable outcomes for the lending institution.

Furthermore, the loan agreement must be legal and not

violate any applicable statutes or regulations. A contract to loan funds for an illegal purpose, such as money laundering or financing unlawful activities, is void and unenforceable. Lenders have a legal and ethical obligation to ensure that the purpose for which the loan is requested is legal and

compliant. This due diligence is critical; ignoring potential red flags can expose lenders to substantial legal and financial risks.

Beyond the fundamental elements, loan agreements typically incorporate a range of clauses addressing various aspects of the loan. These clauses often deal with security interests, repayment schedules, default provisions, and governing law. Security interests, commonly secured by collateral, provide the lender with recourse in the event of borrower default. These security interests must be properly perfected through appropriate filings or other legal actions to ensure their effectiveness. Failure to do so can significantly weaken the lender's position in case of default, resulting in substantial financial losses. The level of security provided impacts the terms of the agreement itself; stronger security may lead to more favorable terms for the borrower, potentially reducing the interest rate.

Repayment schedules, outlining the frequency and amount of payments, must be clearly defined. Any deviations from this schedule should be addressed in the agreement with

Explicit conditions and repercussions. Late payment clauses, specifying penalties for missed or delayed payments, are crucial to protect the lender's interests. However, these penalty clauses must be carefully drafted to comply with applicable usury laws, which regulate maximum permissible interest rates. Excessive penalties may be deemed

unenforceable by a court.

Default provisions specify the actions that constitute a

breach of contract and the lender's remedies in such

circumstances. These provisions should be clearly defined and unambiguous, avoiding any potential for

misinterpretation. The lender's remedies may include

acceleration of the loan, foreclosure on any collateral, and pursuit of legal action to recover the outstanding debt. These remedies are essential to mitigate the lender's risk in the event of default. The clarity and enforceability of these provisions are critical, ensuring that the lender can

effectively protect its interests.

The choice of governing law, specifying which jurisdiction's laws will govern the interpretation and enforcement of the agreement, is another crucial consideration. Lenders

typically opt for jurisdictions known for their established commercial laws and efficient legal systems. The chosen jurisdiction influences legal procedures, dispute resolution, and the enforceability of contractual provisions.

Loan agreements frequently contain representations and warranties, which are statements made by the borrower concerning the accuracy of information provided in the loan application. These representations and warranties form a significant part of the lender's credit decision.

Misrepresentation or breach of warranties can provide the lender with grounds to rescind the agreement or pursue legal

Action. The lender's ability to rely on these representations and warranties is essential.

Covenants, ongoing obligations imposed on the borrower throughout the loan term, are common in loan agreements, especially in commercial lending. These covenants may address financial performance, debt levels, or other aspects of the borrower's business. Breach of covenants can trigger default and provide the lender with grounds to exercise its remedies. The type and stringency of covenants vary

depending on the perceived risk associated with the

borrower and the type of loan. Failure to appropriately monitor the borrower's adherence to covenants can weaken the lender's position.

The process of drafting and negotiating loan agreements requires careful attention to detail and an understanding of applicable laws and regulations. Involving experienced legal counsel is essential to ensure that the agreement protects the lender's interests while remaining legally sound and

compliant. A well-drafted loan agreement minimizes the risk of disputes, protects the lender's investment, and facilitates a smooth and successful lending relationship. The cost of legal expertise is far outweighed by the potential cost of litigation and the risk of financial loss arising from a poorly drafted agreement.

Furthermore, even with a well-drafted contract, effective communication and a collaborative approach between the lender and borrower are critical. Open communication can mitigate potential misunderstandings, fostering a positive working relationship and minimizing the likelihood of disputes. Regular updates and prompt responses to inquiries can contribute significantly to a smooth loan lifecycle. A strong lender-borrower relationship can significantly

improve the odds of successful repayment.

In summary, the foundation of responsible lending rests on a solid understanding and meticulous application of contract law principles. Loan agreements, as legally binding

contracts, require careful drafting, thorough negotiation, and a clear understanding of the relevant legal landscape. By prioritizing legal compliance, employing experienced legal counsel, fostering open communication, and maintaining a collaborative approach with borrowers, lenders can minimize risk, protect their investments, and contribute to a more stable and sustainable financial system. The focus on legal compliance and adherence to best practices is not merely a matter of regulatory compliance, it is a cornerstone of

responsible and successful lending operations.

Bankruptcy Law and Loan Recovery

The previous section detailed the critical role of contract law in structuring and securing loan agreements. However, even the most meticulously drafted contract cannot guarantee repayment. Economic downturns, unforeseen circumstances, and poor management can lead borrowers into financial distress, culminating in bankruptcy filings. Understanding bankruptcy law, therefore, is paramount for lenders, as it significantly impacts their ability to recover outstanding loans and any pledged collateral.

Bankruptcy, in its essence, is a legal process designed to provide debtors with a fresh start by discharging certain debts while allowing creditors to recover as much of their funds as possible. The specific procedures and outcomes depend heavily on the type of bankruptcy filed, primarily Chapter 7 (liquidation) or Chapter 11 (reorganization).

Understanding these distinctions is vital for lenders

navigating the complexities of loan recovery in bankruptcy proceedings.

Chapter 7 bankruptcy involves the liquidation of the debtor's non-exempt assets to repay creditors. This process is

typically initiated when the debtor's liabilities significantly outweigh their assets, rendering reorganization impractical.

A trustee is appointed to oversee the liquidation process, gathering and selling the debtor's assets. The proceeds from the sale are then distributed among creditors according to a pre-determined priority scheme. Secured creditors, those with a perfected security interest in specific collateral, generally receive priority over unsecured creditors. This means that if a lender has a properly perfected security interest in a piece of equipment or real estate, they are more

Likely to recover a substantial portion of their loan than a lender with an unsecured claim.

However, even secured creditors are not immune to losses in Chapter 7 bankruptcy. The value of the collateral may be less than the outstanding loan balance, leaving the lender with a deficiency. Furthermore, the liquidation process can be time-consuming and expensive, potentially incurring legal and administrative costs that further reduce the lender's recovery. The process involves meticulous record-keeping, including the proper documentation and perfection of security

interests, which often require legal expertise to navigate effectively. A deficiency can be substantial, and lenders often must weigh the costs of pursuing further action against the potential recovery.

Chapter 11 bankruptcy, in contrast, focuses on reorganizing the debtor's business to allow for continued operation and eventual repayment of debts over time. This approach is often preferred by businesses facing temporary financial difficulties but possessing viable long-term prospects. A debtor filing under Chapter 11 submits a reorganization plan to the bankruptcy court, outlining how it intends to

restructure its debts and operations to become financially solvent. The plan must be approved by a majority of

creditors and confirmed by the court before it becomes effective. Lenders are usually involved in the negotiation process, seeking to protect their interests while facilitating a successful reorganization. They may even participate

directly in developing the plan, ensuring their repayment terms are reasonable and attainable given the debtor's

reorganized operations.

Negotiating a successful reorganization plan within Chapter 11 often requires extensive financial analysis, legal

expertise, and skillful negotiation. The complexity of such

Agreements necessitate deep understanding of financial modeling, and the ability to assess the feasibility of a

debtor's projections. The lender's legal counsel should

possess experience in bankruptcy proceedings to effectively advocate for the lender's interests throughout the complex negotiation and court process. Successful navigation of this path often hinges on finding a balance between maximizing recovery and facilitating a feasible reorganization that allows the debtor to continue operating and eventually repay debts. Failure to reach a mutually agreeable outcome might result in a conversion of the Chapter 11 case to a Chapter 7

liquidation, where the recovery is less certain.

Regardless of the bankruptcy chapter involved, several key legal and procedural steps are crucial for lenders seeking loan recovery. First, the lender must file a proof of claim, formally documenting the amount owed. This claim must be detailed and accurate, providing supporting documentation to substantiate the debt. Any errors or omissions can

jeopardize the claim's validity and impair recovery efforts. A properly prepared proof of claim, coupled with meticulously kept records, allows the lender to stand firm and effectively press their claim within the bankruptcy proceedings.

Second, lenders with secured interests must take steps to protect and realize their collateral. This may involve

repossessing the collateral, preserving its value, and

liquidating it to recover as much of the loan as possible. This process often requires legal action and court approval,

especially if the borrower resists repossession. The lender's actions must be strictly compliant with all relevant laws to avoid potential liabilities. The legal complexity of

repossession underscores the need for experienced legal representation, capable of navigating the intricacies of state and federal law concerning collateral recovery.

Third, lenders must actively participate in the bankruptcy proceedings. Attending hearings, reviewing the debtor's financial statements, and engaging in negotiations are crucial. Passive participation significantly diminishes the lender's ability to protect their interests and influence the outcome of the proceedings. Understanding the court's schedule and actively participating in all hearings allow the lender to intervene if necessary, challenging issues that might negatively impact their recovery.

Finally, lenders may need to pursue legal action to protect their rights and recover outstanding amounts. This could involve contesting the debtor's bankruptcy petition, objecting to aspects of the reorganization plan, or pursuing legal action to recover deficiencies after liquidation. Experienced legal counsel is invaluable in such cases, ensuring that the lender's actions are legally sound and strategically effective within the confines of the bankruptcy court's jurisdiction. The legal fees incurred in litigating these issues must be weighed against the potential recovery, and prudent financial

decisions are crucial during this process.

The ethical considerations in loan recovery during

bankruptcy are also significant. While lenders have a right to pursue their financial interests, they must act ethically and avoid predatory or exploitative practices. Transparency and fair dealing are essential throughout the process. Attempting to circumvent legal processes or engage in actions designed to maximize profit at the expense of the debtor's recovery can lead to legal repercussions. Ethical behavior, moreover, fosters a positive reputation among courts and within the lending community, impacting future operations and

facilitating future success.

In conclusion, bankruptcy law presents a complex landscape for lenders seeking to recover outstanding loans.

Understanding the distinctions between Chapter 7 and

Chapter 11, the legal procedures involved, and the ethical considerations is crucial for maximizing recovery while mitigating risk. Proactive participation, meticulous record-keeping, and experienced legal representation are paramount in navigating the complexities of bankruptcy proceedings and securing the best possible outcome for the lender. The investment in legal expertise is not merely a cost but a

strategic investment in the protection of assets and the

preservation of the lender's financial stability. The ultimate goal is to balance the pursuit of recovery with ethical

practices that contribute to a stable and sustainable financial ecosystem.

Regulatory Compliance and Enforcement

The previous section explored the legal intricacies of loan recovery within the bankruptcy framework. However, even before a borrower reaches the brink of insolvency, lenders operate within a complex web of regulations designed to protect borrowers and maintain the stability of the financial system. Understanding and adhering to these regulations is not merely a matter of compliance; it's fundamental to the long-term viability and ethical standing of any lending institution. Non-compliance can lead to significant financial penalties, reputational damage, and even criminal charges.

Regulatory compliance in lending encompasses a wide range of activities, from the initial loan application process to the final disposition of defaulted accounts. It demands a

proactive and ongoing commitment to understanding and implementing the relevant laws and regulations at both the federal and state levels. Key areas of regulatory focus

include fair lending practices, consumer protection laws, and anti-money laundering (AML) regulations.

Fair lending practices are central to responsible lending.

These regulations prohibit discrimination based on race, color, religion, national origin, sex, marital status, age, or the receipt of public assistance. Lenders must ensure that their lending criteria are objective and applied consistently across all applicants, avoiding subjective assessments that could inadvertently lead to discriminatory outcomes. This requires robust internal controls to monitor lending decisions,

identify potential biases, and rectify any discrepancies.

Regular audits and training programs for loan officers are critical components of maintaining fair lending practices.

Failure to comply with fair lending laws can result in

Significant fines, lawsuits, and reputational damage that can severely impact a lender's business. The consequences extend beyond financial penalties, eroding public trust and harming the lender's long-term sustainability.

Consumer protection laws are equally critical, aiming to safeguard borrowers from predatory lending practices. These regulations dictate disclosure requirements, interest rate caps, and restrictions on certain types of fees. The Truth in Lending Act (TILA), for example, mandates that lenders provide borrowers with clear and concise information about the terms and costs of their loans. This includes the annual percentage rate (APR), finance charges, and any other fees associated with the loan. Failure to comply with TILA's disclosure requirements can result in significant penalties and legal challenges. Moreover, certain states have enacted stricter regulations that further limit interest rates and fees, underscoring the need for lenders to remain current with all applicable state and federal laws. The complexity of these regulations necessitates dedicated compliance teams who possess a deep understanding of both federal and state laws.

Anti-money laundering (AML) regulations play a crucial role in preventing the use of the financial system for illicit activities. These regulations require lenders to implement robust customer due diligence (CDD) procedures to identify and verify the identities of their borrowers. This includes obtaining and reviewing identification documents,

conducting background checks, and monitoring transactions for suspicious activity. AML compliance demands

significant investment in technology and training to ensure accurate identification and effective monitoring. Institutions failing to meet these requirements face substantial financial penalties and the risk of reputational damage. Moreover, involvement in money laundering can expose a lender to severe legal ramifications, including criminal charges. Thus,

Meticulous compliance with AML regulations is paramount for safeguarding the lender and its clients.

Beyond these core regulatory areas, lenders must navigate a complex landscape of other regulations, including those related to data privacy, cybersecurity, and environmental regulations. The constantly evolving regulatory environment requires ongoing monitoring and adaptation. Lenders must stay abreast of changes in legislation, regulatory guidance, and enforcement actions to ensure their compliance

programs remain current and effective. This necessitates the development of robust internal control systems to ensure ongoing monitoring, internal audits, and continuous

professional development for compliance officers.

Internal controls are the cornerstone of effective regulatory compliance. These controls should encompass all aspects of the lending process, from loan origination to collection and recovery. Strong internal controls involve establishing clear policies and procedures, implementing segregation of duties, and conducting regular audits to identify and correct any weaknesses. These measures not only mitigate the risk of regulatory violations but also enhance operational efficiency and reduce the likelihood of internal fraud. The development of a comprehensive internal control framework should be a top priority for any lending institution.

Responding to regulatory inquiries is another crucial aspect of compliance. Lenders must have in place procedures to promptly and thoroughly respond to any requests for

information from regulatory agencies. This includes

maintaining detailed records, conducting thorough

investigations, and cooperating fully with any inquiries.

Failure to respond adequately can result in escalated

scrutiny, fines, and enforcement actions. Therefore, proactive strategies for information management, including robust

Record-keeping systems and dedicated teams to handle regulatory inquiries, become crucial to avoid escalating consequences.

In conclusion, regulatory compliance is a multifaceted and ongoing process that demands a significant commitment from lending institutions. It necessitates not only a deep understanding of applicable laws and regulations but also the implementation of robust internal controls, ongoing

monitoring, and a proactive approach to responding to

regulatory inquiries. The costs associated with maintaining compliance can be substantial, but the potential penalties for non-compliance are far greater. Ultimately, a strong

compliance program is not just a matter of avoiding legal repercussions; it's essential for maintaining a positive

reputation, building trust with borrowers, and fostering the long-term stability and sustainability of the lending

institution. It underscores the need for a culture of

compliance, deeply embedded within the institution's

operational framework and decision-making processes. This ensures that compliance is viewed not as a burden but as a cornerstone of responsible and ethical lending practices, essential for the sustained growth and success of any

financial institution.

Ethical Considerations in Lending Practices

Beyond the legal framework, ethical considerations form the bedrock of responsible lending. While regulations provide a minimum standard of conduct, ethical lending goes further, demanding a commitment to fairness, transparency, and the well-being of borrowers. This involves not just adhering to the letter of the law, but also embracing the spirit of

responsible lending, prioritizing the long-term interests of both the lender and the borrower. A purely transactional approach, focused solely on profit maximization, often overlooks the crucial ethical dimensions of lending.

One of the most critical ethical considerations revolves around the concept of responsible lending practices. This involves a thorough assessment of a borrower's ability to repay a loan before extending credit. It's not simply about meeting the minimum requirements set by regulatory bodies; it's about a deeper understanding of the borrower's financial situation, including their income, expenses, existing debt, and overall financial stability. Lenders have an ethical

obligation to ensure that borrowers are not burdened with debt they cannot reasonably manage, potentially leading to financial distress or even bankruptcy. This requires a move beyond a purely numbers-driven approach, incorporating a more holistic assessment of the borrower's circumstances. For example, considering factors like unforeseen job losses, medical emergencies, or changes in family circumstances can help lenders make more informed and ethically sound decisions.

Transparency is another cornerstone of ethical lending.

Borrowers must receive clear and comprehensive

information about the terms and conditions of the loan,

Including all fees, interest rates, repayment schedules, and any potential risks associated with the loan. This

transparency extends beyond the legal requirements of disclosure. Lenders have an ethical responsibility to explain complex financial terms in plain language, ensuring that borrowers understand the implications of their borrowing decision. This is particularly crucial for vulnerable

borrowers, such as those with limited financial literacy, who may be more susceptible to exploitative lending practices.

The ethical lender proactively addresses potential

misunderstandings and fosters open communication to ensure that borrowers fully grasp the commitment they are undertaking. Furthermore, lenders should be transparent about their own fees and operational processes, avoiding hidden charges or unnecessarily complex procedures that obscure the true cost of borrowing.

Avoiding conflicts of interest is paramount in maintaining ethical lending practices. Lenders must prioritize the

interests of their borrowers over their own self-interest. This necessitates a commitment to impartiality and objectivity in loan approval decisions, avoiding any undue influence from personal relationships or financial incentives. For example, a lender should not grant a loan based on a personal

connection with the borrower, or prioritize loans from certain clients due to personal gain or other biases. To mitigate conflicts of interest, lending institutions should implement robust policies and procedures that ensure transparency in decision-making, independent reviews of loan applications, and clear guidelines regarding acceptable conduct. Regular audits and ethical training can also help identify and address potential conflicts of interest before they lead to unethical lending practices.

Ethical decision-making requires a commitment to fairness and equity. This necessitates applying lending criteria

Consistently across all applicants, regardless of their background or characteristics. Discriminatory lending practices, such as redlining or steering, are not only illegal but also profoundly unethical. They perpetuate inequalities and deny individuals access to essential financial services based on factors unrelated to their creditworthiness. Fair lending requires a commitment to inclusivity and ensuring equal access to credit for all individuals who meet the lender's objective criteria. This commitment should manifest in proactive measures to promote diversity in loan applications, ongoing training of loan officers to mitigate biases, and transparent review processes to address any discrepancies.

The ethical implications extend beyond individual loan transactions. Lenders play a crucial role in the broader financial ecosystem and have an ethical obligation to act responsibly towards the stability and well-being of the overall economy. This includes avoiding practices that could contribute to systemic risks, such as reckless lending or excessive risk-taking. Ethical lenders should maintain sufficient capital reserves, diversify their loan portfolios, and conduct thorough risk assessments to protect themselves and the financial system from potential shocks. Furthermore, they should actively contribute to the financial literacy of their borrowers and the wider community, empowering individuals to make informed financial decisions. Supporting initiatives that promote financial education can help reduce the likelihood of borrowers falling into debt traps and contributing to greater stability within the financial system.

Moreover, ethical lending also implies a commitment to data privacy and security. Lenders handle highly sensitive personal and financial information, and they have a responsibility to protect this data from unauthorized access, use, or disclosure. This requires robust cybersecurity

Measures, compliance with data privacy regulations, and a commitment to transparent data handling practices. Ethical lenders should inform borrowers about how their data is used, provide clear avenues for accessing and correcting their information, and implement strong security protocols to protect it from breaches.

In summary, ethical considerations in lending are not merely an addendum to legal compliance but a fundamental aspect of responsible business practice. It encompasses a broader commitment to fairness, transparency, and the well-being of borrowers, extending beyond the narrow confines of legal requirements. It demands a proactive approach to

responsible lending, the avoidance of conflicts of interest, and a dedication to fair and equitable treatment of all

borrowers. By prioritizing these ethical principles, lending institutions not only uphold their moral responsibilities but also cultivate a stronger reputation, build trust with their clients, and contribute to a more stable and just financial system. The long-term sustainability and success of any lending institution are inextricably linked to its ethical

standing and its commitment to responsible lending

practices. This commitment should be evident in every stage of the lending process, from loan origination to collection, reflecting a culture of ethical decision-making that permeates the entire organization.

The implementation of robust ethical guidelines requires a multifaceted approach. This includes not only establishing clear codes of conduct and policies but also providing comprehensive training to employees, fostering a culture of ethical awareness, and creating mechanisms for reporting and addressing unethical behaviors. Regular audits and independent reviews of lending practices can help ensure accountability and identify potential weaknesses in ethical compliance. Furthermore, active engagement with industry

Best practices and participation in relevant professional organizations can help lending institutions stay informed about emerging ethical challenges and best practices in the field.

The consequences of unethical lending practices can be severe. Aside from the legal ramifications, reputational damage can be devastating, leading to a loss of customer trust, reduced business opportunities, and ultimately,

financial instability. Conversely, a strong commitment to ethical lending fosters a positive reputation, strengthens client relationships, and enhances the long-term

sustainability of the lending institution. It's an investment in both the financial and moral well-being of the organization and its stakeholders. The pursuit of ethical lending is not just a matter of avoiding negative consequences; it's about

actively cultivating a positive and sustainable approach to business that benefits both the lender and the borrower.

The ethical dimensions of lending are constantly evolving in response to changing social norms, technological

advancements, and economic conditions. Lenders must remain vigilant in adapting their practices and policies to meet these emerging challenges. This requires a commitment to ongoing learning, continuous improvement, and a

proactive approach to identifying and addressing potential ethical dilemmas. The ethical standards of the lending

industry are not static; rather, they are constantly refined through dialogue, debate, and the evolution of best practices. Lenders must remain engaged in this ongoing conversation to ensure that their practices remain aligned with current societal expectations and responsible lending principles.

Active participation in industry forums, adherence to

updated codes of conduct, and ongoing assessment of ethical risk are essential to maintain a high standard of ethical

compliance. Ultimately, the pursuit of ethical lending is a

Continuous journey that requires a persistent commitment to integrity and a dedication to upholding the highest standards of professionalism and responsibility.

Identifying Distressed Loans and Early Warning Signs

The transition from a performing loan to a distressed one is rarely abrupt; it's a gradual deterioration marked by subtle shifts in the borrower's financial health. Effective debt restructuring and workout strategies hinge on early identification of these distressed loans. Proactive monitoring and a keen eye for early warning signs are crucial for minimizing losses and preserving lender-borrower relationships. This involves a multi-faceted approach, encompassing financial statement analysis, industry trend monitoring, and a thorough understanding of the borrower's business operations.

One of the most reliable indicators of potential loan distress is a consistent decline in key financial ratios. A deteriorating debt-to-equity ratio, for instance, signifies increasing reliance on debt financing, potentially highlighting a strained cash flow situation. Similarly, a declining current ratio (current assets divided by current liabilities) suggests a dwindling ability to meet short-term obligations. These ratios, coupled with a persistent decrease in profitability margins, paint a clear picture of financial vulnerability. The lender should delve deeper into the reasons behind these trends, scrutinizing the balance sheet and income statement for underlying issues. Are there specific expenses escalating uncontrollably? Is revenue growth stagnating or declining? Is inventory building up, indicating potential obsolescence or weak sales? These questions demand detailed answers and prompt proactive engagement with the borrower.

Beyond the quantitative analysis, qualitative factors also provide invaluable insights. A shift in management,

Particularly a sudden departure of key personnel, can signal internal turmoil and potential operational challenges.

Similarly, significant changes in the borrower's business strategy, such as a sudden diversification into unfamiliar markets or a drastic expansion without adequate planning, raise red flags. These changes, if not carefully assessed, can significantly increase the risk of loan default. The lender needs to understand the rationale behind such decisions and evaluate their impact on the borrower's financial stability. Open communication with the borrower is crucial during this assessment, fostering a collaborative environment for

addressing potential concerns. This involves regular

meetings, detailed financial reviews, and a willingness to understand the challenges faced by the borrower.

Industry-specific factors also contribute to the identification of distressed loans. Economic downturns, increased

competition, regulatory changes, and technological

disruptions can all significantly impact a borrower's financial performance. A lender must actively monitor industry trends and assess their potential impact on their borrowers. For example, a sudden surge in raw material prices can severely impact the profitability of manufacturing companies,

potentially jeopardizing their ability to repay loans.

Similarly, the emergence of a disruptive technology can render a company's products or services obsolete, leading to a rapid decline in revenue and profitability. Staying abreast of these industry dynamics is crucial for effective risk

management and the timely identification of potentially distressed loans.

Early warning signs are not always explicit. Sometimes, subtle changes in payment behavior can serve as indicators of looming problems. Delayed payments, even if minor, can be a precursor to more significant delinquencies. A history of late payments, especially if accompanied by excuses or

Unexplained delays, warrants immediate attention. Likewise, requests for loan modifications or extensions should prompt a thorough review of the borrower's financial situation.

While these requests can be legitimate responses to

unforeseen circumstances, they can also signal underlying financial weakness. Lenders should exercise caution and avoid automatically granting extensions without a detailed assessment of the borrower's revised financial projections and the viability of the proposed modifications.

The process of identifying distressed loans also involves analyzing the collateral securing the loan. A decline in the value of the collateral, whether due to market fluctuations or deterioration of the asset itself, increases the lender's

exposure to loss. Regular appraisals and monitoring of the collateral's condition are essential to ensure its continued viability as security for the loan. For asset-based lending, where the loan is secured by specific assets, this monitoring becomes even more critical. The lender needs to stay vigilant about the market value of the collateral and its potential susceptibility to damage or obsolescence. Maintaining

detailed records of the collateral's condition and value

ensures a sound basis for assessing the loan's risk profile.

Another critical aspect of identifying distressed loans is maintaining open communication with the borrower. Regular dialogue allows for early detection of potential problems and proactive intervention. This doesn't necessarily involve aggressive collection tactics; instead, it focuses on a

collaborative approach to problem-solving. The lender

should encourage the borrower to disclose any challenges or uncertainties they may be facing, fostering a relationship built on transparency and mutual trust. Open communication allows the lender to gain a deeper understanding of the

borrower's situation and work collaboratively to develop

Strategies for addressing potential difficulties before they escalate into loan defaults.

Beyond individual borrowers, macroeconomic indicators also provide insights into the potential for loan distress. Rising interest rates, inflation, or an economic recession can significantly impact borrowers' ability to repay loans.

Lenders must be attentive to these broader economic trends and adjust their risk assessment strategies accordingly.

Economic forecasting and scenario planning can help lenders anticipate potential risks and develop contingency plans to mitigate potential losses. This proactive approach is essential for navigating turbulent economic environments and

minimizing exposure to loan defaults. Moreover,

understanding government policies and regulatory changes impacting the borrower's industry can help anticipate future challenges.

The importance of a comprehensive credit analysis cannot be overstated. A thorough review of the borrower's financial statements, industry position, and management team is

crucial for identifying early warning signs. This analysis should not be a one-time event but a continuous process that evolves alongside the borrower's business. Regular

monitoring allows lenders to detect subtle shifts in the

borrower's financial performance and to intervene

proactively before problems escalate.

Ultimately, the identification of distressed loans requires a holistic approach, integrating quantitative financial analysis, qualitative assessment of business operations, industry trend monitoring, and a commitment to open communication with borrowers. By employing this multi-faceted approach,

lenders can significantly improve their ability to identify distressed loans early, implement timely interventions, and minimize potential losses. This proactive strategy protects

Both the lender and the borrower, facilitating a more

sustainable and mutually beneficial lending relationship. The transition from a performing to a distressed loan is rarely sudden; it is a process characterized by subtle shifts and indicators that, when carefully observed, offer valuable insights into potential problems and the opportunity for timely intervention. The sooner these signs are detected, the greater the chance of successful restructuring and the

minimization of financial losses.

Negotiating Loan Modifications and Restructuring Agreements

The identification of a distressed loan is only the first step in a complex process. Once a lender has determined that a borrower is facing significant financial challenges and is at risk of default, the next critical phase involves negotiating loan modifications and restructuring agreements. This

process demands a delicate balance of firmness and

understanding, aiming to protect the lender's interests while preserving the borrower's business viability. The ultimate goal is to achieve a mutually agreeable solution that

minimizes losses for the lender and allows the borrower to regain financial stability.

Successful negotiation hinges on a thorough understanding of the borrower's financial situation. This necessitates a deep dive into their financial statements, cash flow projections, and operational details. The lender needs to identify the root causes of the borrower's financial distress. Are there external factors at play, such as a downturn in the market or increased competition? Or are internal factors, such as poor

management or unsustainable business practices,

contributing to the problem? A clear understanding of these factors is crucial for formulating a realistic and effective restructuring plan.

Before entering into formal negotiations, the lender should conduct a comprehensive assessment of the borrower's assets and collateral. This is especially important in asset-based lending, where the loan is secured by specific assets. The lender needs to evaluate the current market value of these assets and their potential for liquidation. This assessment helps determine the lender's exposure to potential losses and

Informs the negotiation strategy. For instance, if the

collateral's value has significantly declined, the lender might need to consider accepting a lower repayment amount or extending the loan term to mitigate potential losses.

Conversely, if the collateral remains robust, the lender might be in a stronger negotiating position. A professional

appraisal may be required to objectively establish current market values.

The negotiation process itself typically involves several rounds of discussions and proposals. The initial phase often involves informal discussions to establish a rapport with the borrower and gain a better understanding of their situation.

The lender should approach these conversations with empathy and a willingness to explore mutually beneficial solutions. This does not, however, imply relinquishing the lender's rights or accepting unfavorable terms.

During these early conversations, the lender should clearly outline the borrower's obligations under the original loan agreement and the consequences of default. This sets the stage for a realistic negotiation, preventing

misunderstandings and unrealistic expectations. The lender should also gather detailed information about the borrower's current financial situation, including cash flow projections, sales forecasts, and plans for addressing the underlying issues contributing to their financial difficulties. This data will form the foundation for evaluating the feasibility of proposed restructuring options. Transparency is key. The lender should openly discuss their concerns and

expectations, fostering a climate of trust and open

communication.

Once a basic understanding of the borrower's circumstances is established, more formal negotiations can begin. This stage involves the presentation of specific proposals for loan

Modification or restructuring. These proposals may involve a variety of options, including:

Extension of the loan maturity date:

This provides the borrower with additional time to repay the loan, easing their immediate cash flow pressures. However, the lender should carefully consider the increased risk associated with

extending the loan term, particularly in light of uncertain economic conditions or industry-specific challenges. The terms of the extended loan should reflect this increased risk, potentially incorporating a higher interest rate or additional security.

Reduction of the interest rate:

Lowering the interest rate reduces the borrower's monthly payments, easing their burden and providing greater flexibility. The feasibility of this option depends on several factors, including the lender's risk appetite and the overall market interest rates. In times of low interest rates, this is a more viable option; however, in a rising-interest-rate environment, the lender might be less willing to reduce rates, seeking alternative solutions.

Modification of payment terms:

This could involve

adjusting the repayment schedule to align with the

borrower's improved cash flow projections. For example, the lender might agree to a period of reduced payments followed by a period of accelerated repayment. This approach requires a thorough review of the borrower's projected cash flows to ensure that the modified payment schedule is sustainable and feasible. The lender should also establish clear performance metrics to monitor the borrower's progress and ensure

adherence to the revised repayment plan.

Capital infusion or equity injection:

In some cases, the lender might agree to provide additional capital to the borrower or accept equity in the company in exchange for

Modifying the loan terms. This option is typically considered when the borrower has strong potential for recovery but needs additional resources to overcome their immediate financial difficulties. The lender needs to carefully assess the risk and potential return on investment associated with this type of intervention. Legal counsel is critical to ensuring that the equity injection is structured appropriately to protect the lender's interests.

Debt-for-equity swap:

This involves converting a portion of the loan into equity ownership in the borrower's company. This reduces the borrower's debt burden while providing the lender with an ownership stake in the business. The success of this approach hinges on the potential for future growth and profitability of the company. Sophisticated valuation techniques are often necessary to determine a fair exchange rate between debt and equity. Legal and financial advisors play a significant role in structuring a debt-for-equity swap that is equitable for both parties.

During negotiations, it is crucial to document all agreements reached in writing. This prevents misunderstandings and ensures that both parties are fully aware of their obligations. The final restructuring agreement should clearly specify the modified terms of the loan, including the repayment

schedule, interest rate, collateral, and any other relevant conditions. Legal counsel should be involved in reviewing and finalizing the agreement to ensure that it protects the lender's interests and complies with all applicable

regulations.

The negotiation process isn't always straightforward. There may be disagreements and points of contention that require careful consideration and compromise. However, a

collaborative approach is critical. Open communication, a willingness to listen to the borrower's perspective, and a

Shared commitment to finding a mutually beneficial solution are essential ingredients for a successful outcome. A skilled negotiator can guide the process, balancing firmness in protecting the lender's interests with empathy and flexibility in considering the borrower's circumstances. Experienced banking professionals understand the importance of patience and persistence in achieving a workable agreement.

Failure to reach a mutually acceptable agreement can lead to several outcomes, including liquidation of the borrower's assets, bankruptcy proceedings, or a protracted legal battle. Each has significant implications for both the lender and the borrower, often leading to substantial financial losses and damage to business reputations. The objective of the

negotiation process is to avoid these undesirable outcomes by proactively seeking a sustainable solution that allows the borrower to recover and fulfill their financial obligations.

Even after a restructuring agreement is reached, ongoing monitoring is crucial. The lender should closely track the borrower's financial performance and adherence to the agreed-upon terms. Regular financial reporting, compliance monitoring, and open communication are all vital elements of post-restructuring management. Early detection of any deviations from the restructuring plan allows for timely intervention, preventing the recurrence of financial distress. This ongoing relationship builds trust and helps maintain a healthy lender-borrower dynamic even in challenging

circumstances. A successful debt restructuring is not merely a single event but a process requiring constant vigilance and ongoing collaboration. It involves building a long-term relationship where shared success becomes the ultimate objective.

Developing Workout Plans and Strategies

Developing a robust workout plan requires a systematic approach, moving beyond the initial negotiations and into a concrete strategy for recovery. This involves a thorough analysis of the borrower's financial health, a clear

articulation of the lender's objectives, and the strategic deployment of available legal and financial tools. The process is not a linear one; rather, it's iterative, requiring adjustments based on ongoing assessments and the

borrower's response to the implemented strategies.

The first step is to conduct a detailed financial analysis of the borrower. This goes beyond simply reviewing the most

recent financial statements. It demands a deep dive into historical performance, identifying trends and patterns that contributed to the current distress. This might involve

analyzing sales data over several years to understand

fluctuations in revenue, scrutinizing expense reports to

uncover areas of inefficiency, and evaluating the

effectiveness of the borrower's inventory management. Cash flow projections are crucial, not just for the next year, but ideally for a three-to-five-year horizon. These projections should be developed collaboratively with the borrower, providing a realistic roadmap for recovery. Discrepancies between the borrower's projections and the lender's own analysis should be addressed thoroughly, aiming for

consensus on realistic expectations.

The lender's objectives must be clearly defined. What is the ultimate goal? Is it to maximize recovery, preserve the borrower's business, or a combination of both? The answer will heavily influence the development of the workout plan. For instance, a lender primarily concerned with maximizing

Recovery might pursue a more aggressive approach, potentially involving a quicker liquidation of assets.

Conversely, a lender prioritizing business preservation might opt for a more gradual approach, focusing on restructuring the debt and supporting the borrower's operational

improvements. This decision-making process necessitates careful consideration of the risks and potential rewards associated with each strategy.

The workout plan itself should be a detailed document

outlining the specific steps the borrower will take to improve their financial position. This will involve a timeline for achieving key milestones, clear performance metrics to measure progress, and a mechanism for ongoing monitoring and reporting. The plan should also include contingency plans to address potential setbacks. For instance, it should incorporate strategies to deal with unforeseen market

downturns or unexpected operational challenges.

This is where the lender's expertise in asset-based lending becomes particularly relevant. A detailed assessment of the borrower's collateral is paramount. This involves a

professional appraisal of the assets securing the loan to determine their current market value. The appraisal should consider factors such as market demand, depreciation, and potential liquidation costs. If the collateral value is

significantly below the outstanding loan balance, the

workout plan needs to address this shortfall. This might involve negotiations to reduce the debt or explore alternative sources of repayment. Transparency is critical in this phase; both lender and borrower must have a clear understanding of the collateral's value and its role in the restructuring process.

The workout plan should also incorporate strategies for improving the borrower's profitability. This might involve operational improvements such as streamlining processes,

Reducing overhead costs, or improving sales and marketing efforts. The plan may include specific recommendations for these improvements, along with deadlines for their

implementation and metrics for measuring their

effectiveness. It's crucial for the lender to understand the borrower's business model, identifying its strengths and weaknesses and suggesting practical solutions. Financial modeling is often employed to test the feasibility of different strategies, allowing for data-driven decision-making.

The legal aspects of debt restructuring cannot be overlooked.

The workout plan should comply with all applicable laws and regulations. Legal counsel is essential to ensure that the restructuring process adheres to these guidelines and protects the lender's interests. Legal considerations extend to the enforcement of the agreements reached during negotiations, and the plan needs to incorporate mechanisms for dispute resolution. Careful documentation of all agreements and communications is essential to avoid future legal challenges.

The lender's role extends beyond the development of the workout plan. Active participation and ongoing monitoring are crucial. Regular meetings with the borrower are

necessary to review progress, address any emerging issues, and make necessary adjustments to the plan. The lender should receive regular financial reports from the borrower, including updated cash flow projections, sales figures, and expense reports. These reports are crucial in identifying potential problems and ensuring that the borrower adheres to the agreed-upon terms.

The success of a workout plan depends heavily on the

borrower's commitment to the process. The plan needs to be realistic and achievable, taking into account the borrower's capabilities and resources. If the borrower demonstrates a consistent lack of cooperation or fails to meet agreed-upon

Milestones, the lender needs to reassess the situation and potentially explore alternative strategies, which may involve more aggressive measures.

In situations involving multiple lenders, the workout plan needs to be coordinated among all parties. Reaching a consensus on the restructuring terms is crucial, and it often requires extensive negotiations. A lead lender or a

coordinating committee can facilitate the process, ensuring that all lenders' interests are considered.

Finally, it's vital to document every aspect of the workout plan and its implementation. This documentation provides a clear record of the agreements reached, the actions taken, and the results achieved. This documentation is not merely for record-keeping; it also serves as a tool for evaluating the effectiveness of the strategy and making informed decisions as the workout process unfolds. Comprehensive

documentation is particularly crucial in case of future

disputes or litigation. The workout plan, then, represents a dynamic document, constantly evolving and adapting to the changing circumstances of the borrower and the market. Its creation and execution are a testament to the lender's

commitment to preserving value and fostering long-term financial stability. The process demands expertise, patience, and a collaborative spirit, ensuring that the ultimate outcome is mutually beneficial and sustainable.

Implementing and Monitoring Workout Plans

Implementing a workout plan is not a passive process; it requires active engagement and continuous monitoring to ensure its effectiveness. The lender's role shifts from

negotiator to active manager, overseeing the borrower's progress and making necessary adjustments along the way. This requires regular communication, detailed performance tracking, and a willingness to adapt the plan as

circumstances change.

Regular communication with the borrower is paramount.

This shouldn't be limited to formal meetings; it should

involve frequent, informal check-ins to gauge the borrower's progress and address any concerns proactively. These

interactions should focus not only on the financial metrics but also on the operational challenges the borrower is facing.

Understanding the nuances of their business and the

obstacles they encounter is crucial for providing timely support and adjusting the workout plan accordingly. Open communication fosters trust and collaboration, increasing the likelihood of a successful outcome. The frequency of these communications should be determined by the complexity of the situation and the borrower's performance. In some cases, weekly meetings may be necessary; in others, monthly

check-ins might suffice. The key is to maintain a consistent dialogue that enables early identification and mitigation of potential problems.

Effective monitoring requires a robust system for tracking key performance indicators (kpis). These kpis should be directly linked to the goals outlined in the workout plan. This might include sales figures, cost reductions, inventory

turnover, and debt reduction milestones. Regular reporting

From the borrower is essential, and the lender should independently verify this information whenever possible.

Discrepancies between reported data and the lender's own analysis should trigger a deeper investigation to identify the source of the discrepancy and address any underlying issues. Sophisticated financial modeling tools can be employed to project future performance and assess the impact of various interventions. This data-driven approach ensures that

adjustments to the workout plan are informed and

strategically sound.

The workout plan itself should not be treated as a static document. The business environment is constantly evolving, and the borrower's circumstances may change unexpectedly.

Economic downturns, shifts in market demand, or

unforeseen operational challenges can all impact the

borrower's ability to meet the agreed-upon milestones. The lender should be prepared to adapt the plan in response to such changes. This might involve adjusting timelines,

revising performance targets, or exploring alternative

strategies to achieve the overall objectives. Flexibility and a willingness to renegotiate are crucial for navigating these unforeseen circumstances. This requires a collaborative approach, with open communication between the lender and the borrower to jointly assess the situation and develop appropriate modifications to the plan.

Monitoring also involves assessing the borrower's overall commitment to the workout plan. Consistent failure to meet agreed-upon milestones or a lack of proactive engagement should raise concerns. The lender needs to understand the reasons for this underperformance. Is it due to external factors beyond the borrower's control, or is it a reflection of a lack of commitment or capacity? This necessitates a

careful evaluation of the borrower's management team, their operational capabilities, and their overall financial stability.

If the borrower demonstrates a consistent pattern of non-compliance or a lack of effort, the lender may need to consider more aggressive measures, such as accelerating the debt recovery process or exploring legal options. This situation requires a delicate balance between support and enforcement, aiming to motivate the borrower while safeguarding the lender's interests.

In situations involving secured lending, monitoring also involves regularly assessing the collateral's value. Market conditions can significantly impact the value of assets, and this change needs to be factored into the ongoing evaluation of the workout plan. Regular appraisals or valuations may be required, particularly in volatile markets. If the collateral value drops below a critical threshold, the lender needs to proactively address this shortfall, potentially through negotiations to adjust the terms of the loan or explore alternative repayment strategies. This ongoing assessment of collateral is vital for mitigating risk and ensuring that the lender's interests are adequately protected throughout the restructuring process.

The monitoring process doesn't end with the borrower's fulfillment of the workout plan. Even after the borrower demonstrates consistent improvement and meets the agreed-upon targets, the lender should continue to monitor their financial health for a period of time. This post-workout monitoring helps to ensure the sustainability of the recovery and to identify any potential signs of relapse. A transitional period of continued observation allows the lender to gauge the borrower's long-term stability and prevent a recurrence of the financial distress that necessitated the workout in the first place. This proactive approach demonstrates a commitment to long-term financial health and can contribute to a stronger and more sustainable borrower-lender relationship.

The use of technology significantly enhances the effectiveness of implementation and monitoring. Dedicated workout management software can streamline the process, providing tools for tracking kpis, generating reports, and facilitating communication between the lender and the borrower. These platforms allow for real-time monitoring of financial performance, enabling timely intervention and adjustments to the workout plan. The data-driven approach facilitates informed decision-making, ensuring that the strategies implemented are both effective and efficient. The use of advanced analytics can also help predict potential challenges and proactively address risks before they escalate. Moreover, such systems provide a comprehensive audit trail, documenting every step of the workout process and minimizing the potential for disputes.

Finally, effective implementation and monitoring require a highly skilled team. The lender's personnel involved in the workout process should possess expertise in financial analysis, credit risk management, and legal compliance.

They must possess strong communication skills and the ability to build rapport with the borrower. Moreover, experience in crisis management is crucial, equipping the team to handle unexpected challenges and adapt quickly to evolving circumstances. A collaborative approach, involving specialists from various departments within the lending institution, ensures a holistic and comprehensive approach to managing the workout process. Regular training and professional development should be provided to keep the team abreast of the latest techniques and best practices in debt restructuring. Investment in human capital is essential for ensuring the successful implementation and monitoring of workout plans and achieving optimal outcomes for both the lender and the borrower. The ultimate goal is not simply to recover the debt, but to help the borrower regain financial

Stability and establish a sustainable business model. A well-managed workout process fosters a collaborative

environment where both parties work together to achieve mutually beneficial outcomes.

Case Studies in Successful Debt Restructuring

This section delves into specific examples of successful debt restructuring, offering practical insights and demonstrating the application of the principles outlined previously.

Analyzing these real-world scenarios reveals crucial lessons and best practices applicable to a wide range of situations. While confidentiality often restricts the disclosure of specific company names, the core elements of these cases remain instructive, revealing how various strategies were

implemented and the challenges overcome.

Our first case study focuses on a mid-sized manufacturing company facing severe liquidity issues stemming from a rapid decline in demand for their core product. This

company, heavily reliant on short-term credit, found

themselves unable to meet their payment obligations. Initial negotiations with creditors proved unsuccessful, primarily due to a lack of a clear and comprehensive restructuring plan. The intervention of a specialized debt restructuring firm proved pivotal. This firm conducted a thorough

assessment of the company's financial position, including an analysis of its assets, liabilities, and projected cash flows.

Based on this analysis, they developed a multi-faceted restructuring plan that incorporated several key strategies.

First, they negotiated an extension of existing credit lines, providing the company with temporary breathing room to implement other elements of the plan. Secondly, they worked with the company to streamline operations,

significantly reducing overhead costs and improving efficiency. This involved identifying non-essential

expenditures and renegotiating contracts with suppliers. Third, they helped the company diversify its product line,

Mitigating future reliance on the declining core product. This involved market research, product development, and the identification of new market opportunities. Finally, they secured additional equity financing from existing

shareholders to provide a more solid financial foundation for the company. The combination of these actions allowed the company to stabilize its financial situation, eventually

leading to a successful repayment of its debts and a return to profitability. This case highlights the importance of a holistic approach to debt restructuring, encompassing operational improvements, financial engineering, and strategic

adjustments to the business model. The involvement of external expertise proved crucial in developing and

executing a comprehensive and effective plan. The initial failure to articulate a clear plan underscores the critical role of strategic planning and a strong team capable of executing it.

In contrast, our second case study features a real estate development company encountering difficulties due to an over-leveraged balance sheet and an unforeseen downturn in the property market. The company possessed valuable assets but was struggling with high levels of debt servicing. The approach taken in this case differed significantly from the previous one. The primary strategy here focused on asset-based lending and the skillful renegotiation of existing debt obligations. The restructuring team, comprised of

representatives from the company and its creditors, worked together to identify and prioritize assets that could be

monetized. This involved a rigorous valuation process to establish a realistic market price for each property.

The team then engaged in strategic negotiations with

creditors. They proposed a plan that involved the sale of a portion of the company's assets to repay a significant portion of the outstanding debt. They also negotiated an extension

On the remaining debt, lowering the interest rates and

adjusting repayment schedules to align with projected cash flows from the remaining assets. A key element of this

success was the close collaboration between the company and its creditors. Open and transparent communication

fostered a sense of trust, allowing all parties to work towards a mutually acceptable solution. The willingness of creditors to participate in a collaborative effort demonstrates the

importance of maintaining strong relationships and building a collaborative framework for navigating financial

difficulties. This approach contrasts with adversarial

strategies and underscores the benefits of a collaborative and transparent restructuring process. The ultimate success

underscored the importance of understanding asset values accurately and leveraging these to secure better terms with creditors.

A third case study demonstrates the effectiveness of pre-emptive restructuring. A technology company, anticipating a challenging period following a significant shift in market dynamics, proactively engaged with its lenders to restructure its debt. Instead of waiting for a crisis to unfold, the

company sought to mitigate future risk and maintain its financial stability. This early intervention allowed for a more controlled and less stressful restructuring process. They presented a detailed financial forecast demonstrating the anticipated challenges and proposed several preventative measures. These measures included adjusting their growth targets, streamlining their operations, and seeking additional funding to strengthen their capital position. Their proactive engagement with lenders fostered a positive relationship and resulted in a favorable restructuring agreement that allowed the company to navigate the challenging period without significant disruption to its operations.

The successful implementation in this scenario highlights the critical advantage of early intervention. Acting before a financial crisis develops allows for more strategic planning and greater flexibility in negotiations. This approach not only minimizes the impact on the company's operations but also allows it to preserve its reputation and maintain its relationships with lenders and other stakeholders. The

proactive stance demonstrated a commitment to transparency and financial prudence, resulting in a smoother and more successful restructuring compared to reactive measures taken during times of distress. This serves as a strong argument for proactive financial management and early engagement with creditors to avoid more extensive crises later.

The cases presented above illustrate that successful debt restructuring involves a thorough understanding of the

borrower's financial situation, a comprehensive restructuring plan, strong communication, and a willingness to adapt strategies as circumstances evolve. There is no one-size-fits-all solution; the optimal approach depends on the specific circumstances of the borrower, the nature of the debt, and the willingness of all stakeholders to collaborate effectively.

However, consistent themes emerge: accurate financial assessment, transparent communication, and a focus on achieving a sustainable solution for all involved parties are key drivers of successful debt restructuring. The success of these efforts underscores the significant role of proactive financial planning, the utilization of skilled professionals, and a collaborative approach in navigating challenging financial circumstances. Furthermore, the examples

emphasize that successful restructuring often involves not only addressing immediate financial pressures but also implementing fundamental changes to the business model to ensure long-term sustainability and resilience.

Developing Effective Portfolio Management Strategies

Developing robust portfolio management strategies is paramount for mitigating risk and maximizing returns within commercial and asset-based lending. A well-structured portfolio isn't merely a collection of loans; it's a dynamic ecosystem requiring constant monitoring, analysis, and strategic adjustments. This necessitates a multifaceted approach that incorporates diversification, rigorous credit analysis, proactive risk management, and continuous performance evaluation. Let's delve into the key elements of building an effective portfolio.

Diversification is the cornerstone of any sound lending portfolio. Concentrating loans within a single industry, geographic area, or borrower type exposes the portfolio to significant systemic risk. A downturn in a specific sector can trigger a cascade of defaults, severely impacting the portfolio's overall performance. Effective diversification involves spreading risk across various industries, geographic regions, and borrower profiles. For example, a well-diversified portfolio might include loans to manufacturers, retailers, technology companies, and healthcare providers, located across different geographic regions. This approach reduces the likelihood of concentrated losses from a single event.

Furthermore, diversification extends beyond merely the number of borrowers. It also includes the types of loans within the portfolio. A balanced portfolio may incorporate various loan structures, such as term loans, lines of credit, and asset-based loans. This mixed approach helps manage risk by limiting exposure to specific types of credit risk. For

Instance, a heavy reliance on asset-based lending, while offering collateral protection, might leave the portfolio vulnerable to fluctuations in asset values. Conversely, a portfolio solely comprised of term loans could lack the flexibility to respond to changing market conditions. The optimal mix of loan types will depend on various factors, including the lender's risk appetite, market conditions, and the overall strategic goals. Regular reviews and adjustments of this mix are crucial for adapting to evolving

circumstances.

Beyond diversification, rigorous credit analysis forms the foundation of sound portfolio management. Thorough due diligence is vital before extending any credit. This involves meticulously reviewing the borrower's financial statements, conducting industry research, assessing the quality of

management, and evaluating the overall business model's sustainability. The process must go beyond simple numerical analysis; it requires understanding the underlying business dynamics and assessing the borrower's resilience to

unforeseen economic shocks. Detailed financial modeling should be used to predict potential cash flow scenarios, stress testing the borrower's ability to service the debt under various economic conditions. Sophisticated credit scoring models and early warning systems can provide valuable insights into potential credit deterioration, allowing for proactive intervention.

The assessment of collateral is also critical in asset-based lending. A detailed appraisal of the assets pledged as

collateral is necessary to accurately assess their market value and liquidity. Moreover, the lender should consider factors such as the storage, insurance, and maintenance costs

associated with the collateral. In some cases, independent valuations might be required to ensure objectivity and

accuracy. The importance of collateral extends beyond

Simple loan security; it can significantly impact the lender's ability to recover losses in case of default. Therefore, a robust collateral management system, including regular monitoring and valuation updates, is crucial.

Proactive risk management involves continuously

monitoring the portfolio's performance and identifying potential risks before they escalate into significant problems.

Regular reporting and analysis are essential to track key metrics such as delinquency rates, loan loss reserves, and the overall portfolio's concentration levels. Early warning

systems, which flag potential problems based on predefined thresholds, can provide valuable early indications of

emerging risks. For example, a sudden decrease in a

borrower's sales or an increase in their days sales outstanding could indicate potential financial distress. Furthermore, proactive communication with borrowers is crucial. Regular contact allows lenders to identify potential issues early on and work with borrowers to develop solutions before they trigger a default. This collaborative approach not only helps manage risk but also strengthens lender-borrower

relationships.

Stress testing the portfolio is another vital aspect of proactive risk management. This involves simulating various

economic scenarios, such as a recession or a significant industry downturn, to assess the portfolio's resilience to adverse events. Stress testing allows lenders to identify

vulnerabilities and adjust their risk management strategies accordingly. For example, a stress test might reveal that the portfolio is overly exposed to a particular industry. This information allows the lender to take appropriate action, such as diversifying the portfolio or strengthening credit requirements for borrowers in that sector.

Effective portfolio management requires a sophisticated system for tracking and monitoring loan performance. This includes a robust loan servicing system, capable of tracking key performance indicators (kpis), such as delinquency rates, recovery rates, and interest income. Accurate and timely data are critical for making informed decisions about portfolio strategy. Furthermore, the system must facilitate efficient reporting, providing lenders with up-to-date

information on the portfolio's overall health. This data is critical for informing decisions about risk appetite, capital allocation, and future lending strategies. Regular portfolio reviews, conducted by senior management, are vital to ensure alignment with overall business objectives and to identify any potential issues early. These reviews provide an opportunity to assess the effectiveness of risk management strategies and adjust them as needed.

Finally, developing a strong credit culture within the lending institution is paramount. This involves establishing clear lending guidelines, implementing rigorous credit approval processes, and providing training and development for credit officers. The credit culture must foster a culture of risk awareness and accountability. Regular audits of the lending process are essential to ensure compliance with regulations and internal guidelines. Furthermore, the institution should establish a clear escalation process for addressing

problematic loans, ensuring prompt and effective

intervention. This rigorous approach minimizes the

likelihood of significant losses and protects the institution's financial stability.

In conclusion, effective portfolio management for

commercial and asset-based lending requires a

comprehensive and multifaceted approach. Diversification, rigorous credit analysis, proactive risk management, and a strong credit culture are all essential components.

Continuous monitoring, regular review, and proactive

adjustments are key to navigating the dynamic landscape of credit risk and achieving sustainable, long-term success in this competitive industry. Failure to adopt these strategies can lead to significant financial losses and potentially

jeopardize the institution's stability. The principles outlined above, when implemented diligently, provide a solid

foundation for building a resilient and profitable lending portfolio.

Implementing Key Risk Indicators kris

Implementing a robust Key Risk Indicator (KRI) framework is crucial for effective portfolio management. Kris are

quantifiable metrics that provide early warnings of potential problems within a lending portfolio. Unlike Key

Performance Indicators (kpis), which focus on measuring overall performance, kris are specifically designed to

identify and signal emerging risks. A well-designed KRI system provides a proactive, data-driven approach to risk management, allowing for timely intervention and mitigation of potential losses. The selection of appropriate kris is critical and should be tailored to the specific characteristics of the portfolio and the institution's risk appetite.

The process begins with a thorough understanding of the portfolio's composition and the types of risks it faces. This involves analyzing the concentration of loans by industry sector, geographic location, and borrower type. It also requires assessing the diversity of loan structures, including term loans, lines of credit, and asset-based financing. A portfolio heavily concentrated in a single industry, for example, is inherently more vulnerable to sector-specific shocks. Similarly, a reliance on a specific loan type exposes the portfolio to the unique risks associated with that

structure. For instance, asset-based lending, while offering collateral protection, is susceptible to fluctuations in asset values.

Once the portfolio's risk profile is understood, relevant kris can be identified and implemented. These indicators should provide timely signals of emerging problems, allowing for early intervention and corrective action. Here are some

Examples of critical kris for commercial and asset-based lending portfolios:

Delinquency Rate:

This metric measures the percentage of loans past due by a certain number of days (e.g., 30, 60, 90 days past due). A rising delinquency rate indicates potential credit deterioration and requires immediate attention.

Analyzing the delinquency rate by borrower segment (e.g., industry, geographic region) can reveal specific areas of concern within the portfolio. Furthermore, tracking the trend of delinquency rates over time provides valuable insights into the overall health of the portfolio and the effectiveness of existing risk management strategies. A sudden,

unexplained spike in delinquencies should trigger a thorough review of the affected loans and borrowers.

Loan Loss Reserve Coverage:

This KRI measures the adequacy of loan loss reserves relative to the estimated losses in the portfolio. A low coverage ratio indicates

potential under-provisioning and exposes the institution to unexpected losses. Regular review and adjustment of loan loss reserves are essential to ensure adequate coverage based on changes in the credit quality of the portfolio and evolving economic conditions. Factors influencing the required level of loan loss reserves include the overall economic outlook, industry-specific risks, and the performance of individual loans.

Portfolio Concentration Ratios:

These ratios measure the concentration of loans within specific industry sectors, geographic regions, or borrower types. High concentration ratios indicate heightened systemic risk, as a downturn in a concentrated sector could significantly impact the overall portfolio performance. Monitoring these ratios allows lenders to identify and manage exposure to concentrated risks proactively. Regular review of these ratios helps

Maintain an appropriate level of diversification, thereby mitigating the impact of potential losses from a single sector or borrower.

Average Days Sales Outstanding (DSO):

This metric

measures the average time it takes for a borrower to pay their invoices. A significant increase in DSO can indicate

potential financial difficulties for the borrower, as it may suggest difficulties in collecting receivables. Monitoring DSO, particularly in conjunction with other indicators like sales trends, provides early warning of potential problems. A sudden and substantial increase in DSO, without a clear explanation, warrants immediate investigation to assess the borrower's financial stability and the potential impact on the loan.

Debt Service Coverage Ratio (DSCR):

This ratio measures a borrower's ability to service debt obligations from its operating income. A declining DSCR suggests weakening cash flow and an increasing risk of default. This metric is particularly relevant for asset-based lending, where the borrower's ability to generate cash flow is directly linked to the value of the collateral. Monitoring DSCR across the portfolio allows lenders to identify borrowers experiencing financial stress and take timely intervention measures. A significant and sustained decrease in DSCR requires

immediate attention, potentially necessitating renegotiation of loan terms or the implementation of stricter monitoring procedures.

Collateral Value to Loan Ratio:

In asset-based lending, this KRI measures the ratio of the collateral's market value to the outstanding loan balance. A declining ratio indicates

increased credit risk, as the collateral might not fully cover the loan balance in case of default. Regular appraisals and monitoring of collateral values are vital to ensure the

Adequacy of collateral coverage and maintain an acceptable level of risk. Significant declines in this ratio could signal the need for additional collateral or stricter monitoring procedures.

The effective implementation of kris requires a robust data infrastructure and reporting system. This involves collecting accurate and timely data on loan performance, borrower financial health, and market conditions. The data needs to be readily accessible and easily analyzed to facilitate timely decision-making. Furthermore, the KRI system should be integrated with existing risk management processes,

allowing for seamless identification, assessment, and

mitigation of emerging risks.

Regular monitoring and review of kris are essential to ensure their continued effectiveness. Management should regularly analyze KRI trends and deviations from established thresholds. This involves identifying potential patterns and understanding the underlying causes of any adverse trends.

Furthermore, the KRI framework should be periodically reviewed and adjusted to reflect changes in the portfolio composition, market conditions, and the institution's risk appetite. This ongoing refinement ensures the KRI system remains relevant and effective in identifying and managing evolving risks.

The implementation and regular monitoring of kris are not merely technical exercises; they are integral to a proactive risk management strategy. They provide valuable insights into the health and performance of lending portfolios,

allowing for early identification and mitigation of potential problems. A well-designed KRI system, coupled with robust data analysis and informed decision-making, significantly enhances the institution's ability to manage credit risk and protect its financial stability. Ignoring or underestimating the

Importance of kris can lead to significant financial losses and reputational damage. Therefore, investing in a

comprehensive KRI framework is not an expense; it's a critical investment in the long-term health and success of the lending institution. The development and ongoing

refinement of a robust KRI system is an iterative process, requiring continuous attention and adaptation to changing circumstances.

Stress Testing and Scenario Planning

Building upon the robust Key Risk Indicator (KRI)

framework previously discussed, a critical next step in

effective portfolio management is the implementation of comprehensive stress testing and scenario planning. These techniques are not merely supplementary; they are essential components of a proactive and resilient risk management strategy, providing a deeper understanding of the portfolio's vulnerability to a range of potential shocks. Unlike kris, which focus on the ongoing monitoring of current

performance, stress testing and scenario planning allow for a forward-looking assessment, examining the potential impact of future events on the portfolio's financial health.

Stress testing, at its core, involves subjecting the lending portfolio to hypothetical but plausible adverse scenarios.

These scenarios can range from relatively mild economic downturns to more severe, catastrophic events. The objective is to simulate the impact of these scenarios on key portfolio metrics, such as the delinquency rate, loan loss provisions, and overall portfolio profitability. This process helps identify vulnerabilities within the portfolio and assess the institution's capacity to withstand financial stress. A well-executed stress test provides a realistic estimate of potential losses under different stress conditions, allowing for proactive

adjustments to risk mitigation strategies and capital

allocation.

The methodology employed in stress testing can vary

depending on the complexity of the portfolio and the

sophistication of the institution's risk management

capabilities. A common approach involves using quantitative models that incorporate macroeconomic factors, industry-

Specific risks, and borrower-level characteristics. These models may include historical data, econometric projections, and expert judgment to generate plausible stress scenarios.

The specific macroeconomic variables included in the models might vary widely, encompassing elements such as interest rate changes, inflation rates, unemployment levels, and commodity price fluctuations. Industry-specific factors, such as changes in demand, technological disruption, and regulatory changes, can be incorporated to produce more accurate scenarios related to specific portfolio

concentrations. Finally, borrower-level characteristics, including credit scores, leverage ratios, and cash flow

patterns, are crucial inputs to assess individual loan

vulnerabilities under stress.

For example, consider a commercial lending portfolio

heavily concentrated in the real estate sector. A stress test might involve simulating a sharp decline in property values, reflecting a potential market correction or economic

downturn. The model would then project the impact of this decline on the value of collateral securing real estate loans, estimating the potential increase in delinquencies and loan losses. This allows the institution to gauge the adequacy of its loan loss reserves and identify any potential capital shortfalls. Simultaneously, a stress test could incorporate rising interest rates, potentially squeezing the cash flows of borrowers and further increasing the probability of defaults. This dual stress event (declining property values and rising interest rates) provides a far more realistic view of the potential challenges than a single-variable stress test.

Scenario planning is a complementary technique that

complements stress testing by exploring a broader range of potential future events, both positive and negative. While stress testing focuses on quantifiable impacts of specific adverse scenarios, scenario planning takes a more qualitative

Approach, exploring the potential implications of a range of future developments. This may involve considering events such as geopolitical instability, pandemics, technological disruptions, or changes in consumer behavior that could impact the performance of the lending portfolio. These scenarios can be developed through a combination of expert opinions, internal discussions, and external research. The aim is not just to quantify the impact of each scenario but also to build a range of possible futures to assess a wide scope of risk exposure. This approach supports strategic decision-making, enabling institutions to anticipate potential disruptions and develop proactive mitigation strategies.

In the case of asset-based lending, scenario planning is particularly valuable. The value of the underlying collateral is paramount, and unforeseen events such as supply chain disruptions, changes in commodity prices, or shifts in

consumer preferences can dramatically affect the value of the assets securing the loans. A scenario planning exercise might explore the potential impacts of a sudden decrease in demand for a specific type of asset, or the emergence of a disruptive technology that renders existing assets obsolete.

This broader perspective can inform strategies to diversify the portfolio, adjust lending criteria, and implement

improved monitoring of collateral values. For instance, a lender with a significant concentration of loans secured by inventory might incorporate scenario planning to account for a possible prolonged production slowdown due to

unforeseen supply chain issues. This could involve exploring scenarios ranging from minor delays to total supply chain collapses, allowing the bank to prepare contingency plans, including tighter monitoring, and possibly higher loan loss reserves.

The integration of stress testing and scenario planning with the KRI framework is crucial. The kris provide early

Warning signals of potential problems, while stress testing and scenario planning provide a more comprehensive

assessment of the portfolio's resilience to various shocks. The results of stress testing and scenario planning can inform the selection and adjustment of kris, ensuring that the

monitoring system remains relevant and effective. For

example, if a stress test reveals significant vulnerability to interest rate increases, the institution might add or adjust kris focusing on borrower debt service coverage ratios and interest rate sensitivity. Conversely, scenario planning may suggest the need for new kris to monitor exposure to

emerging risks or specific industry developments.

The output of both stress testing and scenario planning should be regularly reviewed and updated. Macroeconomic conditions, industry dynamics, and even the institution's internal risk appetite can change over time. Regular updates to the stress test models and scenario planning exercises, possibly including different economic forecast models, ensures the analysis remains relevant and provides a reliable assessment of the portfolio's vulnerability to potential

shocks. This iterative process, combining continuous

monitoring, proactive assessment, and flexible adaptation, forms the foundation of robust portfolio management.

Furthermore, the results of these analyses should not remain solely within the confines of the risk management

department. They should be communicated effectively to senior management and the board of directors, informing strategic decision-making, capital planning, and risk appetite settings. Transparent communication about potential risks and the institution's preparedness is crucial for maintaining stakeholder confidence and ensuring long-term financial stability. The outcomes can inform capital planning, leading to adjustments in the institution's capital allocation

Strategies, ensuring sufficient reserves to absorb potential losses.

Ultimately, a holistic approach to portfolio management that combines the use of kris, stress testing, and scenario

planning is crucial for maintaining the long-term health and sustainability of any lending institution. These techniques, when implemented and utilized effectively, provide a

powerful toolkit for managing risk, mitigating potential losses, and ensuring resilience in the face of economic uncertainty. The ongoing refinement and adaptation of these tools in response to evolving conditions is not merely

advisable; it's essential for sustainable success within the financial sector. Ignoring these crucial aspects of risk

management can lead to significant financial setbacks and reputational damage, underlining the critical investment these processes represent for the institution's future.

Portfolio Concentration Risk Management

Portfolio concentration risk represents a significant threat to the stability and profitability of any lending institution. This risk arises when a substantial portion of a lending portfolio is exposed to a limited number of borrowers, industries, or geographic regions. A concentration in any of these areas creates a vulnerability; a single adverse event affecting that concentrated area can have a disproportionately large impact on the overall portfolio's performance. For instance, a lender heavily concentrated in commercial real estate loans within a single city becomes highly susceptible to a local economic downturn or a regional real estate market correction.

Similarly, overexposure to a specific industry, like oil and gas, leaves the lender vulnerable to fluctuations in

commodity prices or shifts in regulatory policy affecting that sector.

Effective portfolio concentration risk management requires a multi-faceted approach. This goes beyond simply identifying concentrations; it requires a proactive strategy to mitigate the associated risks and enhance the portfolio's overall

resilience. The first crucial step is comprehensive

identification and measurement of concentrations. This involves analyzing the portfolio across various dimensions:

Borrower Concentration:

This assesses the relative exposure to individual borrowers or groups of related borrowers. A high concentration in a single borrower or a small group of closely linked borrowers creates significant risk, as a default by a key borrower could trigger a cascade of failures among related entities. This can be particularly problematic in cases of syndicated loans where a single default can have wide-ranging consequences. Sophisticated

Analytical tools, including network analysis techniques, can help identify interconnectedness between borrowers and assess the potential systemic impact of individual defaults.

Industry Concentration:

Exposure to a specific industry exposes the portfolio to industry-specific risks, such as

cyclical downturns, technological disruptions, or regulatory changes. For example, a portfolio heavily concentrated in the automotive industry is vulnerable to fluctuations in vehicle sales, changes in consumer preferences, or the emergence of disruptive technologies like autonomous vehicles.

Diversification across multiple industries is crucial to

mitigate this risk. Detailed analysis of industry trends, future forecasts, and potential regulatory changes are essential aspects of this mitigation strategy.

Geographic Concentration:

Concentration within a specific geographic region exposes the portfolio to regional

economic downturns or localized events like natural

disasters. A lender with a large concentration of loans in a single city is vulnerable to local economic problems, while regional concentrations can be impacted by broader events affecting those areas. Diversification across multiple

geographic regions is essential for mitigating geographic concentration risk. This often necessitates a thorough

understanding of regional economic dynamics, including unemployment rates, population growth, and infrastructure development.

Once concentrations are identified, the next step is

developing strategies to mitigate them. These strategies vary depending on the specific nature of the concentration and the risk tolerance of the lending institution. Common approaches include:

Diversification:

This is the cornerstone of concentration risk management. Diversification involves spreading loans across a wider range of borrowers, industries, and geographic

regions. This reduces the impact of any single adverse event. However, blind diversification is inefficient; diversification strategies should be informed by a thorough understanding of the risk profile of each potential borrower, industry, and region.

Credit Risk Rating:

A comprehensive credit risk rating system is vital for evaluating the credit-worthiness of

borrowers and industries. This allows for the identification of high-risk borrowers and industries, permitting the bank to either reduce or manage its exposure. Regular review and updating of credit ratings, considering macro-economic factors, industry trends, and borrower-specific financial information, is critical.

Loan Sizing and Limits:

Establishing appropriate loan sizing and concentration limits are pivotal in mitigating concentration risk. These limits should be determined based on factors such as the borrower's credit quality, industry concentration, and geographic exposure. Regularly

reviewing and adjusting these limits, reflecting updated market conditions and risk assessments, is paramount.

Collateralization:

Secure loan structures with sufficient collateral can offset potential credit losses. This strategy is particularly important when dealing with concentrated exposures. Thorough appraisal and valuation of collateral, together with rigorous monitoring of collateral value in relation to loan balances, are vital to ensure adequate protection.

Loan Covenants:

Including robust loan covenants in credit agreements can help manage concentration risk. These

Covenants can impose specific restrictions or requirements on borrowers that reduce the possibility of default. Examples include financial ratios, debt service coverage ratios, and limitations on additional debt. Regular monitoring of

compliance with these covenants is crucial for early detection of potential problems.

Hedging:

In certain circumstances, financial instruments such as derivatives can be used to hedge against specific types of concentration risk. For instance, interest rate swaps can mitigate the risk of rising interest rates, impacting debt service capacity. However, hedging also comes with its own risks and should be carefully evaluated and employed under guidance from experts.

Active Portfolio Management:

Proactive portfolio

management involves continually monitoring and adjusting the portfolio's composition to minimize exposure to

concentrations. This requires a sophisticated system for tracking key risk indicators (kris), monitoring market

trends, and responding to emerging risks effectively. Regular portfolio reviews, involving a thorough assessment of credit risk and concentration, are crucial to actively managing the portfolio and promptly adjusting exposures.

In the context of asset-based lending, effective concentration risk management is especially critical. The value of the underlying assets securing the loans plays a central role in assessing risk. Concentrations in specific asset types or industries can expose the portfolio to dramatic fluctuations in asset values. For instance, a high concentration in loans secured by oil and gas inventory exposes the lender to price volatility in the energy market. Effective management

therefore requires detailed monitoring of asset values, using valuation models that reflect market conditions and

Incorporating various stress scenarios that could impact asset values.

The process of managing concentration risk is iterative and requires regular review and adjustment. Market conditions, industry trends, and even internal risk appetites evolve continuously. Regular portfolio reviews, combined with ongoing monitoring of key risk indicators, allows for the early identification of emerging concentrations and potential problems. Moreover, the use of stress testing and scenario planning, as discussed earlier, provides a valuable

framework for assessing the potential impact of various adverse events on the portfolio's performance. This allows for proactive risk mitigation strategies. Stress tests should simulate various scenarios, including industry-specific shocks, macroeconomic downturns, and unexpected events like pandemics, examining the potential impact on portfolio composition and the effectiveness of mitigation strategies.

The importance of transparent reporting and communication cannot be overstated. The results of risk assessments and concentration analysis should be clearly communicated to senior management, the board of directors, and other

stakeholders. This fosters transparency and accountability, and allows for informed decision-making regarding risk appetite, capital allocation, and strategic adjustments to lending policies. Failing to effectively communicate these findings risks not only potential financial setbacks but also significant reputational damage, damaging relationships with stakeholders and creditors.

In conclusion, managing portfolio concentration risk is an ongoing and essential aspect of sound lending practice. It requires a comprehensive approach, encompassing thorough identification and measurement of concentrations, the

implementation of effective mitigation strategies, ongoing

Monitoring of key risk indicators, and regular review and adjustment based on changing market conditions and risk assessments. The commitment to managing these risks is not merely a compliance issue; it is a crucial element of long-term financial stability, ensuring the health and sustainability of the lending institution. Neglecting this critical aspect of portfolio management can expose the institution to

substantial financial losses and reputational harm.

Regular Portfolio Reviews and Reporting

Regular portfolio reviews are not merely a compliance exercise; they are the lifeblood of effective risk management and a cornerstone of sustained profitability in commercial and asset-based lending. These reviews provide a crucial mechanism for monitoring the health of the loan portfolio, identifying emerging risks, and proactively adjusting strategies to maintain optimal performance. The frequency of these reviews should be dictated by several factors, including the complexity of the portfolio, the volatility of the underlying assets, and the institution's overall risk appetite. For highly concentrated or volatile portfolios, more frequent, perhaps even weekly, reviews may be warranted. Less volatile portfolios might necessitate monthly or quarterly reviews. Regardless of frequency, a consistent and disciplined approach is essential.

The review process should be structured and comprehensive, employing a standardized methodology to ensure consistency and comparability across different portfolios and time periods. It should incorporate both quantitative and qualitative assessments, utilizing data analytics and expert judgment to provide a holistic view of portfolio performance and risk. Quantitative analysis might involve calculating key performance indicators (kpis) such as loan delinquency rates, loss given default (LGD), exposure at default (EAD), and probability of default (PD). These metrics provide a numerical snapshot of the portfolio's health and offer early warning signals of potential problems. For example, a sudden and significant spike in delinquency rates could indicate an impending credit crisis, prompting a deeper investigation into underlying causes. Similarly, monitoring changes in LGD, EAD, and PD allows for a dynamic

Assessment of the credit risk within the portfolio, enabling proactive measures to limit potential losses.

Qualitative assessments, on the other hand, involve a more nuanced evaluation of the underlying risks within the

portfolio. This includes a careful examination of individual borrower creditworthiness, industry trends, and

macroeconomic conditions. This part of the review process necessitates a deep understanding of the borrowers' financial situations, paying close attention to their financial

statements, operational performance, and market dynamics affecting their businesses. For example, a sudden downturn in a specific industry sector, such as oil and gas or

technology, can necessitate a reassessment of the

creditworthiness of borrowers operating within that sector and require proactive measures to mitigate potential losses.

Similarly, macroeconomic events like unexpected interest rate hikes or recessions can significantly impact the ability of borrowers to service their loans. Identifying and evaluating these qualitative factors is crucial for making informed

decisions regarding loan modification, loan restructuring, or other interventions needed to mitigate risk and protect the institution's interests.

The review process must also incorporate an assessment of concentration risk, as outlined in the previous section. This necessitates a rigorous analysis of borrower, industry, and geographic concentrations, identifying potential

vulnerabilities. For instance, the portfolio's exposure to a specific industry should be compared to industry

benchmarks. If the concentration exceeds established limits, the review should highlight this exposure and prompt a discussion on the necessary mitigation strategies. This may involve diversifying the loan portfolio, establishing tighter loan covenants, or increasing collateral requirements for loans within the concentrated sector.

Beyond the quantitative and qualitative aspects, regular reviews should incorporate a comprehensive assessment of the effectiveness of existing risk mitigation strategies. Are the established loan covenants sufficient to protect the institution in case of borrower default? Are the collateral values adequately protecting the loans against potential market downturns? Are the risk ratings assigned to borrowers still accurate in the face of changing market conditions? These are critical questions that must be addressed during regular portfolio reviews. The answers often necessitate a revision or recalibration of existing strategies, ensuring their continuous effectiveness in mitigating risks.

The output of these portfolio reviews must be meticulously documented and translated into comprehensive reports. These reports serve as a vital communication tool, informing decision-makers throughout the institution regarding the overall health of the portfolio and potential risks. Reporting protocols should be standardized, clearly defining the information to be included, the frequency of reporting, and the dissemination channels. These reports should not be mere summaries of data; they should provide insightful analysis, highlighting potential concerns and recommending appropriate actions. A crucial aspect of reporting is the clear communication of the key findings and their implications, ensuring clarity for all stakeholders. In addition to quantitative metrics and qualitative assessments, reports should include explanations of any significant changes in the portfolio's composition, performance, or risk profile.

Effective reporting also requires clear communication of the overall risk appetite of the institution, which should align with the institution's strategic goals and risk tolerance. Any deviations from the established risk tolerance levels must be

Prominently highlighted in the reports. For example, if a specific segment of the portfolio exhibits a significantly higher risk profile than expected, this should be promptly reported to senior management for immediate attention and potential remediation. The reports should also communicate any changes in risk profile related to specific borrowers, such as a decline in their financial performance or an increase in their debt levels. This transparency allows the institution to take swift action to limit potential losses and protect its interests.

The structure of the reports should be clear and concise, using visual aids such as charts and graphs to make complex data easier to understand. They should also clearly identify potential vulnerabilities and recommend specific actions to mitigate risks. The reports should be disseminated regularly and promptly to relevant stakeholders, including senior management, the board of directors, and other relevant committees. This ensures that appropriate attention is given to emerging risks, allowing timely intervention and preventing potential problems from escalating. The distribution should be controlled and well-documented, with confirmation that the report was received and acknowledged.

Furthermore, the reporting structure must follow relevant regulatory requirements and compliance standards, ensuring transparency and accountability.

Beyond the regular reports, ad hoc reporting might be necessary to address specific events or concerns. For example, in times of economic uncertainty or when a major borrower experiences financial difficulty, additional reports might be required to provide a more detailed analysis of the situation and assess its potential impact on the portfolio. This responsiveness is crucial for proactive risk management, allowing swift adaptation to the changing environment and minimizing potential losses. In such instances, timeliness of

Information is of paramount importance, so systems should be in place to gather and analyze information rapidly. These ad-hoc reports should also be carefully documented and disseminated within the defined reporting protocols.

The development and implementation of these reporting protocols requires collaboration between different

departments within the institution, including lending, risk management, and compliance. This necessitates a robust communication framework and a well-defined process for data gathering, analysis, and reporting. A dedicated team responsible for overseeing the portfolio review and reporting process should be established, ensuring the consistency and quality of the reports. The team should be composed of individuals with expertise in various aspects of lending, risk management, and data analysis. Regular training and

ongoing professional development should be provided to the team to ensure they maintain the necessary skills and

knowledge to perform their tasks effectively.

Finally, the effectiveness of portfolio reviews and reporting should be regularly evaluated. This could be achieved

through internal audits, management reviews, and external assessments. These evaluations should focus on the accuracy and completeness of the reports, the timeliness of the

information, and the effectiveness of the actions taken in response to identified risks. Continuous improvement is crucial; feedback from the evaluation process should be used to refine the portfolio review and reporting process, ensuring its continued relevance and effectiveness in mitigating risk and promoting long-term financial health. The ultimate goal is a system that facilitates proactive risk management,

informs strategic decision-making, and enhances the overall profitability and resilience of the lending institution.

Emerging Trends and Technological Advancements

The landscape of commercial and asset-based lending is undergoing a rapid transformation, driven by a confluence of technological advancements and evolving market dynamics.

These changes are not merely incremental improvements; they represent a fundamental shift in how lenders assess risk, underwrite loans, monitor portfolios, and manage their

overall operations. Understanding these emerging trends is crucial for lenders seeking to remain competitive and

profitable in this evolving environment.

One of the most significant influences is the rise of big data and advanced analytics. Lenders are increasingly leveraging massive datasets— encompassing financial statements, market data, transactional records, and even social media activity—to gain deeper insights into borrowers'

creditworthiness. This goes beyond traditional credit scoring models, allowing for a more comprehensive and nuanced assessment of risk. Sophisticated algorithms can identify subtle patterns and correlations that might be missed by human analysts, leading to more accurate predictions of default probabilities and improved risk management. For example, analyzing a borrower's cash flow patterns in

conjunction with industry benchmarks and macroeconomic indicators can provide a much clearer picture of their

financial health than simply looking at their balance sheet. Furthermore, the integration of alternative data sources, such as social media sentiment analysis or satellite imagery of a borrower's physical assets, can provide valuable

supplementary information, enhancing the accuracy of credit assessments. The challenge lies not only in acquiring and processing this data but also in interpreting the results

Accurately and avoiding biases that could lead to incorrect conclusions. The development of robust and transparent analytical frameworks is therefore critical.

Artificial intelligence (AI) and machine learning (ML) are rapidly transforming the lending process, automating tasks and enhancing decision-making. AI-powered platforms can streamline the loan application process, automating tasks such as document verification, credit scoring, and fraud detection. This significantly reduces processing time and operational costs, allowing lenders to focus on more

complex aspects of the lending process. ML algorithms can analyze vast datasets to identify patterns and predict

outcomes, leading to more accurate underwriting decisions and improved risk management. These algorithms can adapt and learn from new data, constantly improving their

accuracy and efficiency over time. However, the

implementation of AI and ML in lending requires careful consideration of ethical and regulatory implications.

Ensuring transparency and fairness in lending decisions is crucial, and measures must be in place to prevent

algorithmic bias and discriminatory outcomes. Regular audits and rigorous testing are essential to ensure the responsible use of these technologies.

Blockchain technology offers the potential to revolutionize several aspects of commercial and asset-based lending. By providing a secure and transparent record of transactions, blockchain can enhance the efficiency and security of loan origination, servicing, and securitization processes. Smart contracts, self-executing contracts with the terms of the agreement directly written into lines of code, can automate loan payments, collateral management, and other processes. This can significantly reduce operational costs and improve the accuracy and efficiency of these processes. The

immutability and transparency of blockchain can also

Enhance trust and reduce disputes among lenders, borrowers, and other stakeholders. However, the widespread adoption of blockchain in lending is still in its early stages, with

challenges remaining in scalability, interoperability, and regulatory frameworks. The development of robust and standardized protocols is crucial for realizing the full

potential of this technology.

Cloud computing is another transformative force, providing lenders with scalable and cost-effective solutions for

managing their data and operations. Cloud-based platforms offer greater flexibility and accessibility, allowing lenders to access their data and systems from anywhere, at any time. This is particularly important for lenders with geographically dispersed operations or those dealing with large volumes of data. Cloud computing also enables collaboration among different teams and departments, enhancing efficiency and communication. The scalability of cloud-based systems allows lenders to easily adjust their capacity as needed, avoiding the costs associated with maintaining on-premise infrastructure. However, cloud computing also raises

concerns about data security and privacy. Lenders must choose reputable providers with robust security measures in place and adhere to strict data privacy regulations.

Open banking initiatives are promoting greater transparency and competition in the lending market by enabling lenders to access customer data from multiple sources. This allows for a more comprehensive assessment of a borrower's financial situation and can lead to more tailored and competitive

lending products. However, the successful implementation of open banking requires strong regulatory oversight and

safeguards to protect customer privacy and data security.

Careful consideration must be given to the ethical

implications of data sharing and the potential for misuse of customer information.

The increasing use of Robotic Process Automation (RPA) is streamlining many back-office processes, freeing up staff to focus on more strategic activities. Tasks such as data entry, document processing, and customer communication can be automated, improving efficiency and reducing errors. This frees human capital for more complex and relationship-oriented tasks that require human judgment and interaction.

However, the implementation of RPA requires careful planning and integration with existing systems, ensuring seamless workflow and avoiding disruptions.

Finally, the increasing focus on sustainable finance is

impacting commercial and asset-based lending. Lenders are increasingly incorporating environmental, social, and

governance (ESG) factors into their lending decisions,

considering the environmental and social impact of

borrowers' operations. This requires the development of new assessment methodologies and data collection processes, as well as increased transparency and reporting standards. The demand for sustainable financing is growing rapidly,

presenting both opportunities and challenges for lenders willing to adapt to this evolving landscape.

In conclusion, the future of commercial and asset-based lending is being shaped by a dynamic interplay of

technological advancements and shifting market demands.

Lenders who embrace these changes and adapt their

operations accordingly will be best positioned to succeed in this increasingly competitive and complex environment. The ability to leverage data effectively, adopt innovative

technologies responsibly, and integrate ESG considerations into their lending practices will be crucial for achieving long-term success. The effective management of risk and the development of robust, adaptable strategies are essential for navigating this period of rapid transformation and ensuring

The continued health and profitability of the lending industry. Continuous learning, innovation, and a commitment to ethical and sustainable practices will be paramount in shaping the future of this vital sector.

The Impact of Regulatory Changes and Compliance Requirements

The evolving regulatory landscape presents both challenges and opportunities for commercial and asset-based lenders. Increased scrutiny following the global financial crisis and the subsequent rise of fintech have led to a proliferation of new regulations and compliance requirements, impacting every aspect of the lending process, from loan origination to portfolio management. These changes aim to enhance

transparency, protect consumers, and maintain the stability of the financial system. However, navigating this complex regulatory maze necessitates significant investment in

compliance infrastructure, technology, and skilled personnel.

One of the most significant areas of regulatory impact is capital adequacy. Regulations like Basel III and its

subsequent revisions impose stricter capital requirements on banks and other lending institutions, forcing them to hold more capital against their risk-weighted assets. This reduces the amount of capital available for lending, potentially impacting lending volumes and credit availability,

particularly for smaller businesses that may rely more

heavily on asset-based lending. The increased capital

requirements incentivize lenders to rigorously assess risk, refine their underwriting processes, and diversify their loan portfolios. This necessitates the adoption of sophisticated risk management techniques, including advanced analytics and predictive modeling, to optimize capital allocation and minimize losses.

Furthermore, regulatory changes frequently affect the

reporting requirements for lenders. The increased demand for transparency and accountability has led to more stringent

Reporting standards, requiring lenders to provide detailed information on their lending practices, risk profiles, and financial performance. This includes reporting on various metrics, such as loan defaults, recovery rates, and exposure to specific industries or geographic regions. These enhanced reporting requirements demand significant investment in reporting systems and infrastructure, ensuring accurate and timely data submission to regulatory authorities. Failure to comply can lead to significant penalties, reputational

damage, and even operational disruptions. The complexity of these reporting requirements often necessitate specialized expertise, requiring lenders to invest in training and

recruitment to ensure compliance.

Consumer protection regulations are another critical area of regulatory change. Regulations like the Consumer Financial Protection Act (in the US) and similar legislation in other jurisdictions aim to protect borrowers from predatory

lending practices and unfair treatment. These regulations impact the terms and conditions of loans, requiring lenders to provide clear and concise information to borrowers,

ensure fair and transparent pricing, and avoid discriminatory lending practices. Compliance with these regulations

necessitates thorough review and updating of loan

agreements, credit application processes, and customer

communication strategies. Lenders need to implement robust systems to monitor compliance, identify potential violations, and take corrective actions promptly. This involves not only training staff on compliance regulations but also establishing internal audit mechanisms and engaging external consultants to conduct independent assessments.

Anti-money laundering (AML) and know-your-customer (KYC) regulations are increasingly stringent and play a crucial role in preventing financial crime. Lenders are now required to implement robust AML/KYC programs,

Including thorough customer due diligence, transaction monitoring, and suspicious activity reporting. This requires significant investment in technology, training, and

compliance personnel. AML/KYC compliance requires the use of sophisticated software systems to monitor

transactions, detect suspicious activity, and maintain

accurate records of customer information. Moreover, lenders must adhere to ongoing updates and amendments to

AML/KYC regulations, adapting their programs as needed.

Non-compliance can result in significant fines, legal repercussions, and severe reputational damage.

The increasing use of technology in lending also brings forth a new set of regulatory challenges. The rise of fintech and the adoption of artificial intelligence (AI), machine learning (ML), and blockchain technologies introduce new

considerations for regulatory oversight. Regulators are

grappling with how to ensure the responsible use of these technologies, addressing concerns about data privacy,

algorithmic bias, and the potential for market manipulation. New regulations may be enacted to govern the use of AI and ML in lending, requiring lenders to implement measures to ensure fairness, transparency, and accountability in their algorithmic decision-making. This necessitates the

development of explainable AI (XAI) methods to provide insights into the reasoning behind automated lending

decisions, ensuring transparency and mitigating the risk of bias.

Furthermore, the use of blockchain technology introduces regulatory uncertainties concerning data security, cross-border transactions, and the legal enforceability of smart contracts. Regulatory bodies are actively working to develop frameworks that address these issues, balancing the potential benefits of blockchain with the need to protect consumers and maintain financial stability. Lenders adopting blockchain

Technology must closely monitor regulatory developments and adapt their practices accordingly, ensuring compliance with evolving standards. The increasing interconnectedness of financial systems also necessitates international

cooperation on regulatory matters, ensuring a consistent approach across jurisdictions and minimizing regulatory arbitrage.

Cybersecurity is another critical area where regulations are becoming increasingly stringent. Lenders are obligated to protect the confidentiality, integrity, and availability of

customer data, requiring significant investments in

cybersecurity infrastructure and personnel. Compliance with cybersecurity regulations necessitates regular security audits, penetration testing, and incident response planning. The failure to adequately protect customer data can result in substantial fines, legal action, and irreparable damage to a lender's reputation. Implementing robust cybersecurity measures is no longer a discretionary choice; it's a

fundamental requirement for operating in the commercial and asset-based lending space.

The impact of these regulatory changes extends beyond compliance costs. It affects strategic decision-making, resource allocation, and the overall competitive landscape.

Lenders that fail to adapt to the evolving regulatory

environment risk facing penalties, operational disruptions, and reputational damage. Conversely, those who proactively embrace these changes and integrate compliance into their core business strategy will be better positioned for long-term success. This requires a culture of compliance, where

regulatory adherence is not viewed as a burden but as a critical component of risk management and responsible business practice. Investing in compliance technology,

training, and personnel is not simply an expense; it's a

strategic investment that protects the lender's interests and

Fosters trust with borrowers, investors, and regulators alike.

Successful navigation of this complex regulatory terrain demands vigilance, adaptability, and a commitment to ethical and responsible lending practices. The future of commercial and asset-based lending will be defined by those lenders who not only comply with regulations but actively contribute to shaping a more transparent, stable, and equitable financial system.

Changing Market Dynamics and Economic Conditions

The confluence of macroeconomic factors and evolving market dynamics will significantly shape the future of commercial and asset-based lending. Understanding these shifts is crucial for lenders to adapt their strategies and maintain profitability and stability. The post-pandemic economic recovery, while uneven, has been marked by significant inflation and subsequent interest rate hikes by central banks globally. This has created a complex environment characterized by higher borrowing costs, increased uncertainty, and a potential slowdown in economic growth. The impact on commercial and asset-based lending is multifaceted.

Firstly, the higher interest rate environment directly impacts borrowing costs for businesses. This leads to reduced demand for loans, especially for projects with lower margins or longer payback periods. Businesses will be more selective in their borrowing, prioritizing essential investments and delaying or canceling less crucial projects. Lenders, in turn, will need to adapt their pricing strategies, carefully evaluating the risk-reward profile of each loan application. This necessitates a more sophisticated approach to credit risk assessment, incorporating macroeconomic forecasts and industry-specific analyses to predict the probability of loan defaults. Furthermore, lenders will need to develop more flexible financing structures to accommodate the varying needs of businesses operating in this volatile economic climate. This could include offering variable interest rate loans with adjustable repayment schedules, or developing hybrid financing structures that combine debt and equity financing.

Secondly, the inflationary environment poses challenges for both borrowers and lenders. Rising input costs, including raw materials, energy, and labor, squeeze profit margins for businesses, reducing their ability to service debt. This

increased credit risk necessitates a more stringent

underwriting process, focusing on cash flow projections, debt-to-equity ratios, and collateral valuation. Lenders may demand higher loan-to-value ratios (ltvs), potentially limiting the amount of financing available to businesses that rely heavily on asset-based lending. Inflation also impacts the value of collateral, leading to potential increases in loan defaults if asset values decline faster than anticipated. This necessitates a proactive approach to portfolio management, including regular monitoring of collateral values and the implementation of robust early warning systems to identify potential problem loans.

Thirdly, the global economic uncertainty resulting from geopolitical tensions, supply chain disruptions, and volatile energy markets contributes to heightened risk aversion among lenders. This leads to a more conservative lending approach, characterized by stricter credit criteria, reduced loan sizes, and a higher focus on security. Businesses may find it more difficult to secure funding, particularly smaller businesses with limited credit history or collateral. This could exacerbate economic inequality and hinder economic growth. Lenders will need to enhance their risk management capabilities, utilizing advanced analytics and predictive modeling to assess the impact of macroeconomic factors on their loan portfolios. Collaboration with economic

forecasters and industry experts is crucial to accurately predict future trends and anticipate potential risks.

Fourthly, the changing competitive landscape will also influence the future of commercial and asset-based lending.

The rise of fintech companies has disrupted traditional lending models, offering faster, more efficient, and often more accessible financing options to businesses. These fintech lenders often utilize technology to automate the lending process, reduce operational costs, and improve customer experience. Traditional lenders need to embrace technology to remain competitive. This includes investing in new technologies such as AI-powered credit scoring models, blockchain-based loan management systems, and advanced analytics platforms to improve efficiency, reduce costs, and enhance customer service.

Furthermore, the increasing use of alternative data sources for credit risk assessment is reshaping the lending landscape. Lenders are exploring the use of non-traditional data points, such as online business reviews, social media activity, and e-commerce transaction data, to better understand borrower behavior and assess creditworthiness. This allows for more accurate risk assessment, particularly for businesses with limited credit history. However, careful consideration must be given to data privacy and regulatory compliance when utilizing alternative data sources. Transparency and fairness in algorithmic decision-making are critical to maintain trust and avoid accusations of bias.

Finally, the future of commercial and asset-based lending will be heavily influenced by regulatory changes aimed at enhancing financial stability and protecting consumers. Stricter capital adequacy requirements, increased reporting standards, and heightened scrutiny of lending practices will necessitate significant investments in compliance infrastructure and personnel. Lenders will need to embrace a culture of compliance, integrating regulatory adherence into their core business strategy. Failure to adapt to the evolving regulatory environment could result in substantial penalties, reputational damage, and even operational disruptions.

In conclusion, the future of commercial and asset-based lending is intertwined with the evolving macroeconomic environment and shifting market dynamics. The higher interest rate environment, inflationary pressures, global economic uncertainty, and the rise of fintech lenders are creating a more complex and challenging landscape for lenders. To navigate this environment successfully, lenders must adapt their strategies, enhance their risk management capabilities, embrace technology, and prioritize regulatory compliance. Those lenders who can effectively manage risk, leverage technology, and adapt to changing market

conditions will be best positioned for long-term success. A proactive and adaptable approach is crucial to not just

survive but thrive in this dynamic and evolving sector.

Furthermore, collaboration within the industry, sharing best practices and insights, will be vital in navigating the

collective challenges and ensuring the continued health of the commercial and asset-based lending sector. Ignoring these dynamic shifts will not only impact profitability but may even compromise the long-term viability of lending institutions in the face of increasing economic volatility and regulatory scrutiny. Understanding these challenges is the first step towards building a robust and resilient lending model for the future. The integration of advanced analytics, predictive modelling and the responsible use of alternative data sources will be critical factors in achieving this. By embracing innovation and prioritizing responsible lending practices, the commercial and asset-based lending industry can continue to play a vital role in supporting economic growth and business development.

Opportunities and Challenges for Lenders

The evolving landscape of commercial and asset-based lending presents both significant opportunities and

formidable challenges for lenders. Navigating this complex terrain requires a strategic approach that balances risk

mitigation with the pursuit of growth and profitability. One of the most significant opportunities lies in the increasing sophistication of data analytics and predictive modeling. The ability to leverage vast datasets, encompassing traditional credit scores, alternative data sources such as online business activity and social media presence, and macroeconomic indicators, allows lenders to build more accurate and

nuanced credit risk profiles. This granular understanding of borrower behavior and market trends enables more precise pricing, more tailored financing solutions, and ultimately, a reduction in loan defaults. This enhanced predictive

capability is not simply a technological advantage; it's a fundamental shift in how lenders assess and manage risk. It allows for a more proactive approach to portfolio

management, enabling early identification of potential

problems and the implementation of timely interventions.

This proactive stance differentiates lenders who embrace data-driven insights from those relying on traditional, often less effective, methods.

Furthermore, the growth of the digital economy presents unique opportunities for lenders to expand their reach and efficiency. The increasing prevalence of e-commerce

transactions, digital payment systems, and online business operations provides a wealth of data for creditworthiness assessment, offering access to previously untapped market segments. Fintech companies have already demonstrated the potential of leveraging these digital footprints to provide

Swift, efficient, and often less expensive financing options to businesses. However, traditional lenders, with their

established networks and regulatory compliance

frameworks, are well-positioned to leverage these digital advancements, adapting their processes and systems to

benefit from the efficiencies and scalability offered by

technology. This includes implementing automated

underwriting systems, deploying AI-powered risk

assessment models, and creating seamless digital customer journeys. The integration of blockchain technology holds the potential to further revolutionize the lending process,

enhancing transparency, security, and operational efficiency.

The increasing emphasis on sustainability also presents significant opportunities for lenders. The growing demand for environmentally friendly practices and the expanding market for green technologies create a burgeoning sector ripe for investment and lending opportunities. Businesses

committed to sustainability are often viewed as more

resilient and less susceptible to certain risks, potentially lowering the overall risk profile for lenders. By actively supporting sustainable projects, lenders can enhance their reputation, attract socially conscious investors, and

contribute to a more environmentally responsible financial sector. This necessitates developing specialized financing products and expertise to cater to the specific needs of

environmentally conscious businesses, fostering a positive relationship with both borrowers and investors looking for impact investments. The creation of green loan products and the establishment of rigorous ESG (Environmental, Social, and Governance) frameworks will become increasingly crucial for lenders to attract investment and retain a

competitive edge.

Despite these opportunities, the future of commercial and asset-based lending is not without its challenges. The current

Macroeconomic environment, characterized by persistent inflation, rising interest rates, and geopolitical uncertainty, presents considerable headwinds. Higher interest rates directly impact borrowing costs, potentially reducing demand for loans and increasing the risk of defaults.

Inflationary pressures squeeze business profit margins, impacting their ability to service debt obligations. The

resultant economic uncertainty leads to increased risk

aversion among lenders, leading to stricter credit criteria and a reduction in lending activity. This increased scrutiny will inevitably make it more difficult for many businesses,

particularly smaller enterprises and those with limited credit histories, to access the funding they need. Lenders will need to carefully balance their risk appetites with their growth ambitions in this volatile climate.

The competition within the lending sector is also

intensifying. The emergence of fintech lenders, armed with advanced technologies and agile business models, is

disrupting traditional lending practices. These companies frequently offer faster, more streamlined, and often lower-cost financing options, putting pressure on traditional lenders to innovate and adapt. Competition is not just about price; it's also about speed, efficiency, and customer experience.

Traditional lenders need to modernize their operations, invest in technology, and enhance their customer service capabilities to remain competitive. Failure to do so risks losing market share to nimbler, more technologically adept competitors.

Furthermore, the regulatory environment is becoming

increasingly complex, adding another layer of challenge for lenders. Increased regulatory scrutiny, stricter capital

adequacy requirements, and heightened reporting standards demand significant investments in compliance infrastructure and personnel. Lenders must maintain a strong compliance

Culture, proactively adapting to changing regulations and adhering to best practices to mitigate reputational and financial risks. Ignoring regulatory requirements not only jeopardizes long-term viability but can lead to severe financial penalties and significant reputational damage.

Another key challenge arises from managing the increasing complexity of collateral valuation. In an inflationary environment, asset values can fluctuate significantly, impacting the value of collateral used to secure asset-based loans. Lenders need robust valuation methodologies and proactive monitoring systems to manage this risk effectively. Underestimating the risk of collateral devaluation can lead to significant losses if asset values decline faster than anticipated. Regular reviews and updated appraisals of collateral are essential to accurately reflect market fluctuations and prevent potential shortfalls.

Finally, the inherent challenge of managing credit risk remains paramount. Accurately assessing and mitigating credit risk is fundamental to the success of any lending operation. In an uncertain economic climate, this task becomes even more critical. Lenders must refine their underwriting processes, incorporating more sophisticated data analytics and robust risk management frameworks to identify and manage potential defaults. This necessitates continuous improvement in risk assessment methodologies, including the use of alternative data sources, advanced statistical models, and scenario planning to accurately predict future outcomes.

In conclusion, while significant opportunities exist within the evolving landscape of commercial and asset-based lending, lenders face equally significant challenges. The successful navigation of this dynamic environment necessitates a multifaceted strategy that combines embracing

Technological advancements, enhancing risk management capabilities, adapting to regulatory changes, and maintaining a proactive approach to portfolio management. Lenders who can effectively adapt to changing market dynamics, leverage data analytics, and maintain a strong focus on compliance will be best positioned to thrive in the future of commercial and asset-based lending. A commitment to innovation,

coupled with a strong understanding of the underlying risks, will be crucial to maintaining profitability, stability, and long-term success in this sector. The ability to anticipate change, not merely react to it, will determine the winners and losers in this evolving landscape.

Adapting to the Changing Landscape

Adapting to the shifting dynamics of the commercial and asset-based lending market requires a proactive and

multifaceted approach. Simply reacting to change is

insufficient; lenders must anticipate future trends and

strategically position themselves to capitalize on emerging opportunities while mitigating potential risks. This

necessitates a thorough understanding of the forces shaping the industry and the development of a robust adaptation strategy.

One crucial element of this adaptation is the integration of advanced technologies. While the benefits of data analytics and predictive modeling have been touched upon, their effective implementation requires a significant investment in infrastructure and personnel. This goes beyond simply

acquiring new software; it requires the development of internal expertise capable of interpreting complex datasets, developing sophisticated algorithms, and translating data insights into actionable strategies. This includes training existing staff and potentially recruiting data scientists,

analysts, and technology specialists. The transition may necessitate a cultural shift within the lending institution, encouraging a data-driven decision-making process at all levels.

Beyond data analytics, the adoption of automated

underwriting systems is crucial. These systems can

streamline the loan application process, reducing processing times and freeing up staff to focus on more complex tasks.

They can also improve consistency and accuracy in credit assessments, reducing the risk of human error. Moreover, the implementation of robust Customer Relationship

Management (CRM) systems can enhance customer service, personalize interactions, and foster stronger client

relationships, which is vital in a competitive market. A seamless digital customer journey is paramount; clients expect convenient and efficient access to information and services, irrespective of their location or preferred method of communication.

The embrace of technology must also extend to

cybersecurity measures. As lenders increasingly rely on digital systems to manage data and transactions, the risk of cyberattacks increases exponentially. Therefore, significant investment in robust cybersecurity infrastructure and

protocols is not merely advisable, but essential. This

includes implementing multi-factor authentication, regularly updating software, conducting penetration testing, and

developing comprehensive incident response plans. Failure to address cybersecurity adequately can result in substantial financial losses, reputational damage, and regulatory

sanctions.

Another critical area for adaptation lies in risk management.

The macroeconomic uncertainties mentioned earlier

necessitate a more rigorous and sophisticated approach to credit risk assessment. This includes diversifying the loan portfolio, carefully monitoring borrower financial health, and proactively identifying potential defaults. The use of stress testing and scenario planning is crucial to understand the potential impact of various economic scenarios on the loan portfolio. Furthermore, establishing clear risk appetite parameters and adhering to them strictly is vital in

preventing excessive risk-taking. Regular review and

refinement of these parameters based on market conditions are essential.

Effective risk management also extends to collateral valuation. The previously mentioned volatility in asset values demands a more proactive and sophisticated approach. Lenders should employ independent valuation specialists to conduct regular appraisals, ensuring that collateral values accurately reflect market conditions. This necessitates a clear understanding of the various valuation methodologies applicable to different types of collateral and the selection of appropriate methodologies based on specific circumstances. Moreover, lenders must establish a system for continuous monitoring of collateral value, triggering early warnings and appropriate actions should asset values start to decline.

The regulatory landscape also requires proactive engagement. Lenders should establish a dedicated compliance function with experienced professionals who can effectively navigate the complexities of evolving regulations.

This includes staying abreast of changes in legislation, implementing appropriate policies and procedures, and ensuring that all lending activities are compliant. Moreover, developing a strong compliance culture within the institution is crucial; this means fostering a mindset where compliance is viewed not as a burden, but as a cornerstone of sound business practice. Ignoring regulatory requirements can lead to significant fines, reputational damage, and even legal action.

Beyond regulatory compliance, Environmental, Social, and Governance (ESG) considerations are rapidly becoming crucial for lenders. Investors are increasingly demanding transparency and accountability in relation to ESG factors, leading to the growth of sustainable finance. This represents a significant opportunity for lenders who can effectively integrate ESG factors into their lending practices.

Developing specialized products and services catering to the

Needs of environmentally conscious businesses can attract both borrowers and investors who are committed to sustainability. This requires internal training and the development of specific expertise in ESG assessment and reporting.

Finally, attracting and retaining top talent is critical for adaptation. In a competitive market, lenders need to offer competitive salaries, benefits, and career development opportunities to attract and retain skilled professionals, especially in areas like data science, technology, and risk management. Creating a positive and supportive work environment is equally important, fostering innovation, collaboration, and a commitment to continuous improvement.

In conclusion, adapting to the changing landscape of commercial and asset-based lending is a continuous process that requires a comprehensive and integrated strategy. By proactively embracing technological advancements, enhancing risk management capabilities, adhering to regulatory requirements, integrating ESG considerations, and prioritizing talent acquisition and retention, lenders can position themselves for long-term success in a dynamic and increasingly competitive market. The ability to anticipate and respond to change effectively will be a key determinant of future success in the commercial and asset-based lending sector. Ignoring these factors risks obsolescence and ultimately, failure to thrive in this rapidly evolving landscape. The strategic integration of these points will ensure not only survival but also a significant competitive advantage in the years to come.

Recap of Key Concepts and Principles

This concluding section synthesizes the core tenets and practical applications explored throughout this book on navigating the complexities of commercial and asset-based lending. We will revisit the crucial lessons learned in each chapter, offering a cohesive understanding of the

multifaceted nature of this dynamic field. The aim is to provide a robust framework for effective lending strategies in an ever-evolving financial landscape.

Our journey began by establishing a foundational

understanding of the commercial and asset-based lending landscape. We examined the diverse range of lending

products available, from traditional term loans and lines of credit to more specialized financing solutions tailored to specific industries and asset types. This initial exploration highlighted the importance of a thorough understanding of the nuances of each product, considering factors such as interest rates, repayment schedules, and associated risks. A clear grasp of these fundamental concepts is the cornerstone of responsible lending practices. We underscored the need for comprehensive due diligence and risk assessment,

emphasizing the crucial role of meticulous underwriting and ongoing monitoring of borrower performance. This early emphasis on due diligence laid the groundwork for the more advanced concepts discussed later in the book. Failing to thoroughly understand the fundamentals invariably leads to difficulties in adapting to the more complex challenges presented in the latter stages of the lending process.

Subsequent chapters delved into the critical area of credit analysis and risk assessment. We investigated various

analytical techniques, including financial statement analysis,

Cash flow projections, and industry benchmarking,

demonstrating how these tools help lenders evaluate the creditworthiness of potential borrowers. The importance of understanding the borrower's business model, management team, and industry dynamics was highlighted. We stressed the necessity of integrating qualitative and quantitative

factors in the credit assessment process, acknowledging that a purely quantitative approach can often overlook crucial qualitative elements that can significantly impact a

borrower's ability to repay debt. This holistic approach, considering both numbers and narrative, is fundamental to mitigating risk effectively. Specific examples of industries with unique risk profiles, such as real estate development, technology start-ups, and agricultural businesses, were

analyzed to illustrate the diversity of challenges in credit assessment across sectors. The discussion extended to the use of sophisticated credit scoring models and the potential pitfalls of over-reliance on automated systems without

human oversight. The human element, interpreting data within the context of market conditions and industry-specific knowledge, remains critical.

Further chapters expanded on the crucial role of collateral management in asset-based lending. We explored various types of collateral, including inventory, accounts receivable, and real estate, examining the unique characteristics and valuation methodologies for each. The significance of

accurate and up-to-date collateral valuations was stressed, underscoring the need for independent appraisals and

continuous monitoring to ensure the collateral's value

adequately supports the outstanding loan amount. We delved into the complexities of collateral perfection, highlighting the importance of understanding legal and regulatory

requirements to protect the lender's interests in case of

default. This involved detailed exploration of relevant legal frameworks and the intricacies of securing liens and other

Forms of collateral protection. The potential impacts of collateral depreciation and market volatility were also discussed, emphasizing the need for proactive strategies to manage these risks. Specific scenarios, such as sudden market downturns affecting real estate collateral or rapid obsolescence of inventory, were examined to illustrate how effective collateral management can mitigate losses.

The ever-changing regulatory landscape formed the

backbone of another significant section of the book. We discussed the key regulations governing commercial and asset-based lending, including those related to fair lending practices, consumer protection, and anti-money laundering (AML) compliance. We highlighted the importance of

maintaining a strong compliance program, regularly

updating policies and procedures to reflect changes in

legislation and best practices. Examples of regulatory

changes and their impact on lending practices were provided, emphasizing the need for continuous monitoring and

adaptation. This included discussion on the increasing

scrutiny on ESG (environmental, social, and governance) factors and the implications for lenders. The integration of ESG considerations into lending decisions is no longer a niche concept; it's becoming a crucial aspect of responsible and sustainable finance. We examined how lenders can

incorporate ESG factors into their due diligence and risk assessment processes, highlighting the potential for both reputational and financial benefits for institutions that

actively embrace sustainable lending practices. The potential penalties and reputational damage from non-compliance were also explicitly addressed.

Technological advancements and their integration into

lending operations were discussed in detail. The

transformative power of data analytics, predictive modeling, and artificial intelligence (AI) in credit risk assessment and

Portfolio management was explored. We also discussed the importance of cybersecurity and the need for robust systems to protect sensitive data. The implementation of automated underwriting systems and their potential to streamline the loan application process was examined, while

simultaneously addressing the ethical considerations and potential for bias in AI-driven decision-making. Examples of effective technology implementation in lending institutions, along with the potential pitfalls of poorly implemented

systems, were included to provide practical guidance. This included discussions on data privacy regulations and the implications for lenders handling sensitive customer

information.

The final chapters emphasized the crucial role of effective risk management and crisis preparedness in navigating

unexpected economic downturns and market volatility. We highlighted the importance of diversifying loan portfolios, monitoring economic indicators, and implementing stress testing to assess the resilience of the loan portfolio under various adverse scenarios. Specific crisis management

strategies, including proactive communication with

borrowers and the development of contingency plans, were explored. The importance of maintaining sufficient liquidity and capital reserves was also emphasized. Detailed case studies were included, examining real-world examples of financial crises and how effective risk management

strategies helped lenders navigate these tumultuous periods. The role of proactive communication with stakeholders, both internally and externally, during periods of economic

uncertainty was also stressed.

In essence, this book has underscored the dynamic nature of commercial and asset-based lending, requiring a constant adaptation to evolving market conditions, technological advancements, and regulatory requirements. The successful

Lender of tomorrow will be one that not only understands these fundamental principles but also actively embraces continuous learning and innovation. The ability to anticipate and respond effectively to change is no longer a desirable trait; it's a critical factor for survival and sustainable growth in the commercial and asset-based lending sector. A holistic approach integrating financial acumen, technological

proficiency, regulatory compliance, and robust risk

management is essential for sustained success. The journey from understanding the fundamentals to implementing sophisticated strategies is a continuous one, demanding both expertise and adaptability. The information and guidance provided in this book are designed to equip lenders with the knowledge and tools needed to navigate the complex

landscape and thrive in this ever-evolving environment.

Practical Applications and Implementation Strategies

This section translates the theoretical frameworks and analytical tools explored throughout this book into practical, actionable steps for improving your lending practices and crisis management capabilities. We will move beyond abstract concepts and delve into specific implementation strategies, offering real-world examples and case studies to illustrate how these strategies can be effectively integrated into your daily operations.

Firstly, let's revisit the foundational elements of due diligence. Remember the emphasis placed on thorough underwriting and the importance of a holistic approach encompassing both quantitative and qualitative factors. In practice, this means developing a robust due diligence checklist. This checklist should not merely be a generic template; it must be tailored to the specific industry and type of borrower you are assessing. For example, a due diligence checklist for a technology start-up will differ significantly from one designed for an established manufacturing company. The start-up checklist might place greater emphasis on intellectual property valuation, market analysis, and management team experience, while the manufacturing checklist might focus more on production capacity, supply chain stability, and inventory management. Furthermore, regularly update this checklist to reflect evolving industry trends, emerging risks, and regulatory changes. Consider incorporating specific questions related to environmental, social, and governance (ESG) factors, aligning with the increasing importance of sustainable finance. Don't just collect data; critically analyze it, looking for inconsistencies or red flags that might indicate higher risk.

Next, we address the practical aspects of credit analysis and risk assessment. While sophisticated credit scoring models and predictive analytics offer valuable insights, they should not replace human judgment. These technologies are

powerful tools, but they are only as good as the data they are fed. Garbage in, garbage out, as the saying goes.

Furthermore, these models may not fully capture qualitative factors, such as management integrity or the overall market sentiment towards a specific industry. Therefore, the

integration of human expertise remains paramount. This necessitates ongoing professional development for your credit analysts, ensuring they possess the up-to-date skills and knowledge needed to interpret data effectively within the broader economic context. Invest in training programs that cover advanced financial statement analysis, cash flow

forecasting techniques, and industry-specific knowledge. Encourage your team to participate in industry conferences and networking events to stay informed about the latest trends and best practices.

Effective collateral management is equally crucial,

translating into proactive monitoring and valuation. This requires a robust system for tracking collateral value, including regular appraisals conducted by independent, qualified professionals. The frequency of these appraisals will depend on the nature of the collateral and market volatility. For instance, real estate appraisals might be conducted annually, while inventory appraisals could be more frequent, especially for rapidly changing industries.

Moreover, establish clear protocols for handling collateral depreciation. This involves establishing triggers for

intervention, such as predetermined thresholds for acceptable collateral-to-loan ratios. When these thresholds are breached, a defined action plan must be activated, which might involve discussions with the borrower about refinancing or other

Restructuring options. In addition, understand and adhere to the legal and regulatory requirements for collateral

perfection in your jurisdiction to protect your lender's interests.

Regarding regulatory compliance, developing a robust

compliance program is not a one-time exercise; it's an

ongoing process. This involves maintaining an up-to-date understanding of all applicable regulations, including those related to fair lending, consumer protection, and anti-money laundering (AML). Designate a dedicated compliance

officer, or team, responsible for monitoring regulatory

changes and ensuring that your lending practices align with all applicable laws. Implement a robust training program for all staff involved in lending operations to ensure that they are fully aware of the legal and ethical requirements of their roles. This training must be regularly updated to reflect any changes in legislation or best practices. Finally, regularly conduct internal audits to identify and address any potential compliance gaps. A proactive approach to regulatory

compliance is not just about avoiding penalties; it's about upholding ethical standards and building trust with your clients and stakeholders.

Technological integration necessitates a strategic approach. The adoption of new technologies should not be driven by hype alone; it must be aligned with your organization's overall strategic goals. Before investing in new systems, thoroughly assess your needs and determine which

technologies can effectively address those needs. Consider the potential costs and benefits of various options, including both the initial investment and the ongoing maintenance costs. Proper training is essential for ensuring that your staff can effectively use and maintain these technologies. Equally important is the establishment of robust cybersecurity

measures to protect sensitive data. This involves

Implementing strong password policies, conducting regular security audits, and maintaining up-to-date antivirus

software.

Finally, crisis preparedness is not a luxury; it's a necessity.

Develop detailed contingency plans for various scenarios, including economic downturns, industry-specific crises, and natural disasters. These plans should outline clear

communication protocols for stakeholders, procedures for assessing the impact on your loan portfolio, and strategies for mitigating potential losses. Regularly test these plans to ensure their effectiveness and identify any areas for

improvement. Diversify your loan portfolio to reduce your exposure to any single industry or borrower. Actively

monitor economic indicators and conduct regular stress tests on your loan portfolio to assess its resilience under various adverse scenarios. Early identification of potential problems allows for proactive intervention, mitigating losses and preserving relationships with borrowers.

In conclusion, implementing the strategies outlined in this book requires a commitment to continuous learning,

adaptation, and investment. It's about building a culture of risk awareness, proactive management, and technological innovation. The successful lender of tomorrow will be one that integrates these practical strategies into their daily

operations, positioning themselves for continued growth and resilience in the ever-evolving financial landscape. By

embracing a holistic approach that encompasses due

diligence, credit analysis, collateral management, regulatory compliance, technological integration, and crisis

preparedness, you equip your institution to not only survive but thrive in the dynamic world of commercial and asset-based lending. Remember that effective implementation is an iterative process. Regularly review your processes, seeking areas for improvement and adapting to changes in the market

And regulatory landscape. The journey towards excellence in lending is a continuous one, demanding constant vigilance and a commitment to best practices.

Future Directions and Emerging Trends

The preceding chapters have laid out a robust framework for navigating the complexities of commercial and asset-based lending and effectively managing crises within the financial sector. However, the financial landscape is dynamic,

constantly evolving with technological advancements,

shifting regulatory environments, and unforeseen economic shocks. Therefore, understanding and adapting to future directions and emerging trends is crucial for continued

success. This section explores these critical areas, offering insights and strategies for navigating the evolving landscape.

One of the most significant emerging trends is the increasing influence of technology, particularly artificial intelligence (AI) and machine learning (ML). These technologies are revolutionizing various aspects of lending, from credit

scoring and risk assessment to fraud detection and customer service. AI-powered credit scoring models can analyze vast datasets, identifying subtle patterns and correlations that might be missed by traditional methods. This leads to more accurate risk assessments, enabling lenders to make more informed lending decisions and optimize their portfolio allocation. Moreover, ML algorithms can automate various aspects of the lending process, such as loan application

processing, document review, and underwriting, significantly improving efficiency and reducing operational costs.

However, the implementation of AI and ML requires careful consideration. Data quality is paramount; inaccurate or biased data will lead to flawed models and potentially

discriminatory outcomes. Furthermore, the "black box"nature of some AI algorithms can make it difficult to

understand their decision-making process, potentially

creating challenges for regulatory compliance and

Transparency. Lenders must adopt a responsible and ethical approach to the implementation of these technologies, investing in robust data governance frameworks and

ensuring the interpretability and fairness of their models. Ongoing monitoring and evaluation are also essential to ensure the continued accuracy and effectiveness of these systems.

Beyond AI and ML, other technological advancements are transforming the lending landscape. Blockchain technology, for instance, offers the potential to streamline processes such as loan origination and collateral management. Its

decentralized and transparent nature can enhance security and reduce fraud risk. Cloud computing offers scalability and flexibility, allowing lenders to efficiently manage their data and applications. The use of apis (Application

Programming Interfaces) is further facilitating seamless integration between different systems, creating more

streamlined workflows and enhancing efficiency. The

adoption of these technologies, however, requires significant investment in infrastructure and training. Lenders must carefully assess the costs and benefits of adopting new

technologies, ensuring they are aligned with their strategic goals and have the necessary expertise to effectively

implement and manage them. Furthermore, robust

cybersecurity measures are crucial to protect sensitive data from cyber threats.

The regulatory environment is also undergoing significant change. Increased scrutiny on environmental, social, and governance (ESG) factors is driving the growth of

sustainable finance. Lenders are increasingly incorporating ESG considerations into their due diligence processes,

assessing the environmental and social impact of their

borrowers' activities. This requires the development of new methodologies and frameworks for evaluating ESG risks and

Opportunities. Regulatory authorities are also increasingly focusing on responsible lending practices, particularly regarding consumer protection and fair lending. This

necessitates the implementation of robust compliance

programs, ensuring lenders adhere to all applicable

regulations and avoid potential penalties. Staying abreast of regulatory changes and adapting lending practices

accordingly is essential for avoiding legal issues and

maintaining a strong reputation. Proactive engagement with regulatory bodies and industry associations is crucial for navigating these complex regulatory shifts.

Geopolitical instability and macroeconomic fluctuations add further layers of complexity to the lending landscape.

Unexpected events, such as pandemics or natural disasters, can significantly impact borrowers' ability to repay loans. Lenders must develop robust crisis management strategies to mitigate potential losses and preserve relationships with their borrowers. This involves proactive monitoring of

macroeconomic indicators, conducting regular stress tests on their loan portfolios, and developing contingency plans for various scenarios. Diversifying loan portfolios across

different industries and geographical regions can help to mitigate risks associated with concentrated exposure.

Furthermore, establishing clear communication protocols with borrowers during times of crisis is essential for fostering trust and facilitating effective solutions.

In the area of asset-based lending, specifically, we see a shift towards more sophisticated collateral management

techniques. The use of data analytics to monitor collateral value and identify potential risks is increasingly prevalent.

This allows lenders to intervene proactively if collateral value declines, preventing significant losses. Furthermore, advances in technology are enabling more efficient and secure methods of tracking and managing collateral. This

Includes the use of blockchain technology for secure record-keeping and smart contracts for automated collateral release.

The development of sophisticated valuation models,

informed by market data and predictive analytics, is also crucial for accurate assessment of collateral value. However, it is important to ensure that these advanced techniques do not overshadow the importance of human judgment and experience in collateral valuation and management.

Looking ahead, the successful lender of the future will be one that embraces innovation, proactively adapts to changing circumstances, and cultivates a culture of continuous

learning. This requires significant investment in technology, talent, and training. Lenders must invest in developing the skills and knowledge of their employees, ensuring they are equipped to navigate the complexities of the evolving

financial landscape. This includes providing training on new technologies, regulatory changes, and risk management techniques. Furthermore, fostering a culture of data-driven decision-making and collaboration is crucial for leveraging the full potential of available data and insights. Strong

leadership is essential in guiding the organization through these changes, fostering a culture of adaptability and

resilience.

The future of commercial and asset-based lending will be characterized by increased competition, technological disruption, and evolving regulatory requirements.

Successfully navigating this landscape requires a holistic approach encompassing strategic planning, technological innovation, robust risk management, and a commitment to ethical and responsible lending practices. By embracing these future directions and emerging trends, lenders can position themselves for continued growth and success in the dynamic world of commercial and asset-based lending. The path forward requires ongoing vigilance, continuous

Adaptation, and a commitment to excellence in all aspects of the lending process. The financial institution that proactively anticipates and adapts to these trends will be well-positioned to thrive in the years to come, while those who fail to adapt risk becoming obsolete. The key is not simply to keep up, but to lead the way in shaping the future of lending.

Resources and Further Reading

This concluding section aims to equip you with resources to deepen your understanding and continue your professional development in commercial and asset-based lending and crisis management. The dynamic nature of the financial industry demands continuous learning, and the resources listed below represent a starting point for your ongoing journey. We've categorized them for easier navigation, encompassing academic publications, industry associations, regulatory bodies, and online learning platforms.

Academic Publications and Research:

The academic literature provides a rich foundation for understanding the theoretical underpinnings and empirical evidence related to lending practices and crisis management. A thorough review of peer-reviewed journals and academic books is highly recommended. Key journals to explore include the *Journal of Banking & Finance*, the *Journal of Financial Economics*, the *Review of Financial Studies*, and the *Financial Management* journal. These publications frequently feature articles on credit risk assessment, loan portfolio management, financial modeling, and the impact of macroeconomic factors on lending. In addition to these specialized journals, broader economics and finance journals often publish relevant research, providing a wider perspective on market trends and regulatory developments.

Furthermore, academic books dedicated to commercial

lending, asset-based financing, and risk management provide comprehensive overviews of the field, often delving deeper into specific topics than journal articles allow. Searching for books with keywords such as "commercial lending," "asset-

Based finance," "credit risk management," "financial crisis management," and "bankruptcy prediction" will yield a wealth of relevant materials. Pay close attention to the

publication date, as the financial landscape evolves rapidly, and newer publications generally reflect more current trends and best practices. University libraries often provide access to extensive databases of academic journals and books, simplifying access to this essential research.

Beyond formal publications, consider exploring working papers and research reports from prominent universities and think tanks specializing in finance and economics. These often present cutting-edge research before formal

publication, providing insights into emerging trends and future directions.

Industry Associations and Professional Organizations:

Professional associations play a crucial role in providing networking opportunities, continuing education, and industry updates. Membership in relevant organizations can

significantly enhance your professional development.

Organizations such as the American Bankers Association (ABA), the Association for Financial Professionals (AFP), and the Risk and Insurance Management Society (RIMS) offer valuable resources, including conferences, webinars, and publications focused on specific aspects of commercial and asset-based lending and crisis management. These organizations often publish reports and white papers on industry trends, regulatory updates, and best practices.

Many niche associations cater to specific areas of finance, offering highly specialized knowledge and networking opportunities. For instance, organizations focused on

structured finance, asset-based lending, or specific industry sectors (e.g., real estate, healthcare) provide valuable

Insights and connections within their respective fields. Participating in conferences, workshops, and networking events organized by these associations can broaden your professional network and expose you to the latest industry developments. Furthermore, accessing these organizations' member-exclusive resources provides access to detailed information and analyses often unavailable to the general public.

Regulatory Bodies and Governmental Agencies:

Staying informed about regulatory changes and compliance requirements is paramount for anyone working in the

financial industry. Understanding and adhering to regulations are essential for mitigating legal risks and maintaining a strong reputation. Therefore, familiarity with the regulatory landscape is critical. The relevant regulatory bodies vary depending on your geographical location and the specific type of lending activity. In the United States, agencies like the Federal Reserve, the Office of the Comptroller of the Currency (OCC), the Federal Deposit Insurance Corporation (FDIC), and the Consumer Financial Protection Bureau (CFPB) play crucial roles in regulating banks and other financial institutions. Internationally, organizations such as the Basel Committee on Banking Supervision (BCBS) and the International Monetary Fund (IMF) influence global banking regulations and provide valuable insights into

international financial stability.

Monitoring these regulatory bodies' websites for updates, announcements, and publications is essential for staying informed. Many offer guidance documents, faqs, and compliance materials that can help you understand and implement regulatory requirements effectively. Furthermore, subscribing to regulatory alerts and newsletters can ensure you receive timely updates on significant changes. Active

Engagement with regulatory bodies through participation in industry consultations and feedback processes is encouraged to ensure that your perspective is heard and considered in the development of future regulations.

Online Learning Platforms and Resources:

The rapid evolution of the financial industry makes continuous learning essential. Online learning platforms provide convenient and flexible ways to enhance your knowledge and skills. Platforms like Coursera, edx, Udemy, and linkedin Learning offer a wide range of courses on topics relevant to commercial and asset-based lending and crisis management. These courses are often developed by leading academics and industry professionals, ensuring high-quality content and up-to-date information. Many platforms offer certifications upon course completion, enhancing your professional credentials.

Beyond structured courses, a wealth of online resources is available. Websites of reputable financial institutions, research firms, and consulting companies provide insightful reports, articles, and analysis on industry trends and best practices. Following influential thought leaders in the finance industry through their blogs, podcasts, and social media channels can offer exposure to fresh perspectives and cutting-edge ideas. However, it is crucial to critically evaluate the credibility and reliability of online resources, ensuring that the information you consult is accurate and based on sound evidence.

Additional Resources:

Beyond the categories already mentioned, several additional resources can significantly contribute to your understanding of commercial and asset-based lending and crisis

Management. These include industry-specific databases providing detailed financial information on companies, market trends, and economic indicators. Databases like Bloomberg Terminal, Refinitiv Eikon, and S&P Capital IQ offer comprehensive data and analytical tools used extensively by professionals in the financial industry. These tools provide crucial data for credit risk assessment, portfolio management, and financial modeling.

Furthermore, networking with experienced professionals in the field is invaluable. Attending industry events, joining professional organizations, and participating in online forums can connect you with experts who can share insights, mentor you, and provide guidance on your career path. The exchange of knowledge and experience within the professional community is crucial for continuous learning and professional growth. Seeking out mentorship from seasoned professionals can offer invaluable guidance and help you navigate the complexities of the industry.

Finally, remember that continuous learning is not just about acquiring new knowledge, but also about refining your existing skills. Seek opportunities to apply your knowledge in practical settings, whether through internships, projects, or volunteer work. Real-world experience is essential for developing the practical skills and judgment needed to succeed in this challenging and rewarding field. The journey to becoming a proficient professional in commercial and asset-based lending and crisis management is ongoing. By utilizing these diverse resources and actively engaging in the industry, you can equip yourself with the knowledge and skills to excel in this constantly evolving field.

Final Thoughts and Reflections

The preceding chapters have meticulously examined the intricacies of commercial and asset-based lending, delving into the nuances of credit risk assessment, portfolio

management, and the critical role of crisis preparedness.

We've explored various lending structures, analyzed the impact of macroeconomic factors, and dissected the

complexities of navigating financial distress. However, the true essence of success in this dynamic field lies not solely in mastering the technical aspects but in embracing a holistic, proactive approach to risk management and ethical lending.

This concluding section serves as a reflection on the overarching principles that underpin sustainable and responsible lending practices.

Proactive risk management isn't merely a checklist of

compliance measures; it's a fundamental philosophy that should permeate every stage of the lending process, from initial client assessment to loan servicing and recovery. The ability to anticipate potential challenges, assess their

likelihood and impact, and implement mitigation strategies is paramount. This involves a deep understanding of the

borrower's business model, industry dynamics, and the

broader macroeconomic environment. While quantitative analysis is crucial, qualitative assessments of management teams, operational efficiency, and the overall business

climate are equally important. A thorough due diligence process, complemented by robust monitoring and early

warning systems, forms the cornerstone of effective risk management. This proactive approach minimizes the

likelihood of encountering severe financial distress and significantly reduces the potential costs associated with loan defaults or restructurings.

The ability to anticipate and effectively manage crises is a crucial skill for any banking professional. It's not a matter of *if*

a crisis will occur, but

when

. The recent global financial crisis, along with countless other smaller-scale crises, serves as a stark reminder of the potential for unforeseen events to disrupt even the most well-managed institutions. However, preparedness is key to mitigating the impact of such events. This involves developing comprehensive crisis management plans that outline clear procedures for identifying, assessing, and responding to various scenarios. Regular stress testing, scenario planning, and the development of contingency plans are essential for ensuring that institutions can withstand significant shocks. These plans should not gather dust on a shelf; they must be regularly reviewed, updated, and

practiced to ensure effectiveness when needed. Furthermore, fostering a culture of open communication and collaboration across all levels of the organization ensures swift and

coordinated responses in times of crisis.

Responsible lending extends far beyond simply adhering to regulatory compliance. It encompasses a commitment to ethical conduct and a focus on the long-term sustainability of both the borrower's business and the lender's own institution. It involves a thorough understanding of the borrower's needs and a responsible assessment of their ability to repay the loan. It's about fostering a collaborative relationship based on trust and transparency, providing borrowers with the support and guidance they need to succeed.

This often

entails offering tailored financial solutions that meet the specific circumstances of the borrower, while ensuring the protection of the lender's interests. It also involves

acknowledging that sometimes, despite diligent underwriting and monitoring, loans may still fail. In these instances,

responsible lending incorporates processes for fair and

equitable loan workout and restructuring, minimizing the

Adverse impact on both the borrower and the lender. By prioritizing responsible lending, financial institutions not only contribute to the stability of the broader economy but also strengthen their own reputation and long-term viability.

The integration of technology is revolutionizing commercial and asset-based lending. Sophisticated data analytics,

machine learning algorithms, and advanced financial

modeling techniques are transforming the way lenders assess credit risk, manage portfolios, and monitor borrowers. These tools offer enhanced speed, accuracy, and efficiency,

allowing lenders to process larger volumes of data and make more informed decisions. However, it is crucial to recognize that technology is a tool; its effectiveness depends on the expertise and judgment of the professionals using it. Human oversight and critical evaluation are paramount to ensure the responsible and ethical application of these technologies. Over-reliance on automated systems without proper human intervention can lead to unintended consequences and

exacerbate existing biases. Therefore, a balanced approach is essential, integrating cutting-edge technology with the

expertise and judgment of experienced lending professionals.

Looking ahead, the landscape of commercial and asset-based lending will continue to evolve, driven by technological advancements, changing regulatory frameworks, and shifting economic conditions. The capacity to adapt to these changes is paramount for long-term success. This requires ongoing professional development, a commitment to continuous learning, and a proactive approach to staying abreast of industry trends. The resources highlighted earlier in this book – academic publications, industry associations,

Regulatory bodies, and online learning platforms – offer invaluable support for continuous professional development. Engaging with these resources, networking with experienced professionals, and actively participating in industry events

Are essential steps in maintaining a competitive edge in this dynamic field. Furthermore, the pursuit of advanced

certifications and specialized qualifications can further enhance your professional credibility and career prospects.

Beyond technical skills, the development of strong

interpersonal and communication skills is equally crucial for success in commercial and asset-based lending. Building rapport with borrowers, negotiating effectively, and clearly articulating complex financial concepts are essential for establishing trust and fostering successful partnerships. These soft skills, often overlooked, are integral to effective relationship management, which is fundamental in securing deals, managing risk, and navigating challenging situations. Therefore, a holistic approach to professional development should encompass not only the technical aspects of lending but also the cultivation of essential communication and interpersonal skills.

Finally, it is important to emphasize the ethical

considerations that should always underpin lending

decisions. Profitability should never come at the expense of integrity. A commitment to responsible lending practices, transparency, and fair dealings is essential for maintaining a strong reputation and fostering long-term sustainability. Ethical lapses can have severe consequences, impacting not only the reputation of the institution but also the broader economic landscape. The pursuit of short-term gains should never compromise long-term ethical standards. By upholding the highest ethical principles, financial institutions can

contribute to a more stable and just financial system. The financial industry holds a position of significant

responsibility in the wider economy; responsible lending practices are not merely a matter of compliance; they are a moral imperative. By adhering to ethical principles and fostering responsible lending practices, we contribute to the

Overall well-being of both individual borrowers and the wider economic system. The enduring success of any

financial institution rests upon this bedrock of integrity. The journey of a lending professional is a continuous evolution; embracing lifelong learning, adaptable strategies, and strong ethical foundations remains the guiding principle for

navigating the complexities and achieving enduring success within the dynamic world of commercial and asset-based lending.

Appendix

Appendix A: Illustrative Case Studies of Crisis Management in Commercial Lending. This section presents three detailed case studies illustrating different approaches to crisis

management in commercial lending situations. Each case study highlights the challenges faced, the strategies

employed, and the ultimate outcomes.

Appendix B: Sample Loan Agreements and Documentation.

This appendix provides examples of common loan

agreements and supporting documentation used in

commercial and asset-based lending, offering a practical reference for readers. These are simplified examples and should not be considered legal advice. Always consult with legal counsel for specific legal requirements.

Appendix C: Checklist for Proactive Risk Management in Commercial Lending. This appendix provides a

comprehensive checklist to assist lenders in implementing a robust proactive risk management framework. The checklist covers key areas such as due diligence, monitoring, and early warning systems.

Glossary

This glossary defines key terms and concepts used throughout the book.

Asset-Based Lending:

A type of financing where loans are secured by the borrower's assets.

Credit Risk:

The risk of a borrower defaulting on a loan.

Due Diligence:

The process of investigating a borrower's creditworthiness and business operations before granting a loan.

Loan Workout:

The process of resolving a loan default, often involving restructuring or renegotiation.

Non-Performing Loan (NPL):

A loan where the borrower is in default and is unlikely to repay.

Portfolio Management:

The process of managing a lender's loan portfolio to optimize risk and return.

Stress Testing:

A process used to assess the resilience of a loan portfolio to various economic shocks

Author Biography

Pradeep K. Berry is an executive senior management consultant in banking and finance. He has conducted viability studies of thousands of diversified companies to determine whether to loan them money for working capital, mergers and acquisitions, crisis management, and investment banking. He plans to write another book focusing on his life, his professional career, and his wife's professional achievement as well.

Pradeep Berry, after the death of his darling wife, Connie, became a global motivational speaker—sharing his experiences in facing Connie's death, in seeking justice for her, in his pursuit of excellence in the United States, and in promoting humanitarianism.

One thing he never ceases to do is to share his blessings to humanity. Apart from having the heart in writing books, Pradeep Berry has a bigger heart in seeking the welfare of others. Philanthropy is innate in him.

www.ingramcontent.com/pod-product-compliance
Lightning Source LLC
LaVergne TN
LVHW052218200926
848481LV00001B/141